Lybrand Template

1) Engage the audience
2) Expose their need
3) Make a "contra
   to meet that need in
   the message.
4) Explain the text:
   its meaning, implications,
   and illustrations.
5) Clarity: Putting together
   the meaning of the text
   and how it meets the
   need of the audience.
6) Offer actions to take
7) close with a point-on
   illustration

A text — Explores carefully
immediate Context — people your speaking to.
Engage theology — proclaim the good News
clarity / Focus — To be understood
Engage the heart — where the battle resides
= Effective preaching changes the way
      we live

1) Identify the main idea

2) Identify the secondary ideas

3) Ask yourself "What is the secondary idea telling me about the main idea?"

4) Express the relationship between the main and secondary ideas in a sentence that has both a subject and a complement.

"Genre is the key to understanding what sort of information a Biblical author is trying to convey"

Principles
Realistic
Propositional
More words

← LAW ——— Epistle ——— Historical Narrative / Gospel ——— Prophecy / Wisdom Literature ——— →

Poetry
Apocalyptic
Pictures
Imaginative
Metaphorical
Emotive
Less words

Basic Questions of Observation

What does the text say?
When did this happen?
(Who are the characters involved?)
(What places are mentioned?)
What are the important connecting or transition words?
Are there any comparisons or contrasts?
Are there repeated words or ideas?

Essential Questions

What does the author say?
How does the author say it?
What is the tone?
Why does he say it here?
(Why in this way?)
What is surprising about it?
How does it point or speak about Christ?
What is it saying as a whole?
Why did the author say this?
(What response did he hope for?)
What is the response God is looking for from us today?

1. Career
2. Relationships
3. Finances
4. Health
5. Overall well-being

} Familiarity
Comfort
Security
influence
Certainties

INVITATION TO

BIBLICAL
PREACHING

- Orient reader & to subject with an anecdote/
  detailed imagery
- Address the scope
- In place of a thesis, offer:
  - Possible generalizations or speculations (
    maybe, perhaps, something "X" and others think "Y"
  - Raise a question
- reader has a general idea (the topic and the
  direction (the stance) but he does not know your
  bottom line or conclusion
              ...to reason I am telling you this is because...
  " Instead (proving your thesis statement,
    you are building it?

Invitation to Theological Studies

Stimulating the mind and nourishing the soul, each volume in the Invitation to Theological Studies series is written to provide a primary textbook for core graduate-level courses.

INVITATION TO
BIBLICAL PREACHING

Proclaiming Truth with
Clarity and Relevance

DONALD R. SUNUKJIAN

Kregel
Academic & Professional

check

"Preaching with Accuracy"
Randal E. Pelton

Invitation to Biblical Preaching: Proclaiming Truth with Clarity and Relevance

© 2007 by Donald R. Sunukjian

Published by Kregel Publications, a division of Kregel, Inc., P.O. Box 2607, Grand Rapids, MI 49501.

Unless otherwise indicated, Scripture quotations are from the *Holy Bible, New International Version*®. Copyright © 1973, 1978, 1984 by International Bible Society. Used by permission of Zondervan Publishing House. All rights reserved.

Scripture quotations marked NASB are from the NEW AMERICAN STANDARD BIBLE®. Copyright © 1960, 1962, 1963, 1968, 1971, 1972, 1973, 1975, 1977 by The Lockman Foundation. Used by permission. (www.Lockman.org)

Scripture quotations marked KJV are from the King James Version.

ISBN 978-0-8254-3666-6

Printed in the United States of America

07 08 09 10 11 / 5 4 3 2 1

① Preaching the Application
— hearing to demands of the text itself:
ⸯ what is the text calling us to do
ⸯ what is the text calling us to realign with God
ⸯ How is the text shaping us for mission?

ⸯ how is the text enriching us
into community?

② Series that are rooted in biblical books
Book Survey - launch pad (Preparation for)
the series
outline, structure ⸱ main-units = strategic
⸱ sub-units   areas *
* (structure leads to meaning)   The structure

③ Paragraph
Detail analysis ⸱ observation (questions)
⸱ key questions   new with the
⸱ inferences (insight text)
⸱ wider context

Processes	Roles/Participants	Circumstances

Processes

Material = Doing

Mental = Sensing

Relational Attributing

Identifying

Roles/Participants

Affector – Affected
Effector – Effected

senser – phenomenon

carrier – Attribute

Identified – Identifier

Circumstances

Extent
Distance: ... many miles.
Duration: ... many days.

Location
Place: He lives there (Loc)
... in Jerusalem (pl)
Time: she left recently (Ca)
He left at noon (p ...)

Manner (behaviour)(How) adver...
Means: ... with mud br...
Quality: It rained heavi...
Comparison: Elijah speal...
di...lty

Cause   Why? (adve...
motivation Reason: ... because / to
intention Purpose: ... lend for p...
plan design
Behalf: ... on behal...
of the king

Contingency
Condition: In the eve...
Concession: He ran
though he was tire...
Default: In the abs...
of an agreement, ...

Accompaniment
Comitative: David
and Jonathan went
together
Additive: David
went as well as Jon...

Role
Guise: she was con...
as a prophet
Product: He grew into
a man

Affector – Affected ② ↑ of to Subject
He hit the hit The idol

Effector – Effected
She built the house

Sensor – Phenomenon
Eli heard Hannah's crying

Carrier – Attribute
The letter is Nonsense

Identified – Identifier
You are the first person
on earth ③ is the complement
↑

① The Nuance
(who/what/when/where/how =
Means/Manner
Why? = Purpose/reason/result)

Perception - mental images
- Perceive
- keep
- use

The raw stuff of life
Select - The life language (correct wording)

Revision - Getting it just right (Not your first draft... craft effectively.

Contents

Rhetorical Functions

Exclamation
Relationship
Basis
Action
Result
Means
Description
manner/agency
Purpose
Time

"Solid research makes great
story telling."

An Invitation to Biblical Preaching

AFTER PREACHING ONE SUNDAY morning, a man asked me, "Don, how do you see yourself when you're up there preaching? What's your self-image? Do you see yourself as an evangelist? A teacher? A 'kerux'? (I think he knew a little Greek and was showing off.) How do you see yourself?"

I'd never considered that question before, but within a split second I instinctively answered, "I see myself standing with you, under the Word of God, saying, 'Look at what God is saying to us.'"

In my mind's eye, I saw myself as standing, not over the congregation, but among them, holding open a Bible, showing its pages to them, saying, "This is God's Word—inspired, inerrant, authoritative. It tells us what we need to know—what to think, how to act, what's ahead. It gives us truth. Isn't it wonderful? It's what God is saying to us! He's already said it to me; I've already received the benefit from it as I've studied and prepared. And now I'm simply sharing it with you—Look at what God is saying to us!"

As I've reflected over the years on that spur-of-the-moment answer, it has struck me that this is, at heart, the definition of a "biblical preacher"— one who says, "Look at what God is saying . . . to us."

The Bible is God's voice, spanning the ages. The role of the biblical preacher is to echo that voice in this generation. Specifically, the preacher's task is twofold:

- to present the true and exact meaning of the biblical text ("Look at what God is saying . . .")

- in a manner that is relevant to the contemporary listener ("... to us").

THE TRUE AND EXACT MEANING

"To present the true and exact meaning of the biblical text" means the sermon must unfold according to the natural flow of thought of the biblical author. If Isaiah were listening to a sermon from his writings, he should be thinking to himself, "Yes, that's what I was saying, and that's how it fits this crowd." But if Isaiah hears the sermon, shakes his head, and says, "What? No! No!" the preacher is in trouble. Biblical preaching takes great pains to present the ideas and sequence of thought of the inspired biblical author.

A true biblical preacher, for example, would not preach the story of David and Goliath as revealing "six characteristics of a future leader":

- Curious—asking, "What will be done for the man who kills this Philistine?"
- Consistent—asking others the same question after his brother rebukes him.
- Courageous—offering to Saul, "Your servant will go and fight him."
- Careful—taking off Saul's armor because he is not used to it.
- Confident—announcing to Goliath, "This day the Lord will hand you over."
- Conclusive—cutting off Goliath's head with the sword.

Surely the original author did not have such a list in mind when he sat down to write his account![1]

Instead, the preacher's study of 1 Samuel 17 within the historical flow of the Old Testament would observe the following:

---

1. Such preaching is poor communication—and worse theology. First, "asking others the same question" is not being *consistent*, it's being *persistent*. (But the speaker is stuck with his *c*'s.) Second, it's highly debatable whether consistency is a true characteristic of a leader. A business owner in the audience might argue, "If I consistently ran my business the same way I did a decade ago, without changing or adapting, I'd be broke." Finally, it's also theologically debatable whether confidence is a true leadership characteristic. Certain leaders in Scripture resolved to act a certain way even though they had no confidence as to what God would do (e.g., Daniel's three friends who informed Nebuchadnezzar that, whether God rescued them or not, they would not bow to his image of gold [Dan. 3:16–18]). Such a sermon—six alliterated *c*'s of leadership—is not God's truth but rather the speaker's artificial creation.

- David continually refers to Goliath as "this uncircumcised Philistine," emphasizing the fact that Goliath has no covenant right to the land.
- Goliath is from the city of Gath, a Philistine city that should have been defeated by the tribe of Judah years earlier. In Judges 1, God picked the tribe of Judah to set the example for the other tribes: by trusting God's covenant promises they would be able to conquer their allotted territories. But Judah, the chosen leader, faltered in faith, defeating only three of the Philistine cities in its territory. Gath was allowed to remain. And now Gath, in the form of Goliath, has come back to trouble Israel.
- But now a young boy from the tribe of Judah steps forward to do what his tribe did not do, because he believes what his tribe did not believe—that God would be true to his covenant promise and that the land would belong to Israel alone. And thus this boy becomes the leader his tribe was supposed to be, prefiguring the coming "Lion of Judah" who will rule God's people forever.

In this way the expositor, by being true to the meaning of the original author, is able to preach the real point of the passage: "Only those who believe God's Word are qualified to lead God's people."

RELEVANT TO THE CONTEMPORARY LISTENER

This true and exact meaning must then be presented in a manner that is relevant to the contemporary listener. God is revealing truth, not simply to a previous generation, but also to us, right now, right where we live. God intends his Scriptures to span the centuries, addressing each generation in its immediate context.

When the Pharisees challenged Jesus as to why he was allowing his disciples to pick grain on the Sabbath (Matt. 12:1–2), he replied, "Haven't you read what David did when . . . ?" (v. 3). In Jesus' mind, God was giving them the answer to their question through an incident recorded a thousand years earlier.

Similarly, Paul, referring to the historical events of Exodus and Numbers, says, "These things . . . were written down as warnings for us" (1 Cor. 10:11). Through accounts written 1,500 years earlier, God was speaking to Gentiles in Paul's day—and to us, now.

Extrapolation + Application

A biblical message is not so much, "This is what God said *then*," as it is, "This is what God is saying *now, to you*." The purpose of the sermon is not to impart knowledge but to influence behavior—not to inform but to transform. The goal is not to make listeners more educated but more Christlike.

When you come, for example, to Genesis 11–12—Abraham's leaving Ur of the Chaldeans for Canaan—you would not be content to simply "teach" the various details of the passage:

- Ur as a commercial and religious center of the ancient Sumerian culture.
- Abraham's trip up the Euphrates River.
- His stay in Haran until the death of his father, Terah.
- His resumed journey to Canaan.
- His travels down the central mountain ridge, building altars and worshiping wherever he goes.

At the end of all this biblical information, the listener thinks to himself, "So what? The man's been dead for four thousand years. What do I care? Why are you telling me this?"

In genuine biblical preaching, you would go on to say, "The reason I'm telling you this is because God may come to some of you and say the same thing he said to Abraham, 'Leave what is known and familiar, and come with me. Let go of what is comfortable and secure, and follow me without knowing what I will put in its place.'"

Then you would draw pictures of what this contemporary "leaving" might look like for your listeners:

- Leaving the familiarity of American culture for an overseas ministry.
- Leaving the comfort of family and friends to go to college in another state or to take a job in another city.
- Leaving the security of a guaranteed paycheck and benefits to start your own business.
- Leaving a circle of teenage friends who are a bad influence on you.
- Leaving the familiarity of singleness for the uncertainties of marriage.

[Handwritten annotations at top of page:]

historical flaw — 1. What's The question? Reason written emphasis
Meaning → to original INTRODUCTION 2. What's The problem? Main Idea 13 How did we get here!
author
The reason I'm 3. What's wrong with this picture? → truth
telling you this happening

To preach in a manner that is relevant to the contemporary listener is to impress on the listener, "God is saying something today. He didn't just say it long ago. He's saying it now, to us, right where we live."

(1)   (2)   (3)

TEXTUAL, TOPICAL, OR EXPOSITORY?

When talking about this kind of biblical preaching, the old distinctions of textual, topical, and expository are not helpful. Those distinctions were based on *the amount* of biblical material being used, or *where* it was being drawn from—a single verse (textual), passages from different biblical books (topical), or sequential paragraphs through a particular book (expository). ✓

Today, instead, we define true biblical preaching by *how* the biblical material is treated—that is, faithful to the meaning and flow of the original author and relevant to the contemporary listener. *Background & Content* *Context = ?*

Any of the above approaches—textual, topical, expository—can be a biblical message. A biblical textual sermon, based on 1 Timothy 5:1a ("Do not rebuke an older man harshly, but exhort him as if he were your father"), might look like this:

I.   We are not to harshly rebuke an older man
    A. "Harshly rebuke" means . . .
    B. In our experience, a harsh rebuke might be something like:
        1. Example
        2. Example
        3. Example
    C. The reason we are not to harshly rebuke older men is because . . .

II. Instead, we should appeal to him, or exhort him, as if he were our father
    A. The difference between an appeal and a rebuke is . . .
    B. In the examples above, an appeal might sound something like:
        1. Example
        2. Example
        3. Example
    C. The significance of viewing him as our father is that . . .

A textual sermon like this is true biblical preaching—the speaker unfolds the author's flow of thought in a short text (here, two-thirds of a verse), making his concepts clear, believable, and relevant to the contemporary listener.

Similarly, topical preaching can be true biblical preaching. A topical sermon on being a Christian husband might look like this:

I. Be <u>considerate</u> as you <u>live</u> with your wife (1 Peter 3:7).
   A. In the original language, the words "live with" look at the most intimate aspects of life, including sexual intimacy.
   B. To be "considerate" means to act in an understanding and knowledgeable way in this intimate relationship.
   C. "Considerate living" in our marriages might take many forms.
      1. Example
      2. Example
      3. Example

II. <u>Love</u> your wife <u>as Christ</u> loved the church (Eph. 5:25).
   A. Christ's love for the church was such that he gave himself up for her.
   B. In a husband's life, such sacrificial love might take many forms.
      1. Example
      2. Example
      3. Example

Such a topical sermon is genuine biblical preaching—it accurately explains each passage according to its biblical context and applies the truths to everyday life.

THE HARDEST AND BEST THING WE WILL EVER DO

This book is an invitation to biblical preaching. We'll talk about how to determine the true and exact meaning of the biblical author. And we'll talk about how to present that meaning in a clear, believable, and relevant way to the contemporary listener.

<u>Such preaching is the hardest and best thing we will ever do.</u>

It's the hardest, for it will take the most rigorous mental ability and discipline God has given us. We will find ourselves tempted to do anything but the hard study required—we'll schedule meetings, arrange counseling appointments, tackle administrative tasks, clean our fingernails, find a sermon on the Internet, or settle for some superficial approach to our passage—anything to avoid the sheer labor required.

For a man, preaching is probably as close as he will ever come to giving birth. He'll go through the same "labor": "There's something growing inside of me. It's getting larger. It wants to come out. Oh, it's so hard to get it out . . . Aaaugh! . . . It's done; it's over! . . . Tell me that's the prettiest baby you've ever seen!" (And the next day, he has the "postpartum blues"!)

It's the hardest thing we will ever do, but it's also the best. It's the best thing we can do for our ministries. Good preaching does the following:

- It enables us to reach more people in less time with God's truth, since it occurs at the largest gathering of the church.
- It allows us to say things honestly, and sometimes bluntly, knowing that someone, in the anonymity of a crowd, will ponder and receive our words, whereas that person might angrily reject them if said face-to-face.
- It builds our credibility for our other pastoral (e.g., counseling) and leadership (e.g., church board) activities.
- It is usually the initial point of contact that encourages visitors to return.
- It brings excitement and anticipation to the whole church.

Biblical preaching is the best thing we can do for our ministries, and it's the best thing we can do for our own personal lives. To drink deeply of the Word of God, to saturate ourselves with its truths, to have our lives changed by its transforming power, and then to stand before God's people, proclaiming with joy and confidence, "Look at what God is saying to us!"—who could be called to anything greater?

What the question? = Topic

What the problem? = Assertion

What wrong with this picture = Proposition, Central truth, Big idea

Grammatical Dingramming

$\longleftrightarrow$ 10 vocatives / interjections

$\Longleftrightarrow$ 5 conjunctions (Postpositive)

$\longleftrightarrow$ 3 Adjectival modifier

| nominal / verbal (of main clause) —> object

$\longleftrightarrow$ 3 Adverbal mod

$\Longleftrightarrow$ 5 con_

object
||
apposition

$\longleftrightarrow$ 8 .
. Direct discourse
.

Semantic Dingramming

① Coordinates ⌈ the boy went to town
            and
            ⌊ the man went fishing

② Subordinate ⌈— the boy went to town
③ (event)   (purpose) in order to buy greek cacc

④ Coordinate (series) ⌈ The boy went to town
  (sequence) and   ⊢ He bought greek cacls
  (series) and   ⌊ He returned home
  (list) and
            event

⑤ Subordinate   event
   to an object   The man caught ——> an ... fish
                  (identification) angel .
                  (description) that weighed
                                100 pounds

⑥ Parallel
   discussion / Narrative ⌈ The boy went into the small for
   (series)   ⊢ He bought Greek cacls   (parall
                        ⌊ He returned to his little home

            (event)

- Behavioral statements

- Sequence / events or circumstances

- Universal commands or to
   individual leading.

- Which is the purpose of the writing in this book?
- What question is the writer discussing in this immediate section?

Part One

"LOOK AT WHAT GOD IS SAYING . . ."

Movement
~~Movement~~ — details + implications, consequences
seeing what is there)
ask questions about the observation) = What is it about?
answer interprete questions)
apply)

Movement — a journey (a progression./
   becoming comfortable in your
   own skin) — the way the
   kingdom opperates.

Mystery — Parallels and layers

1. People, places, Time, topic (relationship with previous paragraph)

a. To carry forward the previous Thought? To set for another step in a series.

b. To progressively provide additional details?

c. To compare, contrast, oppose, refute, or parallel thought?

d. To illustrate, explain, or virtually repeat a previous thought in more specific terms.

e. To emphasize, offer an alternative to what was previously said, or to offer a choice?

f. From cause to effect, to develop the authors purpose or reason for writing.

g. To further describe what was previously said by pointing out 'what kind? 'Which one?' 'where?' 'when?' 'in what matter?' 'To which extent?' 'Under what condition?' 'Why?'

h. To rename, redefine, or eq-uate something else with what was previously said.

RIDER

R - Read the sentence

I - Make an image or picture in your mind

D - Describe how the new image is different from the last sentence. * relationship with previous paragraph ↑

E - Evaluate the image & make sure it contains everything necessary.

R - Repeat the steps & RIDE as you read the next sentence.

Reinforcement idea, contrast idea, concession (relationship with previous paragraph)

— Dependent words: after, although, as, as soon as, because, before, if, since, unless, until, whenever, wherever, while, because.

— How, what, when, where, which, who, whom, whose, why

Relative Pronouns: who, which, that

THE REAL POINT OF THE PASSAGE

Study the Passage

Read with fresh eyes

KWL
- *What they know*
- *Want to know*
- *Learned and still want to learn*

Sections

THE FIRST STEP IN PREPARING a biblical message is to study the passage. This large step breaks down into several stages: *Where does the passage begin, and where does it end?*

(1) • Read the surrounding context for an overview. *(Overview)*
(2) • Flag the things you don't fully understand. *(Details)*
(3) • Use your skills and resources in the original languages. *(Arcing)*
(4) • Consult good commentaries. *background content*

READ THE SURROUNDING CONTEXT FOR AN OVERVIEW

What does the passage say?

First, read your specific passage and its surrounding context in several different translations in order to get the author's broad flow of thought. Determine how your unit fits into his unfolding sequence of ideas. *People places Time Topics*

For example, suppose you're going to preach on James 1:5–8:

God's job / man's job

If any of you lacks wisdom, he should ask God, who gives generously to all without finding fault, and it will be given to him. But when he asks, he must believe and not doubt, because he who doubts is like a wave of the sea, blown and tossed by the wind. That man should not think he will receive anything from the Lord; he is a double-minded man, unstable in all he does.

TOPIC

If you fail to note the flow of thought in James 1, you might be tempted to preach things very different than what James had in mind. You might find yourself applying James 1:5–8 to a variety of situations:

Moment
Movement
Mystery

Finding the premise: — a statement

- A teenager wanting to know what college he should attend
- A young woman needing to decide which suitor to encourage
- A mother wanting wisdom on dealing with a problem child
- A widow needing direction on how to handle her finances
- A husband weighing a job change

Or, you might preach James 1:19—"Everyone should be quick to listen, slow to speak and slow to become angry"—as "Advice for Parents of Teenagers" or "Guidelines for Lay Counselors" or "How to Be a Man of Discernment."

But as you read the entire chapter several times through in different translations, you realize that throughout the chapter James is talking about what you should do "whenever you face trials of many kinds" (v. 2). His flow of thought is as follows:

- You should face trials with joy and persevere through them, knowing they're producing maturity and Christlike completeness in you (vv. 2–4).
- If you lack wisdom regarding the purpose of the trial or how to persevere through it, ask God, and he'll give it to you. But you must firmly believe in his sovereignty and love in order to receive it (vv. 5–8).
- Both poor and rich ought to be able to discern the purposes and benefits that come through their trials (vv. 9–11).
- If you successfully persevere through the trial, you'll receive the crown of life (v. 12).
- But if you respond sinfully to the trial, don't blame God for pushing you too far. Your sinful failure was due to some evil in you, not because God was tempting you (vv. 13–15).
- God never pushes us toward sin. On the contrary, his every action is only and always for our good—from his initial choice to give us birth to his final welcoming of us in heaven as the highest of all his creation (vv. 16–18).
- Therefore, don't become angry with God or blame him if you respond sinfully in a trial. Instead, "be quick to listen" to the wisdom you asked for and to the "word of truth" within you. Be "slow to speak"—do not accuse God or others of causing you to sin. And

finally, be "slow to become angry, for man's anger does not bring about the righteous life that God desires." An angry, accusatory response will never bring the maturity or completeness or crown of life that God intends through the trial (vv. 19–20).

- Instead of being angry and blaming God, get rid of whatever filth or evil caused you to react sinfully in the first place, and then return to the Word of God, which is able to guide you safely through the trial (v. 21).

- When you return to the Word, however, you must obey it, and not simply listen to it. You must be a "doer" and not merely a "hearer" (vv. 22–25).

By recognizing this flow of thought through James 1, you will then be able to preach the author's true and exact meaning in verses 5 and 19.

FLAG THE THINGS YOU DON'T FULLY UNDERSTAND

Once you have a handle on the large flow of thought, you can then more thoroughly probe your specific passage, flagging things that are unclear to you: customs you don't understand, logical connections that don't make sense to you, a choice of wording that seems strange, apparent doctrinal difficulties, or anything else you need to pin down more precisely. In other words, you're asking the questions that your subsequent study must answer before you can truly preach the meaning of the original author.

For example, in James 1:5–8 you might flag the following:

- Why does James assure me that God "won't find fault"? I wouldn't have thought that he would. If I'm praying and asking God for wisdom, I would think he'd be pleased. Why does James think I would be worried that God will find fault?

- When I ask God for wisdom, I must "believe." Believe what? That God will give me wisdom? If I didn't believe he would give me wisdom, I probably wouldn't be asking him for it in the first place, would I? What must I believe? What should I not doubt?

- What does it mean to be "double-minded"? What are the two minds, or contrasting thoughts, that could be present?

As another example, suppose you're preparing a message on 1 Corinthians 4:1–5:

> So then, men ought to regard us as servants of Christ and as those entrusted with the secret things of God. Now it is required that those who have been given a trust must prove faithful. I care very little if I am judged by you or by any human court; indeed, I do not even judge myself. My conscience is clear, but that does not make me innocent. It is the Lord who judges me. Therefore judge nothing before the appointed time; wait till the Lord comes. He will bring to light what is hidden in darkness and will expose the motives of men's hearts. At that time each will receive his praise from God.

From reading the preceding context (chap. 3), you observe that Paul is rebuking the Corinthians for their unworthy and unfounded infatuations with certain ministers. Then, in the passage you're going to preach on (4:1–5), he tells them how ministers should be regarded instead.

With this surrounding context in mind, you now probe the verses, noting things you don't fully understand, things you will need to get a handle on through your study before you can preach the passage accurately. You might flag the following:

- What are the "secret things of God"? Why would God have secrets? Other translations talk about the "mysteries of God." Has God written whodunits? What are these mysteries, or secrets, and why would God have them?
- The NIV describes ministers as ones who are "entrusted" with something; the NASB calls them "stewards." What does it mean to be "entrusted"? We have been given "a trust," but what is it? What was a steward in that culture? Was it the same as in our culture—for example, an airplane hostess or a dispenser of wine on a ship? Or was it something different?
- There seems to be a slight adversarial relationship between Paul and his readers. Why is that? What in their previous history might have caused that?
- Paul says he cares "very little" about their opinion of him. What

does this do to our contemporary emphasis on small group accountability? It seems like Paul considers himself unaccountable.

- Paul says he doesn't even judge himself. Aren't we supposed to examine our lives to see if we're living worthy of the Lord? Doesn't Paul himself say a few chapters later that "a man ought to examine himself" before he participates in the Lord's Supper (1 Cor. 11:28)? Is he being inconsistent?
- If, as Paul says, "my conscience is clear, but that does not make me innocent," then what hope do I ever have of pleasing the Lord?
- Are we really to "judge nothing"? Don't other verses assume some judgment or discernment on our part that properly leads us to rebuke a sinning brother?
- When is the "appointed time"?
- When we get to heaven, is God going to display our entire lives through some cosmic video, revealing every secret sin and hidden thought for all of heaven to see? If not (and we hope not!), then what does it mean that "he will bring to light what is hidden in darkness and will expose the motives of men's hearts"?

The goal of your subsequent study is to get clear answers to these questions, so that when you speak, your message will confidently and accurately present what God is saying.

USE YOUR SKILLS AND RESOURCES IN THE ORIGINAL LANGUAGES

Once you have the larger flow of thought and have flagged specific things you don't fully understand, you're ready to begin an in-depth study of your passage, hopefully starting with the languages in which the original authors wrote.

Our abilities in the original languages differ, but to the extent that you are able, work your way through the passage in Greek or Hebrew, noting vocabulary, word order, structural connectors, and organizational designs (e.g., chiasmus, inclusio, parallelism).[1] Use whatever computer programs or language aids might help you.

Moving slowly through the material in Hebrew or Greek pays off in

---

1. See pages 70n. 5, 131n. 5, 140–41, 161–63, 182–91, and 247 for explanations and examples of these organizational designs.

Content words carry the meaning in a sentence, and functional words join phrases and sentences

many ways. First, by going slowly and saturating yourself in the text, you build the fire or passion you will eventually want when you preach. You begin to feel the power of the Word. It starts to seep into your soul.[2]

Second, looking up the original vocabulary in the lexicons gives you nuances of meaning that cannot be brought out in the single word or phrase of the English translation.

Third, the original languages contain aids to interpretation that may not be apparent in the English, such as word order to indicate emphasis, or syntactical observations to reveal the organization of thought (e.g., if participles are subordinate to an imperative in the Greek, they indicate the time, manner, means, cause, condition, concession, purpose, or result that attaches to the command being given).

Fourth, the original languages sometimes reveal an ambiguity that the English translators have interpretively resolved (e.g., whether the genitive is objective or subjective). While their resolution might be helpful and accurate, it might also reflect a doctrinal bias or at least an interpretative viewpoint that should be held tentatively until further study is done.

Finally, having the original languages in mind will prepare you to read the commentaries more intelligently and profitably. Your familiarity with the original words or phrases will enable you to immediately understand the points the commentators are making and prepare you for how they play off each other in their various viewpoints.

The three stages so far—reading the surrounding context, flagging what you don't understand, and going through it in the original languages— might take one to two hours, depending on the length of your chosen passage. The next stage will probably add four to six hours to this.

CONSULT GOOD COMMENTARIES

Good commentaries generally are found among those produced in the last few decades. Older works, perhaps in the public domain and therefore inexpensively available, have limited value. Though perhaps written by godly men or women, many are merely random devotional observations

---

2. That may be why God commanded the king "to write for himself on a scroll a copy of this law" (Deut. 17:18). The king wasn't just to read someone else's copy; he had to personally and slowly write one out in longhand for himself—a process that would deeply embed the content in his soul.

without a grasp of the author's true meaning or flow of thought. Others, though written by competent scholars, are dated and lack the benefit of recent cultural, archeological, and grammatical studies.

We're all indebted to scholars who have spent their lives understanding the biblical languages and cultures. As we read and compare their insights, the biblical author's flow of thought begins to take definite shape, and our own understanding of the passage crystallizes further.

Good commentaries tend to fall in one of three categories. The first category is what we might call an expositional, or synthesis, commentary. This type of commentary, often an inexpensive paperback, is written for the intelligent English reader. Its goal is to present the flow of thought of the biblical writer, with some attention to individual words and phrases. This kind of commentary is often a good place to start, since it will quickly give you the large units of thought and the lines of argument of the text.

The second category is what we might call an exegetical, or critical, commentary. Usually in more expensive hardback, this type of commentary is the most detailed and scholarly. It focuses on words, phrases, and intricate issues of grammar and syntax and presents long discussions of culture and background. It has the best chance of resolving the study questions you flagged earlier.

The third category is the sermonic, or homiletic, commentary, which is usually a series of sermons that were first preached to a local congregation and then put into print for a wider audience. The value of this type of commentary is that it might spark applications, titles, special phrasings, or even a creative approach to the message.

Study thoroughly in the first two categories before you read the third. If you start with sermonic commentaries, you may be tempted to prematurely conclude, "That'll preach!" without first determining whether the printed sermon accurately reflects the meaning of the biblical author. Instead, start with the commentaries that have no homiletical ax to grind. Become emotionally wedded to the concepts and flow of the biblical author, and then you'll be more properly selective in how you benefit from someone else's sermon.

A wise preacher will budget money to buy these books. Just as the mechanic has to invest in the latest tools to diagnose complex engines, so you must have the best and latest books to keep up with advances in biblical knowledge and to stimulate your mind.

Stay abreast with what's being published. Two excellent resources are the *Journal of the Evangelical Theological Society*[3] and *Bibliotheca Sacra*.[4] These two journals not only have consistently helpful articles on biblical passages and topics, but also valuable book reviews of the latest commentaries. Published quarterly, their yearly cost is about the price of a nice restaurant meal.

Other resources for commentary recommendations might be a booklist put out by the professors of a seminary, or a published work by a respected scholar evaluating recent works, or a book exclusively focused on how to build an evangelical theological library.[5]

To really stay on the cutting edge of New Testament and Old Testament studies, subscribe to *Old Testament Abstracts* and *New Testament Abstracts*.[6] Modestly priced, these abstracts summarize almost every recent article pertaining to biblical studies that have appeared in hundreds of journals around the world and are an excellent way to stay current with emerging scholarship.

Your first and most essential step is to thoroughly study the passage. Spend the hours reading, taking notes, and learning all you can, so that you can say substantively, accurately, and confidently, "Look at what God is saying."

---

3. *Journal of the Evangelical Theological Society,* 200 Russell Woods Drive, Lynchburg, VA 24502-3574.

4. *Bibliotheca Sacra,* 3909 Swiss Avenue, Dallas, TX 75204.

5. For helpful guidance, see John Glynn, *Commentary and Reference Survey: A Comprehensive Guide to Biblical and Theological Resources* (Grand Rapids: Kregel, 2007).

6. *Old Testament Abstracts* and *New Testament Abstracts,* published three times a year by the Catholic University of America, 433 Caldwell Hall, Washington, DC 20064.

1. what the question?
2. whats the problem?
3. whats wrong with this picture?

–2–

– Outline the Flow –

observation · The Plot tells us what happens – Passage
interpretation · The theme tells us why it happens – Truth

AS YOU THOROUGHLY STUDY the passage—reading it several times, flagging the difficult parts, working through it in the original language, and consulting good commentaries and journals—the author's flow of thought begins to take shape in your mind. Now it's time to put this flow into outline form. The goal is to identify the writer's "big hunk" ideas and his smaller supporting concepts. In succinct fashion, you want to articulate his large umbrella thoughts—what they are and how they unfold—and his internal explanatory details. *(what is the secondary idea telling me about the main idea?)*

VIP
verbal
indirect
preposition

passage
as

Your outline form will eventually progress through three stages—from an outline of the biblical *passage*, to an outline of the timeless *truth*, to an outline of the final *sermon*.

In this chapter, we'll define these three stages and then give an example of how a specific Scripture passage moves through the three stages. In the next chapter, we'll explore the first two stages in detail. We'll save the third stage for a later chapter.

problem that has – what is the main problem?
some the occasion of – what caused the problem?
the author to write
forcing the book

THE THREE OUTLINE STAGES

WHAT? The steps and details the passage
The Passage Outline *takes to get its message across.* ①

You will start with an outline of the biblical passage. In simplest terms, the passage outline tells what happened in time past—"this occurred" or "so-and-so said this."

I. (Complication)

[handwritten top margin: observation of What does the passage say? / what the author writes about Gods people ... at that time — Extent — location — Manner — Cause — Contingency — Accompani / cause meaning by which / Time when / Manner in — Rav which / reason why / result of]

PASSAGE OUTLINE
"happened"

[handwritten: = Biblical Authors outline]

OBSERVATIONS

[handwritten left margin: Main Idea — Background — Reason Written — time when — manner in which — reason why — means by which — cause of]

This passage outline is essentially the outline the original author might have used as he wrote to his original readers. It's what he might have jotted down to guide his thoughts as he penned his original manuscript.

The language or phrasing of this outline reflects the particulars of the biblical world—names, places, events, and cultural practices:

[handwritten: Specific to that Time + observation]

- The reason God did not take Israel on a direct route from Egypt to Canaan was because he knew they would face war on that route and turn back (Exod. 13:17). *[handwritten: Reason why]*
- The time when Jacob had his dream of the staircase between heaven and earth was his last night in the Promised Land, when he was fleeing Esau's anger and fearing that he had lost the promised blessing forever (Gen. 28:10–22).

[handwritten: Who, What, When, Where, Why - Purpose/Reason, How - means/manner / Circumstances]

The passage outline, sometimes called an exegetical or textual outline, often states the points with grammatical precision (e.g., time when, manner in which, reason why, result of, means by which, cause of) and reveals the logical connections between them.

The Truth Outline

[handwritten: WHY? Why did the author write this? Why are you telling me this? Theme tells us why it happens.]

As your preparation progresses, you will change your passage outline into a timeless truth outline. The truth outline tells what happens—"these are the kinds of experiences people have; this is how God deals with us; this is what God reveals about himself." *[handwritten: Process]*

In the truth outline, the historical statements of the passage outline are turned into timeless statements that convey the eternal truths being revealed through the biblical material. The concepts are phrased more generally, more universally, so as to span time.[1]

[handwritten: II (Extrapolation) about God]

---

1. This movement from history to theology is essentially an interpretive step. Your careful study of the passage with the help of good commentaries, and your accurate passage outline, will usually enable you to take this step without difficulty. The process, however, must be

[handwritten bottom: Material = doing / Mental = sensing / Relational = Attributing   Processes = undergoing / Beneficiary = recipient]

Theme: why it happens..
why the author writes
about God... *why is it important?*

what the passage
meant for the Biblical
website... Plot:
what happens...

= Timeless

TRUTH OUTLINE *= God's lessons for humanity*
"happens"

Extrapolation
(The underlying
principle the author
is giving to the
original audience.)

Connect truth
with the
background.

PASSAGE OUTLINE
"happened"

Complication

If the passage outline is *historical,* the truth outline is *theological.* The language or wording of this outline could be spoken to any audience, in any century, in any place. The earlier "passage" sentences might now be phrased as: *Universal truths: Purpose, reason, result, means, manner. (what is the secondary RW when telling me about the NT for us...)*

- The reason God sometimes does not take us on a direct route to his good plans for us is because he knows there is some obstacle on that route that would keep us from reaching the goal (Exod. 13:17).
- When we fear we have forever blown God's plan for our lives, God often comes to us with a reassuring message (Gen. 28:10–22).

The Sermon Outline *Pictures of Contemporary Application.*

Eventually you will shape the outline into its final sermon form. The sermon outline essentially says to the listener, "This is *happening* in our lives today, just as it *happened* in the biblical world, for this kind of thing *happens* as we walk with God."

The sermon outline shows how the truth of the biblical passage will be communicated in a contemporary way to your specific audience. It proclaims the eternal truths, shows how these truths were drawn from

III. (Application)

---

guarded by valid hermeneutical principles. For a helpful summary of these principles, see Timothy S. Warren, "The Theological Process in Sermon Preparation," *Bibliotheca Sacra* 156 (July–September 1999): 335–56.

(I) what's the question?
(II) what's the problem?
(III) what's wrong with this picture?

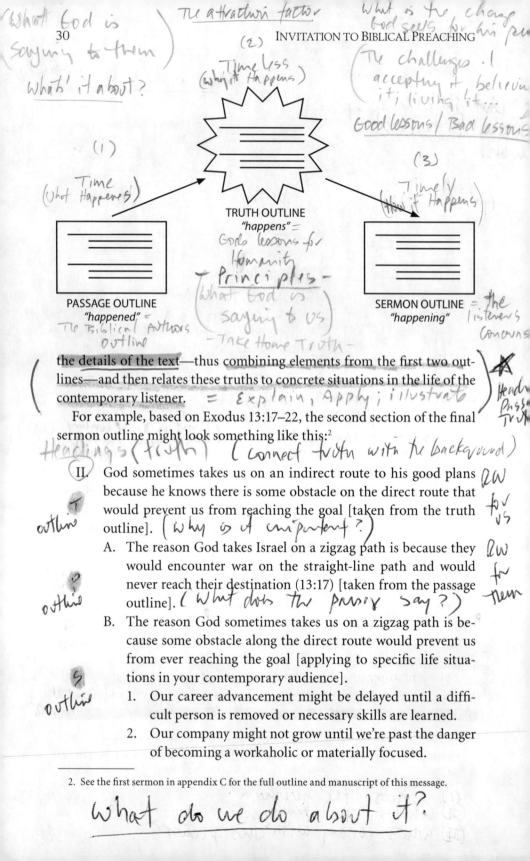

PASSAGE OUTLINE
"happened"

TRUTH OUTLINE
"happens"

SERMON OUTLINE
"happening"

the details of the text—thus combining elements from the first two outlines—and then relates these truths to concrete situations in the life of the contemporary listener.

For example, based on Exodus 13:17–22, the second section of the final sermon outline might look something like this:[2]

II. God sometimes takes us on an indirect route to his good plans because he knows there is some obstacle on the direct route that would prevent us from reaching the goal [taken from the truth outline].

A. The reason God takes Israel on a zigzag path is because they would encounter war on the straight-line path and would never reach their destination (13:17) [taken from the passage outline].

B. The reason God sometimes takes us on a zigzag path is because some obstacle along the direct route would prevent us from ever reaching the goal [applying to specific life situations in your contemporary audience].

1. Our career advancement might be delayed until a difficult person is removed or necessary skills are learned.

2. Our company might not grow until we're past the danger of becoming a workaholic or materially focused.

2. See the first sermon in appendix C for the full outline and manuscript of this message.

3. Marriage might be put off until past issues no longer threaten a stable and long-lasting relationship.
4. Ministry opportunities might wait until pride is less of a danger.

AN EXAMPLE: MARK 4:35–41

Before we examine each type of outline in detail, let's look at how a specific passage of Scripture might move through these three outline stages.

We'll use Mark 4:35–41 where the disciples, terrified that a storm is about to drown them, awaken Jesus from sleep in the back of the boat. Jesus first calms the wind and the waves, and then expresses his disappointment with the disciples because of their fear and lack of faith.

Before we develop the outline, however, let's first study the passage as suggested in the previous chapter. This involves the following four activities:

- Read the surrounding context for an overview.
- Flag the things we don't fully understand.
- Use our skills and resources in the original language.
- Consult good commentaries.

We'll start our reading of the surrounding context in Mark 3:13, where Jesus first selects these twelve men who will later find themselves in the boat with him.

Mark 3:13–19 identifies the Twelve by name and specifies the ministry Jesus intends them to have. He is sending them out to do two things: to preach the message of the kingdom and to defeat any demonic attempts to hinder its acceptance.

These twelve men then hear the significant interchange between Jesus and the religious rulers (3:20–30). The religious leaders try to explain Jesus' ability to drive out demons as being due to satanic power. Jesus shows the foolishness of such an explanation and claims instead that he's able to do his miracles because he's stronger than Satan—he has tied up Satan, who is now powerless to prevent Jesus from robbing him of the men and women who are his possessions.

The religious leaders' explanation, though foolish, nevertheless reveals their deep hostility toward Jesus and their determination to reject him as Israel's Messiah. In attributing the Spirit's work to Satan, they have passed a point of no return. They have so hardened their hearts against him that there is nothing more God can offer them.

Knowing the nation will reject him, Jesus then reveals that the kingdom will no longer be limited to those of Jewish blood but will be available to whoever does God's will (3:31–35).[3]

The parables of the next chapter then expand on this broader mission—the message of the kingdom will now be preached to Gentiles as well as Jews. Though Satan will attempt to thwart this, he won't be able to stop its inevitable, worldwide growth (4:1–34).

The Twelve, much to the dismay of Jesus, don't understand even the first of his many parables. If there's anybody who needs to grasp this most basic parable, it's them, for they are the ones who will encounter satanic opposition as they preach (4:10–15). Despite this opposition, however, they can expect overwhelming success (vv. 20, 26–29), as even the Gentiles find rest in the growing kingdom (vv. 30–32).[4]

A reading of the preceding context has thus emphasized the following:

- The twelve men in the boat have been selected to preach the message of the kingdom and to overcome any demonic opposition to its acceptance.
- Because they've been given a power greater than Satan, nothing will stop the worldwide spread of the gospel to the Gentiles.

Mark 4:35–41 then opens with a command to cross the Sea of Galilee and take the gospel to the Gentiles. The "other side" (4:35) that Jesus wants to reach turns out to be the region of the Gerasenes (5:1)—a region populated mostly by Gentiles (note the pigs!).

As we continue to read the surrounding context in chapter 5, we see Jesus again demonstrating a power greater than Satan's by delivering a man indwelt by a legion of demons (Mark 5:1–20). This Gentile man, once

---

3. In the words of John, "He came to that which was his own, but his own did not receive him. Yet to all who received him, to those who believed in his name, he gave the right to become children of God" (John 1:11–12).

4. The birds of the air perching in its shade represent Gentile nations finding protection under a sovereign's rule (Ezek. 17:22–23; 31:6; Dan. 4:12, 20–22; Zech. 2:11 LXX).

healed, wants to go back with Jesus in the boat to Jewish territory. But Jesus sends him instead to his own family and countrymen. And as the man goes through the Ten Cities (Decapolis), taking the gospel to other Gentiles, Satan is powerless to prevent the spread of the kingdom.

Having thus read the surrounding context, both before and after our primary passage, we're now ready to probe our specific verses, making observations and flagging things that aren't immediately clear to us.

We observe, first, that Mark specifically connects this event—the crossing of the sea—to the daylong teaching that had preceded it. He opens his account with the connecting words, "That day when evening came" (Mark 4:35). Mark is suggesting that Jesus wants to immediately implement the point he has been making—about launching the inevitable growth of the kingdom among the Gentiles. He wants to "go over to the other side" to extend the gospel to the Gentiles.

The Twelve immediately obey him. Jesus has been teaching from a boat to keep the people from crowding against him (cf. Mark 3:7–10; 4:1). Without delay, the disciples immediately pull up anchor, allow the boat to drift away from shore, and then head it toward the other side of the lake.

We flag a curious sentence at the end of verse 36: "There were also other boats with him." This seems odd, because we never hear of these boats again. They disappear from the account. Who was in them? What happened to them? Did they drown in the storm? Why does Mark mention them if he doesn't intend to say any more about them? We'll come back to this. Right now we simply flag it as something that is not immediately clear to us.

The account goes on to describe a furious squall that suddenly comes up. Gale winds hit the lake, driving waves of water into the boat. The Twelve bail as fast as they can, but the water comes in faster than they can throw it out. They're terrified, for the rising level means that in a few minutes the water will swamp and sink the boat, and they will die.

Jesus, fatigued by a long day of teaching, is using the two-hour crossing time to nap on an elevated deck in the back of the boat. Cushioned by a mat, and in the early minutes of a deep-sleep cycle, he appears unaffected by the storm. When the disciples awake him, however, he gets up, rebukes the wind, and commands the waves. These physical forces apparently hear him and immediately obey him.

But the word "rebuke" has caught our attention. It strikes us as a strange word to use under the circumstances. We don't usually rebuke inanimate things. I don't bump into the corner of a desk, bruising my leg, and then slap the desk in revenge, saying, "I rebuke you, desk!" Rebuke is what we do to people, not to things. So we flag the strangeness of this term.

Once the storm is calmed, Jesus turns to his disciples and expresses his disappointment with how they had reacted to the situation: "Why are you so afraid?[5] Do you still have no faith?" (Mark 4:40).

We instinctively sense that his question, "Do you still have no faith?" lies at the heart of the passage's meaning. Whatever the disciples lacked is undoubtedly what we should have, and therefore will most likely be the preaching point of the passage.

But what is this faith that they don't have? If we are too hasty in our conclusion, we might be tempted to answer, "They should have had faith that as long as Jesus was in the boat, nothing bad would happen to them." And if, from this conclusion, we preach a message along the lines of, "As long as Jesus is in the boat of your life, nothing bad will happen to you," then our listeners will undoubtedly have violent internal objections. "Pastor, I don't know what world you live in, but in my world that's simply not true!"

And they would be right. It's not true. All kinds of bad things happen to contemporary believers who have Jesus "in the boat of their life." They give birth to spina bifida babies. Their teenagers have automobile accidents and end up in wheelchairs for the rest of their lives. They get downsized from corporations at age fifty-four—too old and too expensive to be hired by another company, and too young to start drawing retirement. So we must resist our hasty conclusion and flag Jesus' question as something we don't yet fully understand.

The story closes with the Twelve thoroughly dazed and "awestruck"[6] by Jesus' power and control over these physical forces.

So far we've read the surrounding context of our passage and flagged some things that aren't totally clear to us. Along the way we've also, in a limited sense, used our skills in the original languages.

Let's finish our study of the passage, combining our abilities in the

---

5. The Greek word for "afraid" is *deilos*, a relatively rare word that has the meaning of "cowardly" or "timid." Note how the NIV gives the word this meaning in 2 Timothy 1:7 and Revelation 21:8.

6. The Greek word in Mark 4:41 is *phobos*, the normal word for "fear" or "awe," and is different from the "fear" or "timidity" of verse 40.

original language with the help of good commentaries, to clear up those matters we've flagged. Then we'll be ready to outline the flow.

Let's return to the strange use of the word "rebuke" and to the commands Jesus gives these physical forces. With the help of a Greek lexicon or concordance, or good commentaries, we learn that Mark 4:39—Jesus "rebuked the wind"—is Mark's third use of *epitimaō,* the Greek word for "rebuke."

Both of Mark's prior uses of *epitimaō* describe Jesus' rebuke of a demon. The first occurs in Mark 1:21–25a:

> They went to Capernaum, and when the Sabbath came, Jesus went into the synagogue and began to teach. The people were amazed at his teaching, because he taught them as one who had authority, not as the teachers of the law. Just then a man in their synagogue who was possessed by an evil spirit cried out, "What do you want with us, Jesus of Nazareth? Have you come to destroy us? I know who you are—the Holy One of God!" "Be quiet!" said Jesus sternly.[7]

The second occurs in Mark 3:11–12:

> Whenever the evil spirits saw him, they fell down before him and cried out, "You are the Son of God." But he gave them strict orders[8] not to tell who he was.

In fact, in Mark every instance of *epitimaō* on the lips of Jesus[9] occurs in a context of rebuking demonic activity: 1:25; 3:12; 4:39; 8:30, 32–33; 9:25.[10]

This consistency of language now helps us to understand the unusual use of *rebuke* in Mark 4:29—Jesus recognizes the storm as Satan's attempt

---

7. Literally, "Jesus rebuked (*epitimaō*) him." Similarly, Jesus' command to the demon in 1:25 to "Be quiet!" is the same Greek word (*phimoo*) he uses in 4:39 to command the wind to "Be still!" And the response of the demons (1:27) and the winds (4:41) is the same—they "obey" (*akouo*) him.

8. Literally, "he strongly rebuked (*epitimaō*) them."

9. On the lips of others in Mark, *epitimaō* does not relate to demonic activity (10:13, 48).

10. A possible exception might be Mark 8:30, but even there the close connection with 8:31–33 suggests that any attempt to prematurely reveal Jesus' messianic identity, and thus avoid the cross, would be motivated by "the things of men" rather than the will of God.

to prevent him and his disciples from reaching the other side, where the gospel will go to the Gentiles. It is not a natural storm but rather a demonic one.[11]

Perhaps another of our flags—the odd sentence, "There were also other boats with him" (v. 36)—is also a clue that this storm was unnatural, demonic. Perhaps Mark briefly notes these other boats and then dispenses with them, because his sole intent is simply to convey that other experienced sailors interpreted the appearance of the sky and determined that it was fair weather for sailing (cf. Matt. 16:2–3).[12] Men whose lives depended on their ability to predict a storm saw no concern for sailing that day.

Understanding the storm as demonically empowered makes the disciples' reaction of dazed awe even more understandable. To the Hebrew people, the sea was a fearful, chaotic place, controlled by evil forces (variously symbolized as sea monsters, Leviathan [Ps. 74], or Rahab [Ps. 89]). God's ability to subdue these forces was proof of his sovereign rule.[13] As Jesus demonstrates a similar divine power over the forces of evil that are attacking through the physical elements, the disciples are filled with awe as they see new dimensions of his identity.

(Let's summarize our study of the passage to this point: These twelve men in the boat have been selected to preach the message of the kingdom and have been given the power to overcome any satanic opposition to that preaching. They have the ability to "tie up the strong man" and render him impotent. Though Satan will attempt to prevent their preaching to Gentiles in particular, he will not be able to stop the worldwide growth of the kingdom. Jesus commands them to cross the lake for the purpose of preaching in Gentile territory. A storm comes up out of nowhere, threatening to destroy them and their mission. And they respond with fear and dismay.

(We are now ready to consider the key interpretative questions of the passage: "Why are you so afraid? Do you still have no faith?" (Mark 4:40b).

In light of Mark's flow through these chapters, here's what Jesus is saying:

---

11. Job 1:18–20 is another instance of Satan attempting to thwart the purposes of God through a storm.

12. We have a similar ditty in English: "Red skies at night, sailor's delight. Red skies in the morning, sailors take warning."

13. Cf. Job 26:12–13; Psalms 65:7; 74:13–14; 89:8–10; 93:3–4; 107:29–30; Isaiah 27:1; 51:9–10.

"Do you still not grasp what I've been teaching you? Do you still not believe what I've been saying to you—that you have the power to overcome Satan's opposition? You should have recognized this attack for what it was—demonic. I told you it would happen. And I told you that you have the ability to deal with it. Why are you so cowardly, so timid? Do you still not comprehend the power I've given you? Why did you wake me? You should have handled it yourself."

Instead of despairing because of this life-threatening storm, the disciples should have seen it as Satan's attempt to prevent them from accomplishing God's good purpose. They should have had the faith to resist this attack.[14] They should have trusted God's power to carry out the command Jesus had given them—to get to the other side and take the kingdom of God to the Gentiles.

Having thus studied the passage, let's outline the flow. Let's see how a sermon might move through the three outline stages.

The Passage Outline

The passage outline reflects the biblical text—in language and structure. It tells what *happened*:

I. The disciples obey Jesus and find themselves in a life-threatening storm that fills them with despair (4:35–38).

    A. The disciples obey Jesus' command to cross the lake into Gentile territory (4:35–36).

        1. After a day of teaching on the growth of the kingdom, Jesus commands his disciples to cross the lake.

        2. They obey immediately, not going ashore for anything.

        3. The presence of other boats indicates it was a good day for sailing.

    B. As a result of their obedience, the disciples find themselves in an unexpected, life-threatening storm (4:37).

    C. The disciples are filled with fear and despair (4:38).

14. Cf. James 4:7: "Resist the devil, and he will flee from you."

What = Propositions

Why
Headings
Passage = why
How

II. Jesus rebukes the storm and encourages the disciples to trust God's power (4:39–41).

   A. Jesus rebukes the demonically inspired storm, and the lake becomes calm (4:39).

   B. Jesus encourages the disciples to have more trust in their God-given power over Satan's opposition (4:40–41).

Headings   *Grammar*

Note that the material is gathered and stated in big "hunks," or "movements" (i.e., the Roman numerals) that represent the essential flow of the passage. The listeners are not presented with numerous small observations to remember but instead hear a limited number of "large strokes" that take them through the passage.

Why? Re Extrapolation Outline Realities
vs... Interpretation — about God!

The Truth Outline

The truth outline puts the statements of the passage outline into timeless language. This is the theology the author is trying to communicate. This is the eternal truth God was revealing when he inspired the Scripture. This is how God deals with his people. This is what *happens*.

God! Time!/
Why are you telling me this: kinds of experiences people have, how God deals with us,

I. Sometimes we obey God and find ourselves in a difficult situation that fills us with despair.

   A. We obey a command God gives us.

   B. As a result of obeying, we find ourselves in a difficult situation.

   C. The situation fills us with fear and despair.

The answer to the problem the author is trying to convey...

what God reveals about himself

II. When this happens, we should resist Satan's efforts and trust God's power.

   A. We should resist Satan's efforts to prevent us from carrying out God's purposes.

   B. We should trust God's power to enable us to accomplish whatever he has commanded.

The Sermon Outline

How?   *Application Outline*

Though the sermon outline emerges much later in the process of preparation, after the speaker has given thought to interesting and relevant ways of presenting the biblical truth (e.g., an engaging introduction, real-

God is saying something today...
— Pictures of contemporary application.

[handwritten: Organizing = Preaching, explain, Apply; illustr]

life applications, effective wording), we'll include it here for the sake of completeness.

The sermon outline may indent or symbolize a bit differently than the passage or truth outline. It may slightly change the author's structure (but never his meaning!).[15] For example, in the truth outline on page 38, point II reflects the theological interpretation that the storm is demonically inspired. In the sermon outline below, this interpretation is lifted out and made a separate Roman numeral for the sake of focus and clarity.

A sermon outline on Mark 4:35–41 might be as follows:

[handwritten: Organized for clarity]

Introduction

1. Sometimes we obey God, and the bottom falls out of everything.
   a. Example/application
   b. Example/application
2. We despair, and wonder, "God, why is this happening, and what do you want me to do?"
3. Today we'll see the disciples in a similar situation and learn why such things happen and what our response should be.
4. Please turn to Mark 4:35–41.

---

15. For example, the author may have two major points:
   I. Here is the problem we have (vv. 1–3). *[handwritten: Explanation]*
   II. Here is how God wants us to solve it (vv. 4–7). *[handwritten: Application]*

   However, the sermon outline could conceivably have three points:
   I. Here is the problem we have (vv. 1–3). *[handwritten: Explanation]*
   II. Here is how our culture attempts to solve it. *[handwritten: illustration]*
   III. Here is how God wants us to solve it (vv. 4–7). *[handwritten: Application]*

   Someone else may prefer the outline to look like:
   I. Here is the problem we have (vv. 1–3). *[handwritten: Explanation]*
   II. Here is how God wants us to solve it. *[handwritten: Application]*
      A. Not like our culture attempts to solve it. *[handwritten: a.]*
      B. But in the way God specifies (vv. 4–7). *[handwritten: b.]*

In this example, it doesn't make any difference which way it shows up on the outline, since an aural listener would track it the same both ways.

There are other times, however, when a modification of the author's structure may be essential for oral clarity. We'll give examples of this when we talk about the author's thought order (pp. 56–64) and preaching chiastic passages (pp. 185–91).

[handwritten: 10a] *[handwritten: Rewritten for clarity]*

[handwritten: What — Deductive statement]

I.   The disciples obey Jesus and *find themselves* in a life-threatening storm that fills them with despair (4:35–38).

[handwritten: Why — Deductive statement] *[handwritten: what?]*

II. The reason such things happen may be that Satan is attempting to prevent God's purposes.

[handwritten: why?]

A.   The storm is Satan's attempt to prevent the growth of the kingdom.

1.   Jesus has been teaching that his kingdom will grow large and include Gentiles, due to his disciples' preaching and their ability to handle demonic opposition (3:13–4:34).

[handwritten: Explain]

2.   They are now crossing to Gentile territory, where Jesus will rescue a man from Satan's kingdom and send him as a witness to Gentiles (5:1–20).

3.   The storm is a demonic attempt to prevent the growth of the kingdom.

a.   Whenever Mark records Jesus rebuking, it's always of demonic activity.

b.   The command to the wind to "Be still" is the same command given to the demons in Mark 1.

[handwritten: How S]

B.   Our difficulties may be Satan's attempt to prevent what God wants to do through us.

[handwritten: Apply] *[handwritten: illustrate]*

1.   Example/application

2.   Example/application

[handwritten: How — Deductive statement] *[handwritten: Explain]*

[handwritten: what?]

III. We should resist Satan's efforts and trust God's power.

[handwritten: Why P]

A.   Jesus rebukes the demonic activity behind the storm and encourages the disciples to trust God's power (4:39–41).

[handwritten: How S]

B.   We should resist Satan's efforts and trust God's power.

1.   Example/application

[handwritten: Apply / illustrate] *[handwritten: Engage!]*

2.   Example/application

[handwritten: 10b]

Note that the sermon outline usually begins with the listeners, rather than with the text. The introduction probes the contemporary experiences of the audience and gives them a reason to listen to the sermon. Since the passage for the day will be God's Word to them, start with their need for the message.

Note also that in this particular message, the same examples or situ-

[handwritten: Talking points]

I. What
II. Why
III. How

Main point + Explain, Apply, illustrate.

ations used in the introduction would emerge again in points II and III. Each example would be extended or enlarged as the message progressed— the introduction would describe contemporary situations where "obedience leads to disaster"; point II would return to these same explanations and explain them as "due to Satan's opposition"; and point III would then show "how to resist Satan" in them. We'll talk more about how to structure such relevancy in chapter 9.

Now that we've defined and given an example of all three outline stages, let's look more specifically at the first two stages—passage and truth—and talk particularly about how we go from the first to the second.

The Meaning is the message

outlining: the goal is to communicate the ideas in a text and to point out the controlling thought or "big idea"

Whats the question?

(I.) the first point states the idea I want to communicate (but I don't want to state it directly when I begin developing the idea. The idea is/will emerge by the time one's done developing the section.

inductive?

What's the problem? (II.) the second major point is a statement of the sermon's "big idea" state and restate

whats wrong with this picture? (III.)

(if a sentence does not begin with the subject, it may open with an introductory element that tells, when, where, how or why the many actions of the sentence occurs.) = Adverbial Phrase

— the subject of the sentence tells which person, place thing, idea sentence is about.

THE REASON I'M TELLING YOU THIS IS...

Move from History to Timeless Truth

3-

Context
Clarity
Content

— the Eternal truth

IN THIS CHAPTER WE'LL TALK in more detail about two things:

- How to develop an accurate passage outline
- How to move from the history of this passage outline to the theology of the truth outline

observation (statement)

DEVELOPING THE PASSAGE OUTLINE

RW - Background

The benefit of the passage outline is that it anchors the speaker to the text and thus to the intent of the original inspired author. It commits the eventual sermon to the basic content and structure of "what God is saying."

The goal of the passage outline is to identify the author's "big hunk" ideas and to show how they progressively unfold through the passage. The biblical information must be grouped into large units—into umbrella thoughts that cover smaller, supporting details. The sermon must not be a string of unrelated explanations through the verses but instead must show the overall unity and progression of the passage. *(Not preach but chain (in*

Specific to that time (Observations)

1 Corinthians 4:1–5

Let's return to 1 Corinthians 4:1–5 to see how our previous study of the passage[1] would progress to a passage outline:

---

1. See pages 22–23.

42

Context - RW Background
Clarity -
Content - Author's Thought

A

...ught to regard us as servants of Christ and as those
...the secret things of God. Now it is required that
...e been given a trust must prove faithful. I care very
...dged by you or by any human court; indeed, I do not
...self. My conscience is clear, but that does not make
...t is the Lord who judges me. Therefore judge nothing
...ointed time; wait till the Lord comes. He will bring
...s hidden in darkness and will expose the motives of
...At that time each will receive his praise from God.

In chapter 1, we flagged numerous things in these verses that weren't
immediately clear to us. We asked such questions as:

- What are the "secret things of God"? Why would God have secrets? Other translations talk about the "mysteries of God." Has
  God written whodunits? What are these mysteries or secrets, and
  why would God have them?

- The NIV describes ministers as ones who are "entrusted" with
  something; the NASB calls them "stewards." What was a steward in
  that culture? Was it the same as in our culture—for example, an
  airplane hostess or a dispenser of wine on a ship? Or was it something different?

- What does it mean to be "entrusted"? We have been given a "trust,"
  but what is it?

- There seems to be a slight adversarial relationship between Paul
  and his readers. Why is that? What in their previous history might
  have caused that?

- Paul says he cares "very little" about their opinion of him. What
  does this do to our contemporary emphasis on small group accountability? It seems like Paul considers himself unaccountable.

- Paul says he doesn't even judge himself. Aren't we supposed to examine our lives to see if we're living worthy of the Lord? Doesn't
  Paul himself say a few chapters later that "a man ought to examine
  himself" before he participates in the Lord's Supper (1 Cor. 11:28)?
  Is he being inconsistent?

- If, as Paul says, "my conscience is clear, but that does not make me
  innocent," then what hope do I ever have of pleasing the Lord?

- Are we really to "judge nothing"? Don't other verses assume some judgment or discernment on our part that properly leads us to rebuke a sinning brother?
- When is the "appointed time"?
- When we get to heaven, is God going to display our entire lives through some cosmic video, revealing every secret sin and hidden thought for all of heaven to see? If not (and we hope not!), then what does it mean that "he will bring to light what is hidden in darkness and will expose the motives of men's hearts"?

As we learn the answers to these questions, we must be careful not to let these answers become the main points of our outline. This would result in a string of unrelated explanations through the verses:

- The secret things of God are . . .
- In their culture a steward was . . .
- The trust Paul was entrusted with was . . .
- To be faithful means . . .
- When Paul says "I do not judge myself," what he means is . . .
- The reason we can have a clear conscience and yet still not be innocent is because . . .
- The appointed time is . . .

While all of these bits of information will eventually show up in the final sermon, they must be subordinated to the author's "big hunk" ideas and to his unfolding sequence of the thought. The Roman numerals of the outline need to reflect the large movements of the passage.

In 1 Corinthians 4:1–5, it's apparent that Paul's large movements of thought are the following:

- Here's who we are: "So then, men ought to regard us as servants of Christ and as those entrusted with the secret things of God" (v. 1).
- Here's what's required of us: "Now it is required that those who have been given a trust must prove faithful" (v. 2).
- Here's who determines if we meet the requirements: "I care very little if I am judged by you or by any human court; indeed, I do not

even judge myself. My conscience is clear, but that does not make
me innocent. It is the Lord who judges me" (vv. 3–4).

Therefore, here's what you need to do: "Therefore judge nothing
before the appointed time; wait till the Lord comes. He will bring
to light what is hidden in darkness and will expose the motives of
men's hearts. At that time each will receive his praise from God"
(v. 5).

In outline form, this flow of thought would result in the following "big
hunk" points:

I. The Corinthians ought to view Paul and their other teachers as
servants who have been entrusted by Christ, their Master, with
secret things.

II. The requirement for Paul and the other teachers is to be faithful
to their Master and to the trust he's given them.

III. The Lord's evaluation of Paul's faithfulness is the only one that
counts.

IV. The Corinthians, therefore, should stop prematurely evaluating
their teachers and instead wait for the time of the Lord's evaluation and praise.

In point III above, notice how the data of verses 3–4 have been gathered
and stated. Though the phrase, "It is the Lord who judges me," occurs at
the end of the material, it is nevertheless the larger umbrella point of the
two verses, and therefore becomes the "big hunk" statement.

Once you've determined the passage's large concepts and shown the
overall unity and progression of the message, you can then insert the
appropriate subordinate concepts. The full passage outline might look
something like this:

I. The Corinthians ought to view Paul and their other teachers as
servants who have been entrusted by Christ, their Master, with
secret things.

[Handwritten marginal and interlinear annotations:]
study points:
observations — plot tells us what happens — plot summary points = study points
(what happened?)
Content — Author's thoughts
telling point
tueling point
stearing point
tueling core
I. What! (Here's who we are) (Here's who we are)
II. What! (Here's what's required of us)
III. why! (Here's who determines if we met the requirement)
IV. (therefore) The steps and details the passage takes to get its point across...
How!
A to flagged issues
Content — What
Author's support
The steps and details the passage takes to get its point across...

A. The Corinthians ought to change how they've been viewing
    Paul and their other teachers.
B. Paul and the other teachers are servants of Christ who have
    been entrusted with secret things.
    1. A servant/steward is one who . . .
    2. To be entrusted means . . .
    3. The secret things are . . .

> flagged items

What .. II. The requirement for Paul and the other teachers is to be faithful
        to their Master and to the trust he's given them.
        A. The way they show their faithfulness is by . . .
        B. The reason faithfulness is chosen as the requirement and not
            something else is because . . .

> Flagged items

Why III. The Lord's evaluation of Paul's faithfulness is the only one that
        counts.
        A. The Corinthians' evaluation matters very little to Paul.
        B. The evaluation of any other human group has little value.
        C. Paul doesn't even attach much weight to his own self-
            evaluation.
            1. As far as he knows, he has served faithfully and has a clear
                conscience.
            2. But his self-perception may be deceived; he may not be as
                innocent as he presumes.
        D. The only evaluation that really matters is the Lord's.
            1. The Lord is the only one who has sufficient information
                to evaluate.
            2. The Lord is the only one who has the right to evaluate.

How IV. The Corinthians, therefore, should stop prematurely evaluating
        their teachers and instead wait for the time of the Lord's evalua-
        tion and praise.
        A. The Corinthians should stop prematurely evaluating their
            teachers.
        B. They should wait for the appointed time of evaluation.
            1. This time has been appointed by . . .
            2. This appointed time will occur when . . .

> Flagged items

    C. At this time, the Lord's evaluation will bring unknown factors to light.

    D. The result will be praise for each of the teachers.

Exodus 13:17–22

Let's look at another example of how a study of the passage progresses to a passage outline. Since our previous example was from a New Testament epistle, this time we'll take a narrative passage from the Old Testament: Exodus 13:17–22.[2]

In the chapters preceding Exodus 13, the ten plagues have decimated Egypt. The death of the firstborn has caused mourning throughout the land. Pharaoh capitulates (Exod. 12:31–32), and about two million Israelites prepare to leave Goshen where they've been slaves for hundreds of years (vv. 37–42).

There's no question that their destination is Canaan, the Promised Land, the home of their ancestors. They can reach this destination in eight to ten days by following the trade route that runs from Goshen to Canaan—a direct, straight northeasterly route that hugs the Mediterranean coast before it cuts through Philistine territory into Canaan.

But according to Exodus 13:17–18, God does not lead them along this straight route, even though it's shorter and quicker. Instead, God leads the people in the opposite direction, toward the southern desert and the Red Sea:

> When Pharaoh let the people go, God did not lead them on the road through the Philistine country, though that was shorter. For God said, "If they face war, they might change their minds and return to Egypt." So God led the people around by the desert road toward the Red Sea. The Israelites went up out of Egypt armed for battle.

The text gives a reason for this circuitous route: if God took them on the straight path, they would never make it to their destination—they would face some military threat that would cause them to change their minds and return to Egypt.[3]

---

2. See the first sermon in appendix C for the full outline and manuscript of this message.

3. The military threat would come either from the warlike Philistines or from Egyptian forces stationed along the route since this trade route was also the invasion corridor used by northeastern empires (i.e., Syria, Assyria, Babylon) to attack Egypt.

The passage then notes two particular features of this roundabout march to the south—a coffin containing the bones of Joseph (13:19) and a cloud capable of guiding them by day or night as they begin the uncharted journey ahead (vv. 20–22):

> Moses took the bones of Joseph with him because Joseph had made the sons of Israel swear an oath. He had said, "God will surely come to your aid, and then you must carry my bones up with you from this place." After leaving Succoth they camped at Etham on the edge of the desert. By day the LORD went ahead of them in a pillar of cloud to guide them on their way and by night in a pillar of fire to give them light, so that they could travel by day or night. Neither the pillar of cloud by day nor the pillar of fire by night left its place in front of the people.

The coffin contains the bones of their ancestor Joseph. Hundreds of years earlier Joseph, anticipating their exodus from Egypt, had made Israel swear they would take his bones with them and rebury him in the Promised Land (Gen. 50:24–26). As the coffin is lifted each day and carried by strong men, it visibly reminds Israel that though they are heading in the opposite direction, their ultimate destination is Canaan.

The cloud, which comes into their national existence at this unique moment and remains until their travels are complete (Exod. 40:36–38), becomes their guide through the uncharted desert. Later Scriptures will tell us that this cloud also protects them from Pharaoh's chariots (Exod. 14:19–20) and from the desert heat (Ps. 105:39; cf. Isa. 4:5–6) and serves as the visible presence of God in their midst (Exod. 19:16–19; 33:7–10; Num. 12:5; Ps. 99:6–7). A passage outline of Exodus 13:17–22 would represent these concepts and flow somewhat as follows:

I. God purposefully takes Israel from Goshen to Canaan by an indirect route (13:17–18).

    A. When Pharaoh let the people go, they gathered in Goshen, where they had been slaves for four hundred years.

    B. From Goshen, Israel could reach the Promised Land in eight to ten days by means of a direct trade route that went from Goshen through Philistia.

C. But instead of taking them on this direct route, God purposefully leads them in the opposite direction, toward the Red Sea.

II. The reason for God's indirect leading is that Israel would encounter war on the straight-line path and would never reach their destination (13:17).

A. The war might come from Egyptian defenses along the trade route or from the Philistines as they went through their territory.

B. God knows that his people, facing war without military skills or national identity, would return to Egypt instead of continuing to Canaan.

C. God must first take his people into the desert to convince them of his faithfulness (Exod. 16) and commitment (Exod. 19–20) before taking them into Canaan.

III. As Israel embarks on this uncharted journey in the opposite direction, God encourages them in two ways (13:19–22).

A. Joseph's coffin speaks of their eventual arrival in Canaan (13:19).

1. Years earlier Joseph made Israel promise they would take his bones to Canaan when they left Egypt (Gen. 50:24–26).

2. The coffin is a reminder that God will eventually place them in the land he's promised them.

B. The column of cloud is a symbol of God's constant presence.

1. Through this cloud, God leads them on the uncharted journey (13:20–22).

a. As they leave Succoth, they enter uncharted, desert territory.

b. A column of cloud, capable of becoming luminescent at night, gives them round-the-clock direction and visibility for their travels.

c. The cloud remains with them until they finally cross the Jordan River into the Promised Land (Exod. 40:36–38).

2. Through this cloud, God protects them from the Egyptians (Exod. 14:19–20) and the burning sun (Ps. 105:39).
3. Through this cloud, God speaks to them (Exod. 19:16–19).

In this way, the passage outline faithfully reproduces the ideas and flow of the original author. It shows his major concepts in their progressive sequence.[4]

[handwritten: observations —> theology]

GOING FROM THE PASSAGE OUTLINE TO THE TRUTH OUTLINE

[handwritten: statement ——> implication]

A good passage outline anchors you to the text, but it's not usually something you can preach. It's often past tense, ancient history, something that happened long ago. It's not in language that expresses eternal truth; its spiritual value may not be apparent. And it lacks any concrete application to contemporary life.

The passage outline needs to be turned into a truth outline. We need to go from history to theology. How do we do that? We move from the passage outline to the truth outline by modifying the passage outline in two ways:

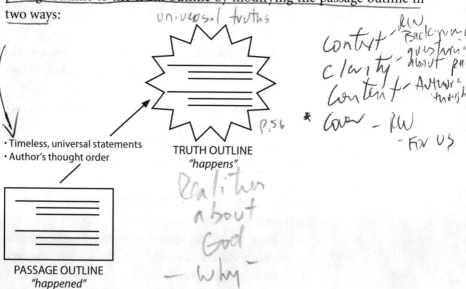

[handwritten: universal truths]

- Timeless, universal statements
- Author's thought order

TRUTH OUTLINE
"happens"

PASSAGE OUTLINE
"happened"

*[handwritten annotations: p.56 * ; Context – Background; clarity – questions about passage; Content – Author's thought; Cover – RW – For us; Realities about God — why]*

---

4. In order to develop good outlines that show the overall unity of the passage and the proper subordination of ideas, you need to follow certain essential outlining procedures. See appendix A for a discussion of these essential guidelines, along with examples.

- We turn its historical statements into timeless, universal ones.
- We put its concepts in the author's original thought order.

Rw - for us...

Turn the Historical Statements into Timeless, Universal Ones

flow if thought -

The first step is to put the "big hunk" statements (i.e., the large stroke movements, not the minor details) of the passage outline in timeless language. Find more general, universal ways of saying what is happening in the text. Move up the ladder of abstraction. Here is an example:

• why does the author tell the original reader this? What is the author's concern?

• why does the audience need to know? what were their original concerns, questions, struggles, strengths, weaknesses, that brought the author's statement here?

• To answer the "why" question, look for the timeless truth being taught.

```
                    Living Thing
                         |
            +------------+------------+
         Mammal                     Tree
            |
      +-----+------+
   Animal         Man
      |
  +---+----+
 Dog       Cow
  |
+-+----+
Collie  Poodle        Haddon Robinson
```

The ladder of abstraction ascends from a specific term to a more general term. The general term must be capable of covering the original specific as well as other similar specifics. For example, if I have the specific term "Collie," the more general term that could cover that specific, as well as other specifics (e.g., poodle, Labrador), is "Dog." "Dog" is more abstract than a specific breed.

If I continued up the ladder of abstraction, looking for a general term to cover the specifics of "Dog" and "Cow," I would come to the more abstract "Animal."

I could keep going up. "Animal" and "Man" would be covered by "Mammal." "Mammal" and "Tree" would have "Living Thing" as the more universal term.

In moving from the passage outline to the truth outline, you want to do something similar. You want to find the language that is more general, more abstract—language that not only describes what is happening in

Truth outline =

Statement ... Time
Implication ... Timeless
Extrapolation ... Timely

the text, but that is also sufficiently broad to describe similar things that might occur in different centuries or cultures.

For example, in historical/passage terms, Exodus 13 says, "God didn't take Israel on a direct route to *Canaan* because some situation of *war* along that route would prevent them from reaching their destination." Moving up the ladder of abstraction to timeless truth, we might say, "Sometimes God doesn't take us on a direct route *to the good plans he has for us* because some *obstacle* along that route would prevent us from reaching that goal."

The language is now sufficiently timeless to cover not only Exodus 13, but also such contemporary obstacles as a corporate vice president who would be an obstacle to our career path, a premature monetary windfall that would derail us from growth in godliness, or a past hurt that would prevent us from entering into a stable and lasting marriage.

The abstraction ladders might look something like this:

```
              Obstacle                    God's Good Plans for Us
              |                           |
      ┌───────┴───────┐           ┌───────┴───────┐
    War             VP          Canaan           Career
                  Windfall                       Godliness
                  Past hurt                       Marriage
```

Compare the following large stroke movements from the passage outline and the truth outline to see the results of turning the historical statements into timeless, universal ones:

Passage Outline

I. God purposefully takes Israel from Goshen to Canaan by an indirect route.[5]

II. The reason for God's indirect leading is that Israel would encounter war on the straight-line path and would never reach their destination.

III. As Israel embarks on this uncharted journey in the opposite direction, God encourages them in two ways.

5. See the first sermon in appendix C for the full outline and manuscript of this message.

[handwritten: 136]

[handwritten top margin: Interpretation: What the author, writes about for (fore knowledge) every people.]

A. Joseph's coffin speaks of their eventual arrival in Canaan.

B. The column of cloud is a symbol of God's constant presence.

Truth Outline *[handwritten: Why — General / Universal (Premise) — Reveals God! Talking points]*

[handwritten left margin: (observation) problem]

I. God sometimes deliberately takes us on a zigzag path to the good plans he has for us. *[handwritten: (The idea I want to communicate.. emerges)]*

[handwritten: — Reveals God]

[handwritten left margin: (implied) Question] [Application] Answer

II. The reason for this zigzag path is because some obstacle on the straight-line path would keep us from reaching the goal. *[handwritten: Why? — state... Reveals God (statement of Sermons, big idea = restate)]*

[handwritten left margin: theology history relevance]

III. As we proceed along this zigzag path, God encourages us in two ways. *[handwritten: What wrong with this picture? How?]*

A. He encourages us with continual reminders of his good intentions.

B. He encourages us with a tangible sense of his presence.

[handwritten: — Reveals God]

Notice how this movement from passage specifics to timeless universals occurs in the example of Mark 4:35–41 given in the previous chapter. The command to cross the lake into Gentile territory becomes, more broadly, a command God gives us to expand his kingdom. The life-threatening storm that results from the disciples' obedience is abstracted to the difficult situation in which we find ourselves as a result of our obedience. Jesus' rebuking the wind, in timeless language, becomes our resisting Satan.

Moving from the passage outline to the truth outline is simpler in the epistles, because most of the material there is already stated in universal terms. The command "Fathers, do not exasperate your children" (Eph. 6:4) is already timeless and universal, and the concept would remain the same as you move from history to theology.

Similarly, in 1 Corinthians 4:1–5, it would take only minor modifications to turn the big strokes of the passage outline into a truth outline:

Passage Outline *[handwritten: — Specific (Point)]*

I. The Corinthians ought to view Paul and their other teachers as servants who have been entrusted by Christ, their Master, with secret things. *[handwritten: What the author said.]*

II. The requirement for Paul and the other teachers is to be faithful to their Master and to the trust he's given them.

[handwritten: Why the author said it.]

III.   The Lord's evaluation of Paul's faithfulness is the only one that counts. *Why the author said it*

IV.   The Corinthians, therefore, should stop prematurely evaluating their teachers and instead wait for the time of the Lord's evaluation and praise. *How the author said it*

Truth Outline — General — p. 56

Why never God

I.   Christians should view their ministers as servants of Christ who have been entrusted with spiritual truths.

II.   The minister's requirement is to prove faithful to his Master and to the trust he's been given.

III.   The Lord's evaluation of the minister's faithfulness is the only one that counts.

IV.   Other believers, therefore, should withhold their judgments and instead wait for the Lord's evaluation and praise.

Occasionally, however, even in the epistles, some specific cultural reference will require you to use the ladder of abstraction just as you do in narrative passages. For example, in 1 Corinthians 8, Paul has a strong conviction that eating food sacrificed to idols is, in itself, a harmless, neutral activity—one that he is free to engage in. But he also recognizes that other Christians have a weak conviction about this—they still believe that eating food sacrificed to idols is sinful. Paul refuses, therefore, to eat such food in front of them, lest he encourage them to do something they believe is wrong.

Moving from the details of the passage to the truth outline, you would turn Paul's refusal to eat food sacrificed to idols into refraining from other activities that might tempt others to sin. Putting the historical statement into timeless, universal language enables you, in the final sermon outline, to apply Paul's words to contemporary situations on which your listeners have differing opinions.

The abstraction ladder might look like this:

Truth outline = Roman Numerals of message (handwritten)

Giving up activities that are harmless
for you, but sinful for others

Specific	General (universal Truth)	Specific
Refusing to eat food sacrificed to idols	theology — timeless — lead statements	Refraining from yoga classes, body piercing, the lottery, etc.

(handwritten annotations: Passage Outline; History — Time — statement; Sermon Outline; Relevance — Timely statements)

A section of the final sermon outline might reflect this flow from *history* to *theology* to *relevance* as follows:

III. We should give up our freedom to engage in a harmless activity whenever it might cause another Christian to sin [theology].

    A. Paul gave up his freedom to eat food sacrificed to idols lest he encourage other Christians to sin [history].

    B. We should give up freedoms we have if they would cause another Christian to sin [relevance].

        1. We should give up the freedom to enroll in yoga classes.

        2. We should give up the freedom to have certain body piercings.

        3. We should give up the freedom to play the lottery recreationally.

The language of the truth outline is general and timeless enough to cover not only the situation of the passage, but also similar situations that might occur in different centuries to different people. This timeless language will eventually serve as the lead statements (the Roman numerals) of the final sermon outline, under which you would develop both the passage specifics and the contemporary applications.

Timeless Theology

A.	B.
Passage Specifics	Contemporary Applications

(Handwritten marginal notes throughout, including: "what? Why How?", "universal / timeless / specific / Passage / specific / contemporary", "Why! What! How!", "Premise", "Point", "God is saying something today — picture of contemporary application — Connection — Relevance", "These are the kinds of experiences people have; this is how God deals with us; this is what God reveals about himself.", "the plot; the steps and details; the passage takes to get its message across; Expressed through — time when, manner in which, reason why, result of, means by which, cause of; names, places, events, cultural practices")

In outline form, it will appear as:[6]

I. Timeless theology
   A. Passage specifics
   B. Contemporary applications

Put the Outline Concepts in the Author's Original Thought Order

The second step in moving from the passage outline to the truth outline is to make sure the concepts are in the author's original thought order, even though this might not necessarily be the written order of the phrases or sentences in the text.

As you look at the passage outline, particularly at its subordinate points, ask yourself, "Which point was the first to occur mentally in the author's thought process? In what order did the concepts or phrases originally come into his mind?" Your goal is to determine how he originally thought it rather than how his pen wrote it.

For example, suppose you're planning to preach on the following two "verses" that are written in this order:

I. You ought not to get mad . . .

II. . . . when the paperboy throws your paper into the bushes.

As a reader you have no difficulty understanding the complete concept of this written order. The complete concept also would be clear to any listener *as long as he or she hears the entire concept in one breath*. A listener can briefly sustain the tension of the above ellipsis as long as the total thought is completed rather quickly.

But, if the speaker chooses to expound or amplify each phrase separately—which is what we do when we preach—thus extending the ellipsis indefinitely, then the listener does not mentally tie the phrases together but instead hears the following, apparently disconnected, outline:

I. You ought not to get mad . . .

II. The paperboy will throw your paper into the bushes . . .

---

6. We'll talk at much greater length about how to structure the final sermon outline in chapter 8.

And the resulting "sermon" can easily become unbiblical, unclear, and repetitive. It might sound something like this:

First, the Bible says, "You ought not to get mad." This means you ought not to get mad when someone cuts you off on the freeway and almost drives you over the guardrail. You ought not to get mad when you learn of severe child abuse in your congregation. You ought not to get mad when you see pictures of children who are starving as Third World dictators divert relief funds into their private Swiss accounts. **[Foolish, unbiblical applications]** The Bible says, "You ought not to get mad."

Second, the Bible says, "The paperboy will throw your paper into the bushes." **[Unclear connection between paragraphs.]** One morning you will look for your paper on the sidewalk but not find it there. As you start back into your house, you will suddenly discover it under the bushes. You know the paper will now have dirt, leaves, and snails on it. And your temptation will be to get mad at the paperboy. But the Bible says, "Don't get mad when the paperboy throws your paper into the bushes." **[With this last sentence, by adding "don't get mad," the speaker has become repetitive, because the brain instinctively recognizes that *this* is the only situation the text has in mind—when paperboys do dumb stunts.]**

The reason for this unbiblical, unclear, and repetitive preaching is because the speaker is making the mistake of following the written order of the phrases while expounding or amplifying the separate clauses.

Instead, the speaker should put the phrases into the author's original thought order. The author's written order was:

I.   You ought not to get mad . . .

II.   . . . when the paperboy throws your paper into the bushes.

However, his original thought order was:

I.   When the paperboy throws your paper into the bushes . . .

II.   . . . you ought not to get mad.

His initial thinking sequence, or reasoning process, went something like this: *Situation, stress, Search, Solution, New Situation*

- He came out to the sidewalk to get his morning paper.
- When he didn't see the paper on the sidewalk, he assumed the paperboy had not yet come.
- But then he noticed his neighbors both had their papers, and so did the guy across the street.
- His next thought was, "The paperboy skipped me. Now I'll have to call the newspaper office and have them make a special delivery."
- But as he turned to walk back into his house, he suddenly saw that the paperboy had thrown the paper under the bushes near his porch.
- This meant his paper would be dirty—with leaves, twigs, and snails.
- In frustration and anger, he shouted, "You dumb paperboy!"
- But then he thought, "No, I shouldn't get angry at him. He's probably just a kid who doesn't realize what he's doing."

As you move from the passage outline to the truth outline, you need to put the phrases in the author's original thought order so that your expanded paragraphs will follow his original reasoning process. In this example, you would preach the second verse before you preach the first one. And the resulting "sermon" will be on-target, clear, and not repetitive:

I.   The paperboy will throw your paper in the bushes.

II.   When this happens, don't get mad.

The "sermon" might sound like this:

Warren says:
most important point last
Second most important point first
Third most important point second.

First, the Bible says in verse 2, "There will be times when the paperboy will throw your paper into the bushes." It may be the morning paper or the evening paper. He may throw it from a Volkswagen or a bicycle. It may land in a gardenia bush or an azalea bush. Whatever the case, there will be times when the paperboy will throw your paper into the bushes. What should you do when that happens? How should you respond?

The Bible gives the answer in verse 1: "Don't get mad." Don't get upset with the paperboy. He's probably just a kid who . . .

This modification—putting the concepts in the author's original thought order—does not in any way change the meaning of the text.[7] It simply recognizes the difference between reading a concept in succinct form or hearing a concept in an expanded form.

Let's look at a few biblical passages where changing the phrases or verses from the written order to the author's thought order allows for a clearer exposition.

James 1:2

Consider it pure joy, my brothers, whenever you face trials of many kinds.

---

7. Often the Greek or Hebrew text itself is in the original thought order but has been changed into a different written order for the English translation. Compare the Greek thought order of Paul's many imperatives in Romans 12:10–13 with the English word order in the NIV and NASB. The Greek word order of Romans 12:12, for example, reflects Paul's original thought order: "In hope, be joyful; in affliction, be patient; in prayer, be faithful." The English translations appropriately change this to a written order easier for reading: "Be joyful in hope, patient in affliction, faithful in prayer." But if you outline and preach each phrase according to the English written order, you run the danger of being unclear and repetitive:

   I. You ought to be joyful.

   II. You have a hope—an expectation of Christ's return.

   III. Live joyfully in this expectation.

On the other hand, if you follow the original thought order, your message will be on-target and clear:

   I. You have a hope—an expectation of Christ's return.

   II. Live joyfully in this expectation.

If preached from the written order of the passage outline, the listener will be unclear on the connection between points I and II:

I. Consider it pure joy.
    A. "Consider" means . . .
    B. We ought to be joyful in life.

II. You will face trials of many kinds.

But James's thought order is first his realization that we will face many trials, followed by his encouragement to maintain a joyful spirit during these trials. So the truth outline would be the following:

I. You will face trials of many kinds.

II. When they come, consider it pure joy.

Philippians 1:3–5

Adverbial Phrase

I thank my God every time I remember you. In all my prayers for all of you, I always pray with joy because of your partnership in the gospel from the first day until now.

If preached from the written order of the passage outline, a subpoint of point III repeats point II:

I. I thank God for you.

II. I remember you.

III. I pray for you.
    A. I pray with joy.
    B. I pray because I remember your partnership.

But Paul's thought order is first his remembering how the Philippians have been part of his life and then his subsequent praying in light of that memory. So the truth outline would be:

I. Whenever I remember you, I remember your partnership.

II. This leads me to give thanks and pray for you.
   A. I give thanks for you.
   B. I joyfully pray for you.

Psalm 1:1–2

> Blessed is the man
>   who does not walk in the counsel of the wicked,
>   or stand in the way of sinners[2]
>   or sit in the seat of mockers.[3]
> But his delight is in the law of the LORD,
>   and on his law he meditates day and night.

When preached from the written order of the passage outline, the subpoints get expounded in the wrong order, and the listener doesn't grasp their connection:

I. The man who wants to be blessed does not look to the ungodly for instruction.
   A. He does not walk in the counsel of the wicked.
      1. The Hebrew word "walk" is . . .
      2. "Counsel" is when someone tells you to . . .
      3. "Wicked" people are those who . . .
   B. He does not stand in the way of sinners.
      1. "Stand" means . . .
      2. "Way" looks at . . .
      3. "Sinners" are those who . . .
   C. He does not sit in the seat of mockers.
      1. "To sit" means you . . .
      2. A "seat" was something used when . . .
      3. "Mockers" are those who . . .

II. Instead, he eagerly looks to the Word of God.
   A. His spirit is one of "delight."
   B. In his day "the law of the Lord" meant the wisdom found in the Torah.

C. He meditates on this law day and night.

But the psalmist's thought order is first to point out certain people in his society—wicked, sinners, mockers. Then he notices how these people try to instruct or influence others to join them. And finally he urges us not to be swayed by them if we want to be blessed. In the second "hunk," he first contemplates the wisdom of God's law and then finds himself delight-ing in it and meditating on it. So the truth outline would look like this:

I.   The man who wants to be blessed does not look to the ungodly for instruction.
     A. He does not walk in the counsel of the wicked.
         1. There are certain "wicked" people.
         2. These wicked people will try to "counsel" you.
         3. You must not "walk" in their way.
     B. Etc.
     C. Etc.

II. Instead, he eagerly looks to the Word of God.
     A. In his day "the law of the Lord" meant the wisdom found in the Torah.
     B. He delights in and meditates on this law.
         1. He delights in this wisdom, eagerly seeking it.
         2. He meditates on it.

Ephesians 1:13

Having believed, you were marked in him with a seal, the prom-ised Holy Spirit.

If this verse is preached in the written order, you end up talking about *when* we are sealed and *in whom,* before actually defining *what* the seal is:

I.   Believers are sealed when they believe.

II. Believers are sealed in Christ.

III. Believers are sealed with the Holy Spirit.

The more logical reasoning of the thought order would be:

I.   Believers are sealed with the Holy Spirit.

II.   This sealing occurs when they believe.

III.   This sealing is in Christ.

Colossians 1:9

[For this reason,] since the day we heard about you, we have not stopped praying for you and asking God to fill you with the knowledge of his will through all spiritual wisdom and understanding.

If you preach the written order, your encouragement to pray will be wide-ranging and undefined, and you will be repetitive (because you'll instinctively revert to the thought order):

I.   We ought to continuously pray for other believers.

II.   We ought to ask God to fill other believers with the knowledge of his will.

III.   We ought to pray continuously for this filling.

The more natural thought order would be to first preach *what* the prayer is, and then preach *how often* it is to be prayed:

I.   We ought to pray for other believers to be filled with the knowledge of God's will.

II.   Our prayer for this filling should be continuous.

We preachers can easily overlook this second step—making sure the concepts are in the author's original thought order—when moving from the passage outline to the truth outline. Since we are so familiar with the passage and intuitively understand how the points connect with each other, it doesn't occur to us that the listener will have any difficulty with the flow of concepts regardless of the sequence in which we develop them. But the listeners have not had our prior study of the material, and their entire comprehension depends on that single moment in time when our words are spoken to them. So we must intentionally look through our passage outline for sections where the thought order may be different from the written order and adjust accordingly. *NASB*

There's one final way of checking to see if you're unfolding the concepts in their proper thought order: as you rehearse the final sermon prior to preaching it, if you find yourself repeating something you said earlier, there's a good chance you're not yet using the author's thought order.

The resulting truth outline—in timeless, universal language, and in logical thought order—could conceivably be preached to any audience, in any century, in any location. But it is still not a sermon outline. It still needs focus and relevancy and effective language and engaging delivery. We will see the benefits of these in the chapters ahead.

The trick to keeping people on track when your sermon is more conversational is to craft effective transitions. Transitions stitch blocks of ideas together, showing relationships between them.

Paragraph transitions:

therefore	furthermore	in spite of this	in the next place
consequently	however	accordingly	as might be expected
as a result / this	similarly	finally	an example of this
besides	lastly	nevertheless	also on the contrary
meanwhile	soon	after all	in other words on the other hand
such	in addition	likewise	then again

A timeless truth is a principle to believe in and to live by, and that is valuable for all christians for all times.

— Take away truth

Taking people whose minds are anywhere and focus them onto a specific question they may not have realized they needed

The Proposition : the answer to...

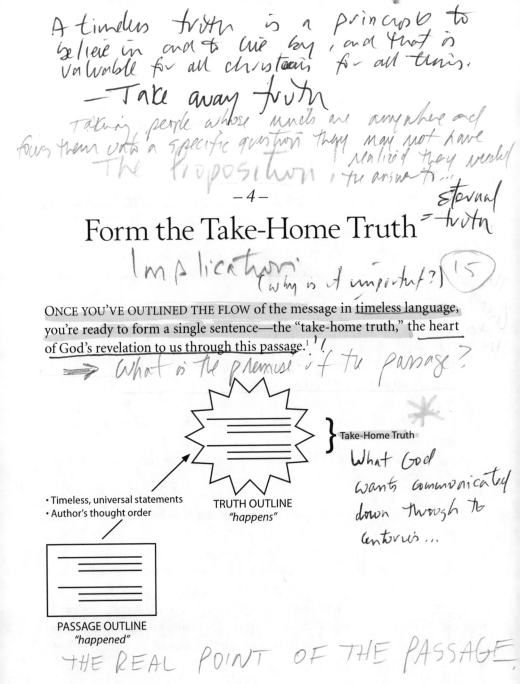

—4—

Form the Take-Home Truth *= Eternal truth*

Implication : (why is it important?) 15

ONCE YOU'VE OUTLINED THE FLOW of the message in timeless language, you're ready to form a single sentence—the "take-home truth," the heart of God's revelation to us through this passage.[1]

⟹ What is the premise of the passage?

} Take-Home Truth

What God wants communicated down through the centuries...

• Timeless, universal statements
• Author's thought order

TRUTH OUTLINE
"happens"

PASSAGE OUTLINE
"happened"

THE REAL POINT OF THE PASSAGE

---

1. While it is possible to form a single sentence to express what is happening in the passage outline (e.g., an "exegetical idea"), the value of this sentence is most apparent once the truth outline has been determined. The passage outline is simply history, while the truth outline is theology, reflecting what God wants communicated down through the centuries. Working from this truth outline, therefore, we state the core of what he's revealing in a single timeless sentence.

THE DOMINANT IDEA

This sentence will not necessarily be a summary of all the major points of the truth outline. It won't include every thought in the passage. (Such a sentence might require two semicolons and four commas!) Rather, this sentence is the essential core of what the author is saying. It's the idea that dominates all other ideas—it's the "Big Idea,"[2] the central truth the author is trying to get across. It's the truth you want the listeners to take home and remember even if they forget everything else. Weeks later they may not remember what passage it came from, but hopefully the wording of this sentence will still come to mind and work its godliness in them.

In this chapter we'll talk about the necessity of a take-home truth and how to go about forming it.

THE NECESSITY OF A TAKE-HOME TRUTH

It's essential that your sermon have this take-home truth. At some deep mental and emotional level, the listeners are searching for it. As they listen to you preach, they are subconsciously asking, "What is it you want me to get from this message? What do you want me to 'take home' from this sermon?"

If the preacher doesn't have a single sentence, the listeners will do one of two things:

- They will create a sentence of their own, based on some small point or story in the sermon. They will form a "truth" in their mind from some minor part of the message. At best, such a truth is partial. At worst, something the speaker said is twisted or garbled into something far different from what the speaker intended.[3]
- Or, they will simply leave the service in a contented fog, mentally blank but unconcerned about it. They didn't really expect to get anything focused or lasting out of the message (and they weren't disappointed).

---

2. Haddon W. Robinson, *Biblical Preaching: The Development and Delivery of Expository Messages*, 2d ed. (Grand Rapids: Baker, 2002), 33–50.

3. This explains why speakers are sometimes baffled when, weeks later, someone says to them, "Remember when you preached on such-and-such?" and the speaker has absolutely no idea what the person is referring to! That's because the listener has unrecognizably grabbed some small concept and made it the theme of the whole message.

Each of Paul's sermons in the book of Acts revolves around one central truth. Each sermon—whether given to Jews (Acts 13), Gentiles (Acts 17), or Christians (Acts 20)—crystallizes into a single sentence that states the sum and substance of the whole message. Everything in the sermon either leads up to, develops, or follows from this single unifying theme.[4]

In Acts 13, speaking to a synagogue audience, Paul's central truth is that "God has brought to Israel the Savior Jesus, as he promised" (v. 23). This key sentence occurs early in the sermon and is Paul's way of synthesizing his entire message:

Introduction
1. God has been delivering Israel since the beginning of her history.
2. God has used individuals to deliver Israel.
3. God promised to climax his deliverance of Israel through David and his descendants.
4. God has brought to Israel the Savior Jesus, as he promised [central truth].

I. God has fulfilled his promise to prepare the nation for the Savior's coming.

II. God has fulfilled his promise to provide the nation with a powerful Savior.

III. God has fulfilled his promise to provide the nation with an eternal Savior.

Conclusion
1. Through Jesus as Savior you can have forgiveness of sins and justification from everything.
2. Be careful to believe this greatest deliverance that God has provided for Israel.

---

4. The following analyses are drawn from my "Patterns for Preaching: A Rhetorical Analysis of the Sermons of Paul in Acts 13; 17; and 20" (unpublished Th.D. dissertation, Dallas Theological Seminary, 1972).

In Acts 17, at a gathering of the Greek Areopagus, Paul builds his sermon around his introduction's promise to make the Unknown God known. What the Athenians worship but do not know, he will proclaim to them. His central truth is the summary of his two major points: "The Unknown God is the Creator of the universe and the Father of all people."

Introduction
1. You are very religious.
2. I observed an altar to the Unknown God.
3. I will proclaim him to you.

I. He is the Creator of the universe [central truth].
A. He made the world and everything in it.
B. He is not, therefore, confined in man-made shrines or served by human hands.

II. He is the Father of all people [central truth].
A. He created people as his offspring.
    1. He made people to seek him.
    2. He helps people to find him.
        a. He determined the times and places for them.
        b. He remains very near to them.
            i. People are dependent on him.
            ii. People are descended from him.
B. He ought not, therefore, be thought of as an image.

Conclusion
1. He now commands all people everywhere to repent of idolatry.
2. He has set a day when he will judge the world by the man he has raised from the dead.

In Acts 20, speaking for the last time to the elders of the Ephesian church, Paul wants to persuade them to guard themselves and the church against the dangers that are going to come. His central truth is stated in Acts 20:28: "Guard yourselves and all the flock."

What!

Introduction
1. You yourselves know my example among you.
   a. You know how I served the church in the face of external trouble.
   b. You see how I am presently denying myself in the face of internal temptation.
2. My life and example are now coming to a blameless end.
3. As overseers of the church, you must follow the example I have set: guard yourselves and all the flock [central truth].

That!

I. Guard the flock against external trouble.
   A. You will be troubled by false teachers from without and within.
   B. So shepherd the church and remember my example of service.

How!

II. Guard yourselves against internal temptation.
   A. You will be tempted to profit financially from the ministry.
   B. So look to the Lord for your reward, and remember my example of self-denial.

Why!

Regardless of the demographics of his audience—Jew, Gentile, or Christian—Paul always had a central and unifying theme in each of his sermons. And since we believe his preaching was guided by the Spirit, then perhaps his pattern is a divinely intended model for our preaching as well—we too must be able to state the core truth of our sermon in a single sentence.

Our sermons must not be a series of isolated comments or unconnected truths. Instead, they should have a progressive and orderly flow of ideas (the outline) and be embodied in a single sentence (the take-home truth).

Here's what a "sermon" would look like as a sequence of unrelated ideas:

The Premise

The Central Truth

- Everything we have is because of Christ.
- The message we preach is "good news"—it is true and will save you.
- The Holy Spirit seals you.
- The Holy Spirit was promised to you.
- You have a future inheritance.

- God always makes good on his promises.
- *Redemption* means "buying back and possessing a second time."

Without a central take-home truth, the listener will either focus on one of the small points or leave in despair at the bewildering array of apparently unrelated ideas.

Sadly, all of the above thoughts have been randomly lifted from two verses of Scripture—Ephesians 1:13–14:

> And you also were included in Christ when you heard the word of truth, the gospel of your salvation. Having believed, you were marked in him with a seal, the promised Holy Spirit, who is a deposit guaranteeing our inheritance until the redemption of those who are God's possession—to the praise of his glory.

In the previous "sermon" the speaker simply makes miscellaneous, unconnected comments on the words or phrases of the verses, without any attempt to see the author's progression of ideas or to fashion the truth into a single sentence.

But Paul's thought in Ephesians 1 is very orderly, and verses 13–14 have a singular, focused truth. In Ephesians 1:3–14, Paul talks about the work of the Trinity in our salvation. Verses 3–6a describe the work of God the Father, verses 6b–12 the work of God the Son, and verses 13–14 the work of God the Holy Spirit. Paul sections off each unit with the identical phrase—"to the praise of his glory."[5]

---

5. It's also possible Paul has structured verses 3–14 in a chiastic arrangement:
   3 Praise
      3b Blessed in the heavenly realms with every blessing from the Spirit
         4–5 Us Jews: chosen, adopted
            6a Praise
               6b–8 Hope in Christ, redemption
                  9 The mystery of his will
                     10 To bring all things under Christ
                  11 The purpose of his will
               12a Hope in Christ
            12b Praise
         13 You Gentiles: included, marked
      14a The Holy Spirit guarantees our inheritance
   14b Praise

Within verses 13–14—the work of the Holy Spirit in our salvation—
Paul makes two essential assertions:

- When you Gentiles believed the gospel and were included in Christ,
  God marked you as his by "sealing" you with the Holy Spirit.
- When you Gentiles believed the gospel and were included in Christ,
  God gave you the Holy Spirit as a "deposit," a sample down pay-
  ment guaranteeing your eventual full inheritance.

The truth outline of verses 13–14 would be something like this:

I. When we believe, we are made secure through the sealing of the
   Holy Spirit.

II. When we believe, we are given the Holy Spirit as a sample down
    payment guaranteeing our future inheritance.

III. Receiving this twofold ministry of the Spirit should lead us to
     praise God.

From this orderly flow of thought, the take-home truth for verses 13–14
emerges: "God is to be praised for making us secure through the sealing
of the Holy Spirit, and for giving us the Spirit as a sample and guarantee
of our future inheritance."[6]

Your sermon must have this kind of "sermon-in-a-nutshell" sentence.
The biblical author had a "truth" from God that he was trying to develop,
and this is the truth you want your listeners to take home.

Occasionally someone asks, "Is there more than one central truth that
can be preached from the same passage?" For example, someone might
argue that instead of the Ephesians 1:13–14 central truth given above, one

---

Assuming this chiastic structure, the point of the V becomes the dominant idea of the
combined three sections of verses 3–14—i.e., the ultimate purpose behind the Triune God's
work to save both Jew and Gentile is "to bring all things in heaven and on earth together under
one head, even Christ." This dominant idea is certainly the focus of the first three chapters of
Ephesians. We'll talk about how to preach such chiastic structures in chapter 10.

6. Eventually this single sentence, based on the truth outline, will be expressed in even more
   contemporary and memorable language in the final sermon outline, perhaps something like:
   "Isn't God wonderful for marking us as his and giving us a taste of what's ahead?" We'll talk
   more about this final sermonic phrasing of the take-home truth in chapter 7.

could preach "The gospel is true" as the central truth ("And you also were included in Christ when you heard the word of truth, the gospel of your salvation.").

But these are not really two different central truths from the same passage. Instead, they are two different central truths from two different passages—the first central truth comes from Ephesians 1:13–14, the second from Ephesians 1:13b. It's even possible to have a third central truth, from Ephesians 1:13a—"Gentiles, as well as Jews, are included in Christ."[7]

The dominant idea, or take-home truth, for any given message depends on how large or small a unit of Scripture you are preaching. A subpoint in one sermon can be the central truth in another:

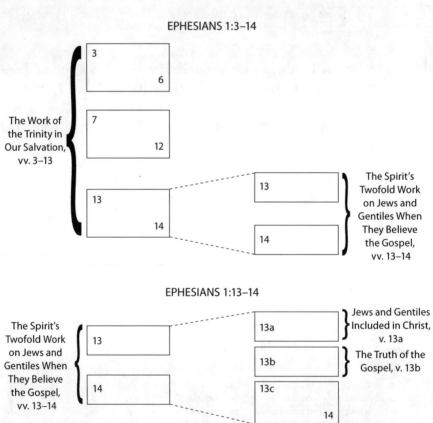

---

7. The same careful distinction should be made if someone asks, "Can't you preach three different central truths from the parable of the prodigal son, in Luke 15—one on the younger son's repentance, one on the father's forgiveness, and one on the older brother's resentment?" But

[handwritten top margin: (if a sentence does not begin with the subject it may open with an introductory element that tells, when, where, how, or why the main action - (the sentence occurs.)] *[circled: 15g]*

[handwritten left margin: F]

Ideally there's only one central truth that can be preached from any given section of Scripture. <u>Whatever the original author was saying within the boundaries of your defined unit</u> is what you also want to reflect in your central truth.

[handwritten left margin: Passage - within] *[handwritten: The plot tells us what happens - Passage outline / The theme tells us why it happens - Truth outline]* *[circled: 15 H]*

HOW TO FORM THE TAKE-HOME TRUTH

[handwritten: The Premise / Central truth]

Once you've determined the precise limits or boundaries of your section of Scripture and <u>have a truth outline</u> that covers that material, you're ready to form your single sentence.[8] *[handwritten: (the fewer less language) , 1)]* *[handwritten: *]*

[handwritten left margin: FCF main]

To form the take-home truth, look at your truth outline and ask, "What is the largest question the biblical author is addressing with this flow of thought, and what answer is he giving to that question?" *[handwritten: - Central truth]* *[circled: 15 I]* *[handwritten: F]*

[handwritten circled: 1] Your question will give you your sermon *topic*—what you're talking *[handwritten: stress]* *[handwritten circled: 2]* about. And your answer will give you your *assertion*—what you're saying *[handwritten: solution]* about your topic. Put the two of them together—question and answer, or *[handwritten: FCF]* topic and assertion—and you have your <u>central truth.</u>

For example, in Luke 1:1–4:

[handwritten left margin: What's the question? - What's the problem = THT] *[handwritten right margin: what's wrong with this picture? FCF]*

> Many have undertaken to draw up an account of the things that
> have been fulfilled among us, just as they were handed down to *[handwritten: Subject +]*
> us by those who from the first were eyewitnesses and servants of *[handwritten: object =]*
> the word. Therefore, since I myself have carefully investigated ev- *[handwritten: FCF]*
> erything from the beginning, it seemed good also to me to write
> an orderly account for you, most excellent Theophilus, so that you
> may know the certainty of the things you have been taught.

[handwritten left margin vertical: why would you compose = The THT / The answer = The THT]

---

again, these are not three different central truths from the *same* passage. They are three different central truths from three *different* passages: the younger son's repentance (vv. 11–20); the father's forgiveness (vv. 11–24), and the older brother's resentment (vv. 11–32). While one of the first two messages could conceivably be preached and would be true to what Jesus is saying in that limited portion of the story, ideally our sermon should focus on the third, the whole passage, for Jesus originally told the parable so that the Pharisees would see themselves in the older brother (cf. vv. 1–3). *[circled: 15 J]*

8. Don't attempt to form the take-home truth until after you've completed the sequence we've been talking about—thoroughly study the passage, anchor yourself to the author's flow of thought through a passage outline, and then turn this passage outline into a truth outline. *[handwritten: fewer less]* Speakers sometimes make the mistake of reading the passage and trying to come up with some single sentence without first having a solid grasp of the flow of concepts in the passage. You can't accurately determine an author's central truth until you've first crystallized his progression of thought.

[handwritten bottom: Context - RW Background / Clarity - questions about the passage / Content - Authors thought / Cover - RW for us (what, why, how?) / Central - question & answer]

[handwritten lower left margin: what / why / how]

The truth outline might look something like this:

Cover
Topic

I. Many accounts, using eyewitness reports, have been written of the life of Christ. *(Situation)* *What*

Cover
What

Question...

II. Luke, having carefully investigated everything, has written an orderly account. *(Stress)* *How*

Why

Answer
Assertion

III. His purpose in writing is to assure us that what we've been taught is really true. *(Solution)* *Why* *Truth* *How* *(it ma a challen*

(Isk) *The Proposition (Pulled from the outline)*

(1) To determine the central truth of this passage—and to form the single sentence that captures the essential core of what the author is saying—ask, "What is the largest question that is being answered through this flow of thought?" You will rather easily settle on: "Why did Luke write his orderly account?" *Pick a point from the outline... The dominant idea* *= Why*

Why?

(2) Then ask, "What is the answer to this question?" And you'll immediately realize it's, "to assure us that what we've been taught is really true." *= How the Assert*

(3) Then turn the question into a "dot-dot-dot" incomplete sentence ("The reason Luke wrote his orderly account was to . . ."), attach the answer to finish the sentence, and you have the central truth: "The reason Luke wrote his orderly account was to assure us that what we've been taught is really true." *Why + How = Central Tr*

As another example, 1 Peter 1:17–19:

Cons Word

Since you call on a Father who judges each man's work impartially, live your lives as strangers here in reverent fear. For you know that it was not with perishable things such as silver or gold that you were redeemed from the empty way of life handed down to you from your forefathers, but with the precious blood of Christ, a lamb without blemish or defect.

The truth outline for this passage would be:

The central truth = question

I. We should live on earth as strangers, in reverent fear. *What?*

II. There are two reasons why we should live this way. *Why?*

stress/solution = "Sermon in"

(Turn the solution into a question Nutshell" incomplete sentence... "to" - gives us the Fallen Condit Fac

A. We should live this way because our Father judges impartially.

B. We should live this way because our redemption was so very costly.

It's obvious the largest question Peter is answering in these verses is, "Why should we live on earth as strangers, in reverent fear?"[9] And he gives a twofold answer to this question. Turning the question into an incomplete sentence, and putting together question and answer, we have the take-home truth: "The reason we should live as strangers on earth, in reverent fear, is because . . . our Father judges impartially and because our redemption was so very costly."

In some passages it may seem that the author is answering lots of questions. These smaller questions, however, are probably just concepts or movements (i.e., Roman numerals) toward the dominant larger question that the entire unit is designed to answer.

For example, the truth outline of 1 Corinthians 4:1–5 might suggest several smaller questions:

I.   Christians should view their ministers as servants of Christ who have been entrusted with spiritual truths. (How should we view ministers?)

II. The minister's requirement is to prove faithful to his Master and to the trust he's been given. (What is required of ministers?)

III. The Lord's evaluation of the minister's faithfulness is the only one that counts. (Who should evaluate ministers?)

IV. Other believers, therefore, should withhold their judgments and instead wait for the Lord's evaluation and praise. (What is our role in evaluating ministers?)

Though several small questions are addressed, Paul's overall purpose in this biblical unit is to answer the third question: "Who should evaluate ministers regarding their faithful service?" Turning this largest question

---

9. Peter answers the smaller question, "*How* should we live on earth?" But the larger question he's answering is, "*Why* should we live this way?"

into an incomplete sentence and giving Paul's answer, we have: "The only one who should evaluate Christ's servants for their faithfulness in service is . . . the Lord."

In smoother English, this central truth might be stated, "Only the Lord has the right and knowledge to evaluate his servants for their faithfulness." And since the question underlying point IV is an important implication for Paul's readers, you also might want to capture its imperative in your central truth: "Let the Lord alone evaluate his servants for their faithfulness." This is the take-home truth for God's people to remember.

This question-answer approach also works for narrative passages. For example, here's the truth outline of the Mark 4:35–41 passage we looked at earlier:

I.   Sometimes we obey God and find ourselves in a difficult situation that fills us with despair.
    A. We obey a command God gives us.
    B. As a result of obeying, we find ourselves in a difficult situation.
    C. The situation fills us with fear and despair.

II. When this happens, we should resist Satan's efforts and trust God's power.
    A. We should resist Satan's efforts to prevent us from carrying out God's purposes.
    B. We should trust God's power to enable us to accomplish whatever He commanded.

If we ask, "What is the largest question the author is addressing through this flow of thought," it easily crystallizes for us: "How should we act when our obedience has led us into difficulty?" Once this question is determined, it becomes easy to add the answer, forming the take-home truth—"When obedience leads to difficulty, resist Satan's efforts and trust God's power."

If we come up with the wrong question, our attempt to answer it will not do justice to the entirety of the passage flow, and we'll know we've not yet found the largest question. For example, in Mark 4:35–41, if we came up with the question, "What sometimes happens to us when we obey God?" we would probably answer it with something like, "Sometimes when we obey God, we find ourselves in difficult situations." But this clearly does not reflect the entirety of the passage material and is therefore not the central truth. We know we've found the right question when, as soon as we ask it, the entire passage falls into place, and we have that "Aha, Eureka! I've found it!" moment. Don't be discouraged if it takes you a few attempts to pinpoint the right question; it'll eventually fall into place

In the truth outline of Exodus 13:17–22, the passage addresses two questions through the second and third outline points—"Why does God take us on indirect, zigzag paths to the destination he's promised us, and what will he do for us en route?"

I. God sometimes deliberately leads us on a zigzag path to the good plans he has for us.

II. The reason for this zigzag path is because some obstacle on the straight-line route would keep us from reaching the goal.

III. As we proceed along this zigzag path, God encourages us in two ways.
   A. He encourages us with continual reminders of his good intentions.
   B. He encourages us with a tangible sense of his presence.

You could attempt to combine the answers to both questions into one central truth: "God leads us on a path of his choosing in order to safely get us to our promised destination, and along the way he gives us continual reminders of his good intentions and a tangible sense of his presence."

But this long sentence would probably be too much for the listener to "hang on to." And since the take-home truth doesn't necessarily have to include all the thoughts of the passage, but only the thought that you want the listeners to remember even if they forget everything else, you might decide that the second outline point is the more critical one. While the material of point III would certainly be a large section of the message proper and a tremendous encouragement on the day it was preached, for the sake of brevity and memorability, you might limit the take-home truth to: "God leads us on a path of his choosing in order to safely get us to our promised destination."

Let's take one more narrative example, and use it to review the entire
process thus far—studying the passage, determining the passage outline,
moving from the passage outline to the truth outline, and then forming
the central truth. We'll use Matthew's account of the feeding of the five
thousand.

When Jesus heard what had happened, he withdrew by boat privately to a solitary place. Hearing of this, the crowds followed him
on foot from the towns. When Jesus landed and saw a large crowd,
he had compassion on them and healed their sick.
    As evening approached, the disciples came to him and said,
"This is a remote place, and it's already getting late. Send the
crowds away, so that they can go to the villages and buy themselves some food."
    Jesus replied, "They do not need to go away. You give them
something to eat."
    "We have here only five loaves of bread and two fish," they
answered.
    "Bring them here to me," he said. And he directed the people to
sit down on the grass. Taking the five loaves and the two fish and
looking up to heaven, he gave thanks and broke the loaves. Then
he gave them to the disciples, and the disciples gave them to the
people. They all ate and were satisfied, and the disciples picked up
twelve basketfuls of broken pieces that were left over. The number
of those who ate was about five thousand men, besides women
and children. (Matt. 14:13–21)

After studying the passage and context of Matthew, we are able to establish the following:

- Matthew's overall purpose of his gospel is to show Israel that Jesus
  is their promised King.
    — His genealogy traces Jesus' ancestry back to David and
      Abraham, focusing on God's promise to provide a Davidic
      king to Abraham's descendants. Jesus is the Son of David,
      with the royal right to Israel's throne.
    — Matthew is the only gospel to relate the visit of the Magi, who

go through the streets of Jerusalem asking, "Where is the one that is born king of the Jews?"

— Matthew's account of the Sermon on the Mount—a message about the kingdom—is the longest of any gospel writer, covering three chapters (Matt. 5–7). It's the King talking about his kingdom.

- The extensive miracles of Matthew 8–9 authenticate Jesus' claim to be King. Their climax comes in Matthew 9:27–34 with the shout of the blind men ("Son of David!"), the amazement of the people, and the religious leaders' rejection of Jesus.
- In chapters 10–11, Jesus formally offers the kingdom to Israel (10:5–7) but anticipates that it will be rejected and that discipleship will become costly. There will be woe for those who reject him but rest for those who come to him.
- In chapter 12 the rejection becomes official: the religious leaders plot to kill Jesus (v. 14), specifically denying his claim to be King (vv. 23–24). Jesus replies that they are a "wicked generation" (v. 45), and pronounces that the kingdom from that point forward will not be limited to natural ties or Jewish blood but will be available to "whoever does the will of my Father in heaven" (vv. 46–50).
- Chapter 13 then reveals in parabolic form what the kingdom will be like as it reaches out to include Gentiles.
- Chapter 14 (which is where the feeding of the five thousand occurs) opens with the beheading of John the Baptist. The voice that originally announced the King is silenced; Jesus' cousin is executed. The rejection is becoming overt and tangible.
- "When Jesus heard what had happened, he withdrew by boat privately to a solitary place" (14:13). His intent is to spend time preparing his disciples for the events to come. What follows (chaps. 14–20) is focused no longer on large crowds but instead on Jesus' efforts to prepare the Twelve for his death, resurrection, and ascension, and ultimately for the Great Commission he will give them—a seemingly impossible command to "go and make disciples of all nations" (28:19).
- A "large crowd,"[10] however, temporarily interrupts Jesus' plan to

---

10. Perhaps ten to fifteen thousand people; Matthew 14:21 puts the men alone at five thousand, not counting the women and children.

spend time with the Twelve (14:14). As the hours of healing unfold, it occurs to Jesus how he can still use the situation to teach his disciples a lesson that will stand them in good stead. And so, when the disciples come to him with the suggestion that he draw the healing to a close so that people can buy food before the markets shut down, he's ready. "You give them something to eat!" he says. He knows how his disciples will react to such an impossible command, and he knows what "truth" he will teach them for the time when they will have to carry out even more impossible commands (i.e., the Great Commission) without him.

With this understanding of the context and passage, we now develop the passage outline. We commit ourselves to the biblical author's ideas and flow of thought—his unfolding hunks, or major concepts.

I. Jesus commands the disciples to feed ten to fifteen thousand people.

II. The disciples reply that they are unable to do what he has commanded.

III. Jesus directs them to bring to him the five loaves and two fish that they do have.

IV. Jesus multiplies the loaves and fish until they are more than sufficient to feed the people.

To move from this passage outline to the truth outline, we turn the historical statements into timeless, universal ones; moving up the ladder of abstraction:

I. God sometimes gives us a seemingly impossible task.

II. We object that we lack the ability to do what he has asked.

III. He instructs us to make whatever resources we have available to him.

What, why, how...

IV. He will expand and empower those resources until they are more than sufficient for the task he has given us.

Implied Topic, implied question, implied answer (152)

What is the take-home truth from this timeless flow of thought? To form the central truth, we ask, "What is the largest question that is being addressed through this flow of thought?" — *Application dominant idea*

We can try the question, "What will God sometimes ask us to do?" Then we turn that into an incomplete sentence, and attach the answer— "God will sometimes ask us to do . . . impossible tasks." However, the resulting sentence will not fit the entirety of the biblical material. (153)

If we pose the question, "How can we accomplish the impossible tasks God gives us?" the whole passage immediately falls into place. "The way to accomplish the impossible tasks God gives us is to . . . make whatever resources we have available to him and let him make them sufficient for the task." This central truth will emerge clearly as the sermon moves through points III and IV.

who?, what?, where?, when?, why?, how?

In forming the central take-home truth, two important notes must be added to what has been said.

First, the question you ask should not be a yes-or-no type of question. For our purposes, any question that can be answered with either a *yes* or a *no* is not really a question but rather an implicit assertion that is asking for either agreement or disagreement.

For example, the yes-or-no question, "Will God sometimes give us impossible tasks?" is not a means of finding a truth but instead is seeking an affirmation or denial of an already assumed truth—"God will sometimes give us impossible tasks. Right? True?"

The question you ask to find the central truth should begin with one of the interrogatives—who, what, when, where, why, how. This kind of question can be turned into an incomplete sentence, and you can test whether the entire passage fits it as an answer or not. (155)

Second, this use of an interrogative to find the central truth is not the same as the "interrogative key word" approach of a generation ago. The interrogative key word approach was used to manufacture the sermon *outline*, not find a passage's *central truth*. The process was as follows.

Before the speaker had an outline of any kind, he would look at the biblical material, and identify some theme that he thought was in the passage—for example, salvation, prayer, or ministry. Then he would select a

outline to talking points

key word around which he would plan to organize his sermon. This key word was always a noun and always plural:

- The *benefits* of salvation
- The *reasons* we should pray
- Some *principles* for ministry

Next he would ask an interrogative question:

- *When* do we get the benefits of salvation?
- *Why* should we pray?
- *What* are some principles for ministry?

Finally, in constructing the sermon outlines, the major points would always be a list—all of the points phrased in parallel language, and all providing an answer to the question.

When do we get the benefits of salvation?

I.   We get some benefits of salvation the moment we believe.

II. We get other benefits of salvation as we walk in obedience.

III. We get the final benefits of salvation when we go to heaven.

Why should we pray?

I.   We should pray because of the faith it shows God.

II. We should pray because of the testimony it shows others.

III. We should pray because of the results it brings us.

Using the feeding of the five thousand, the speaker might ask the question, "What are some principles for ministry?" with the resulting sermon outline:

Phrase the proposition

I. A first principle for ministry—occasionally seek solitude.

II. A second principle for ministry—allow others to change your plans.

III. A third principle for ministry—have compassion.

IV. A fourth principle for ministry—involve others.

V. A fifth principle for ministry—seek closure with a wrap-up.

This interrogative key word approach was a means of creating the *speaker's* outline, rather than a means of finding the central truth in the *author's* outline. Unfortunately, all too often the speaker's resulting outline was artificial and arbitrary, masking the biblical author's real flow of thought and missing the true theology of the passage.[11]

Finding the author's central truth can be done only after you have anchored yourself to the unfolding progression of the passage outline. The biblical author's outline then stays inviolate as you turn it into a truth outline, reflecting its timeless theology. Only then do you ask, "What is the largest question the author is addressing with this flow of thought, and what answer is he giving to that question?" Putting these together—question and answer, or topic and assertion—gives you the author's dominant take-home truth.

When you have completed these steps—study, outline, and take-home truth—you have "What God is saying." You're now ready to consider how he's saying it "to us."

---

11. The biblical authors simply did not sit down to write lists in each of their chapters.

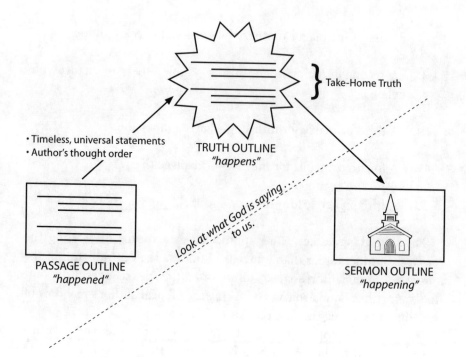

• Timeless, universal statements
• Author's thought order

TRUTH OUTLINE
"happens"

} Take-Home Truth

Look at what God is saying . . . to us.

PASSAGE OUTLINE
"happened"

SERMON OUTLINE
"happening"

Part Two

"LOOK AT WHAT GOD IS SAYING . . . TO US!"

The THT furthered by asking
- What do I need
  to Explain?
- Do we buy it?
- What does it look
  like in real life?

Topic Sentence (TS)

The TS introduces the primary point of the paragraph. It tells the hearer what you will be discussing. Thus, your TS should be direct to the point so that your listener will easily understand your topic.

Concrete Detail (CD)

The CD is a sentence that states evidence facts; illustrations, examples, and other supporting statements for the topic sentence. The CD typically begins with any one of these "signal" words: "for example", "as a matter of fact", "for instance."

Commentary (CM)

The CM provides the analysis, opinion or interpretation. It is the sentence that shows how the CD is linked to the TS. The CM is basically your personal take.

Concluding / Closing Sentence (CS)

The CS summarizes the whole point of the paragraph while serving as a transition sentence for the next paragraph. A common way to start a CS is by using the "signal" phrase, "as a result, therefore, or in effect."

– 5 –

what: a) Explanation (state)
- understands
Why: b) Application p106 120 (Restate)
- belief
where: c) Illustration (illustrate)
- behavior

what do I need to explain about the main point?

How does this apply to the people in front of me? (specific situation)

How can I better help them understand by an analogy, or story that is memorable or clear. (an area outside our personal lives) i.e word study

Relevance = Application of to info-how truth not on illustration.

Ask the Right Questions
Read with critical eyes.

HOW DO YOU EXPAND ~~FIFTEEN~~ sentences into thirty minutes? How do you go from your truth outline to a full message? How do you expand the bare-bones statements of "What God is saying" so that your listeners will realize he is saying it "to us"? You do it by asking three developmental questions:

I. God sometimes gives us a seemingly impossible task.
II. We object that we lack the ability to do what he has asked.
III. He instructs us & under whatever resources we have available to him.
IV. He will expand and empower those resources...

1. What do I need to explain?
2. Do we buy it?
3. What does it look like in real life? *ie: p. 80*

Probing the take-home truth and each statement in the outline with these three questions causes the biblical text to expand and develop into a full sermon.

} Take-Home Truth

Relevance
• What do I need to explain?
• Do we buy it?
• What does it look like?

• Timeless, universal statements
• Author's thought order

TRUTH OUTLINE
"happens"

PASSAGE OUTLINE
"happened"

SERMON OUTLINE
"happening"

where's the friction, the rub, the discomfort?

Ask / the truth outline these questions to expand the message... to a sermon outline.

While there are many different ways to phrase these developmental questions, they all address the three essential areas regarding biblical material: understanding, belief, and behavior.

166

Understanding *WHAT IS SAID?*

what is essential for the listener to know in order to understand what God is saying

- What do I need to explain? *- visual picture* *(behavioral) statement*
- What does this statement mean? *(sequence of events or circumstances)*
- What won't my listeners understand? *(universal command or individual leading)*

clear *(what is essential to know in order to understand what God is saying?)*

Belief *WHY ITS TRUE?*

- Do we buy it?
- Why is this statement true?
- Why does the cause-effect relationship hold true?
- What could cause my listeners not to accept or act on this statement?
- Do I need to prove or defend this statement?

Convincing *- (cause/effect) - contrary to life - not important*

WHERE IS IT, OR CAN OPERATE IN OUR LI[FE]

Behavior *- Relevancy*

- What does it look like in everyday situations?
- Where does it show up in real life?
- What are the implications, the practical applications?
- How, exactly, would my people carry this out in the daily events and circumstances of their lives?
- How can I specifically visualize this for my listeners?
- What ought to happen?
- What ought to change?

Relevant *visualize scenarios this this* *what shows up*

As you ask these questions of each assertion in the biblical outline, you discover what you need to say further about each point in order to make it clear, convincing, and relevant to your contemporary listener.

Let's consider a few of these developmental questions.

WHAT DO I NEED TO EXPLAIN? *- Understanding*

In every biblical message, there are some obvious things that you'll need to explain. Here, for example, is a sermon outline for Colossians 1:9–12:

I. We should continually pray for our Christian friends to know God's will.
   A. Paul continually prays for the Colossians to know God's will (1:9).
      1. More than anything else, he wants them to fully know God's will through all spiritual wisdom and understanding.
      2. He continually prays, therefore, for this to happen.
   B. We should continually pray for our Christian friends to know God's will.

II. When our friends know God's will, they will live worthy of and pleasing to the Lord in every way (1:10–12).
   A. When they know God's will, they will live worthy of the Lord (1:10a).
   B. When they know God's will, they will live pleasing to the Lord (1:10b–12).
      1. They will please him by being productive in good works.
      2. They will please him by growing in knowledge.
      3. They will please him by developing endurance and patience.
      4. They will please him by giving thanks.

One obvious thing you'd need to explain in this message is what Paul means by "God's will." Does he have in mind the behavioral statements God has given us (e.g., "It is God's will that you should avoid sexual immorality" [1 Thess. 4:3])? Or is he referring to the sequence of events or circumstances God has in mind for their life/church (e.g., "Those who suffer according to God's will should commit themselves to their faithful Creator and continue to do good" [1 Peter 4:19])? Obviously you would need to explain whether God's will refers to universal commands or to individual leading.

It also would be helpful to explain what Paul meant when he spoke of continually praying. Your listeners might be thinking, "I can't continually pray; I have to go to work." You would need to explain what it means to continually pray.

Other explanations might include:

- Paul's relationship to these people whom he has never met (cf. v. 9).
- The precise meaning of "spiritual wisdom and understanding" in verse 9.
- The difference between "worthy of" and "pleasing to" (the former may be a horizontal assessment by others, while the latter may be a vertical assessment by God).
- The difference between "endurance" and "patience" in verse 11 (the former may relate to events and the latter to people).

As you answer the question, "What do I need to explain?" be as picturesque as possible in your explanations. Avoid dictionary definitions and abstract descriptions that cause eyes to glass over. Instead, create a visual picture in the listener's mind.

For example, Matthew 6:21, "Where your treasure is, there your heart will be also," could be explained in picture terms:

We usually have it backward, opposite from what Jesus said. We think, "If you get a man's heart, you get his treasure."

Suppose someone visits the seminary where I teach. I show him around campus, pointing out the wonderful diversity of ethnic backgrounds and church traditions. I show him the special homiletics lab and the postings on the bulletin board, where more churches are requesting graduates and workers than we can possibly fill. I get him excited about the ministry of the school.

He says, "Wow, you guys are doing a great job." "Yeah, why don't you consider giving to the school?" "Maybe I will!"

That's usually how we think: "Where the heart is, the treasure will follow."

But Jesus puts it the other way around: "Where the treasure is, the heart will follow." Where a person puts his money is where his heart will focus. Have you invested in a stock or a mutual fund? I bet you look up that stock every day on the financial listing, even before you turn to the comics. Do you support a missionary in some obscure Third-World country? I bet you know more about that country than you do about other countries surrounding it. That's because your heart follows your treasure.

Do you want your heart to be overwhelmed and enthralled with God? Then give your money to the things of heaven, for where your treasure is, your heart will follow.

Matthew 10:29, "Are not two sparrows sold for a penny? Yet not one of them will fall to the ground apart from the will of your Father," also can be explained in picture terms:

Tomorrow morning, downtown, a pet store owner is going to open shop. He'll go to the glass area against one of the walls, take out two parakeets, and put them in a cage with a sign, "Sale, 2 parakeets, $5.95." Later that morning a woman will come into the store to buy a pet for her grandchildren. Because her son-in-law will not tolerate dogs or cats, she'll settle on the parakeets. She'll write out a check—"Two parakeets, $5.95"—put the cage in the back seat of her car, and drive off.

A few blocks later a car will suddenly swerve in front of her. To avoid a collision, she'll jam on the brakes. And in the back seat of the car the cage will tumble to the floor amid a flutter of "brreet, brreet, brreet." And God in heaven will know that it happened.

Isn't that what Jesus says in Matthew 10:29? "Are not two sparrows sold for a penny"—a penny, an assarion, a small copper coin worth one-sixteenth of a denarius, one-sixteenth of a daily wage? Are not two parakeets sold for $5.95? "Yet not one of them will fall to the ground apart from the will of your Father."

The concept of trust, or faith, can be explained by calling up members of the audience and asking them to stand rigid and fall back, trusting your promise to catch them. See if they really will trust you, or whether at the last minute they will thrust back one of their feet to protect themselves from falling. *(1)*

We're usually good at this first developmental question: "What do I need to explain?" Explanation is easy; it's our strong suit. Our hours of study in the passage and in the commentaries provide us with the information we need to develop this area.

In fact, we're so good at explanation that sometimes it takes over the message. We end up explaining everything we've learned about the passage. We're like the TV weather reporter who has to fill up ten minutes on the nightly broadcast. The reporter tells us more than we're interested in—barometric pressures rising or falling, jet streams from the east, high-pressure troughs, offshore depressions, snow flurries in states half a continent away. We don't want or need all this explanation. All we want to know is, "How hot will it be tomorrow?" or "Do I need to take an umbrella with me?"

Likewise in preaching, we should be guided by "What do I *need* to explain?" What is essential for the listener to know in order to understand what God is saying?

We need to make sure explanation doesn't take over the message, not only because it might numb the listener, but also because explanation alone is seldom enough to bring about spiritual change in our hearers. It's not necessarily true that, "If we explain it, they will do it." Knowledge doesn't always produce godly behavior. We need to go on to the second developmental question.

DO WE BUY IT? – *Belief*

Knowing something does not necessarily mean that we buy it or that we will do it. We must first be convinced that it is true.

Our own experience confirms this. For example, many of us probably had some secular theory or body of knowledge explained to us in college. Maybe in a class on child psychology the professor explained that spanking was the least desirable method of discipline for a child: at worst it was child abuse; at best it taught the child that "might makes right" and that when the child got bigger he too could impose his will on others by force. The professor may then have gone on to advocate distraction or isolation as preferable methods of child discipline.

1) Fact – something that can be proven to exist via some sort of evidence.

2) Opinion — something that may or may not be a fact. Until I verify it, it remains an opinion.

As we listened to his explanations, however, something in our spirit said, "That's not true. The Bible says that sparing the rod will do great harm to a child'" (Prov. 13:24; 22:15; 23:13–14).

When the time came for the final exam and we saw the question, "Compare and contrast different methods of child discipline," though we *knew* the answer, we didn't *buy* it. (We got our A on the exam while preserving our integrity, by writing something like, "According to the material presented in class . . ." That meant, "I know what you want me to know, but I don't necessarily accept it as truth for my life.")

In a similar way, our people know many biblical teachings: that wives are to be submissive to their husbands; that husbands are to treat their wives with consideration and respect; that we all are to avoid lustful fantasies, give generously to the Lord's work, marry Christians, intercede for others, and on and on. In fact, our people probably already know 90 percent of any biblical instruction we plan to give them. The reason they are not yet obeying biblical truth is not because they don't know it but because they don't yet buy it.

We could simply explain it to them again for the eighteenth time, but this probably won't have any more effect on them than the previous seventeen times. Instead, along with our explanation we should begin to probe whether they buy it. Do they accept the biblical statement as an authoritative and energizing truth for their lives? Do they own it deep in their souls? If not, why not?

In order to probe and expand the biblical outline points with this second developmental question, it helps to know the three reasons why people don't buy something. What we'll need to say to convince them to own God's truth will depend on the reason why they may not yet have accepted it.

1. The first reason people don't buy something is because they don't see the cause-effect connection. (why is the statement true?)

People often don't buy the truth of the message because they don't understand the cause-effect connection. For example, in the statement "Be nice to your grandfather; it will help you have babies," all the words and phrases are clear. The explanation is obvious. But the validity of the cause-effect connection is not. The listeners don't buy the assertion because they don't see how being nice to an elderly gentleman will have the effect of them getting pregnant.

3) Principle — something that is true in all cases. An example of a principle is the principle of percussion. i.e. When I throw a stone in water, there will always be ripples or waves. Certainty . . .

In other words, how does one half of the statement affect the other half? What is the dynamic that causes the statement to be true? Until the listeners buy the reality or truth of the cause-effect relationship, the statement as a whole will have no authoritative or energizing force in their lives.

In such situations the listeners are not hostile or argumentative. They're willing to be persuaded if the speaker can simply answer the question, "*Why* is this statement true?"

In order for the listeners to be truly motivated to be nice to their grandfathers, the speaker will have to show the cause-effect connection.

He could do this, for example, by pointing out that their grandfather's secret recipe for BBQ sauce is an aphrodisiac, and if they are nice to their grandfather, he may give them his secret recipe, and this will help them have babies.

More likely, the speaker will remind his listeners that "the prayer of a righteous man is powerful and effective" (James 5:16). He will then explain that their kindness to a godly grandfather may lead him to pray to the Lord on their behalf to open the womb and that such a prayer may enable them to conceive.

 Our preaching will inevitably touch on the many cause-effect statements of Scripture. The Bible continually uses language that implies causation: "this leads to this," "this results from this," "this produces this," "this follows from this," "this brings about this."

For example, 1 Timothy 5:1 teaches that it is detrimental to a young man's ministry to harshly rebuke an older man. This is essentially a cause-effect statement: "Harshly rebuking will *cause the effect* of a weakened ministry." But *why* is this true? On the surface, a young pastor may nod in agreement. But later, under pressure, he will blow up at an elder in a meeting, justifying it by thinking, "Somebody needs to tell this man the truth." And from then on the young pastor's ministry will suffer because he never did see or buy the connection between a harsh rebuke and a diminished ministry. We need to show why the statement is true.

Similarly, in Colossians 1:9–11, one of Paul's exhortations can be stated, "You should desire to know the will of God, for this will lead you to be more patient with other Christians." You could explain what Paul means by "will of God." And you could define and give examples of patience. But until you also show how one leads to the other—how knowledge of God's will causes the effect of patience—the statement will have little motivating force in the listener's life. What is the internal dynamic that joins the two halves of the statement?

The promise of Ephesians 6:2–3 is that honoring our parents causes us to live longer. What is the connection between honoring and longevity?

The Word of God constantly has such cause-effect statements at the heart of its teaching. In order for your listeners to fully buy these truths, you must explain the dynamic that joins the two halves together. Simply put, you must answer the question, "Why is this statement true?"

But what if your text doesn't give the answer? How do you surface the correct cause-effect connection when neither your passage nor a cross-reference spells it out? The answer or insight you are looking for may come from one of several sources.

- Your own life experiences sometimes reveal the connection—for example, a time when you harshly rebuked an older man and saw why it set back your ministry.
- Quiet reflection, combined with prayer for the Spirit's help, often can yield an understanding—for example, if we know "God's will," God's intentions for our ministry, we will not fear that someone's resistance will derail his plan but instead will wait "patiently" for God to bring that person along.
- Friends, wives, older people in the congregation, devotional commentaries, outside reading, or members of a small group who help us think about each week's sermon also can give us insights into this cause-effect connection.

Obviously you will offer your cause-effect insights in language that is a bit more tentative than "thus saith the Lord." Since the text itself does not amplify the connection, you will lead into your explanations with such phrases as: "Perhaps the apostle has in mind . . ."; "It seems to me that . . ."; "One explanation might be . . ."; "Maybe the biblical author has observed what you and I have observed, that . . ." This kind of language helps convey that you are making your best attempt at explaining God's inerrant Word.

Granted, you will not have absolute certainty that your cause-effect connection is the one the biblical writer had in mind. But as the insight satisfies your heart, and as the Spirit affirms it during the sermon to the hearts of God's people, you will have a high degree of confidence that you are presenting God's truth.

2. **A second reason people don't buy something is because it seems contrary to real life.** *(show the ultimate truth, or reality behind the words of God.)*

People might not buy the message because it doesn't seem to line up with real life. Their attitude is "That's not how it is in the real world!" For them, the statement simply is not true because their life experiences contradict it.

For example, a woman's response to 1 Peter 3:1–2, "The way to win your husband is through a gentle and quiet yieldedness," might be:

> I tried that, and it didn't work. When I let him do what he wanted, he joined five different softball leagues, and the kids never saw him at night. I didn't win him; he only got worse. And if I let him handle the money, he'd take our savings and invest in the dumbest Ponzi scheme you ever heard of. Our family would be bankrupt. Maybe some other woman can win her husband that way, but not me. For mine, I have to lay down the law and then stay on his case.

Similarly, when a man hears he should "honor his father and mother," he might think:

> If you knew my parents, you wouldn't tell me to do that. If you knew their vices . . . if you knew how manipulative they were . . . if you knew what my father did to my sisters as they were growing up . . . if you knew how my siblings and I are still trying to get rid of the baggage from living in that dysfunctional home, you wouldn't tell me to honor my parents.

In such situations, the listeners are hostile to what the speaker is saying. They flat-out disbelieve the biblical truth and have no intention of living according to it. Based on their life experiences, the statement simply is not true. They don't buy it.

These unspoken objections must be addressed before anything can be accomplished in the message. The listeners sit with the attitude, "Yeah, but . . ." and the "but" deflects anything you say from entering their hearts.

The first step in addressing the objections is to make sure you and the listeners have the same meaning in mind for the key words or terms. Make sure, for example, that when the wife hears "yielding," she hears it as something that occurs *after* objecting, arguing, and pleading, and not as something that expects her to keep her mouth shut and do as she's told. Similarly, when the man hears you say "honor," make sure he knows you mean, "speak politely and respectfully to," and not "publicly praise."

Even after you've made the concepts clear, however, the objections may still remain. Therefore, the second and more critical step in dealing with them is to show that the listeners' life experiences ultimately are *not* contrary to the biblical truth.

This does not mean you deny their life experiences. You can't imply, "Oh, it wasn't really that bad." They could rightly respond, "Were you there?"

But you can show that, while their life experiences and attitudes may be real, they do not invalidate God's truth. You might suggest, for example, that their experience of doing it God's way simply needs more time in order to arrive at the desired outcome.

More helpfully, you might probe the alternative course of action they have chosen instead. You could show that their contrary behavior is actually leading to worse consequences than those they feared had they done it God's way. Since disobedience to God's Word inevitably leads to some measure of sorrow and disintegration, it would not be too difficult for you to illustrate this for them.

For example, you might show that when a wife fails to yield, instead of winning her husband, she actually drives him further away. You might say something like this:

> You know, when a man and woman come to marriage, each one of them has some thoughts deep within. When a man marries, he has the thought, "I'm supposed to be the leader in this marriage." That's strange, because he never has that thought in any other area. A man doesn't go to work and say, "I'm supposed to be the leader in this company." He doesn't look at the government and say, "I'm supposed to be in charge of the country." He doesn't go to church and say, "I'm supposed to be

the leader of the congregation." But when a man marries, something deep within him says, "I'm supposed to be the leader in this marriage." God has put that thought inside him; it is part of his "maleness."

Similarly, when a woman marries, her thoughts are, "I want this man to be my protector. I want him to be my knight in shining armor. When children come, I want him to stand guard and protect us from the world. I want to count on him to keep us safe." These thoughts are part of her "femininity," created by God.

Now, because we are sinners, we often don't act consistent with these thoughts. Because a man is a sinner, he sometimes doesn't lead as he should. Instead of caring for the best interests of his wife and family, he sometimes thinks only of himself and acts self-centeredly.

And because a woman is afraid when she sees this happening, and is fearful of the consequences to the family, she sometimes tries to force the man to act as he should. "No, you can't do that," she says. "You have to act right!"

But in the process of compelling the behavior she wants him to have, she adopts a morally superior position. In essence, she stands over him with a scolding finger and says, "I will tell you what to do. I know better than you do. You will do as I say."

This raises the man's hackles, because now she's taking the leadership position in the marriage. She's acting as his mommy, telling him what to do. But she's not his mommy; she's his wife.

Therefore, in the early stages, a man will resist her attempts to compel his behavior. "Don't tell me what to do!" he will shout. He will argue, fight, slam doors, and, if he's really a sinner, he may even strike her. He will try to hang on to his leadership, even though it is bad leadership.

But as this arguing and fighting continues over months, eventually, the Bible says, a man will kick into a second response—he will shut down and become passive. He will conclude, as Solomon did on more than one occasion, "Better to live on a corner of the roof than share a house with a quarrelsome wife" (Prov. 21:9; 25:24).

He'll retreat to his hobbies or the television set. He'll go run his Fortune 500 company. His attitude will be, "I don't want to argue anymore. I want peace. You can do whatever you want. You can decorate the house any way you want; you can send the kids to whatever schools you want; you can join whatever clubs you want. I don't care!"

> And you will have lost your knight in shining armor. Instead of winning him, you will have driven him away.
>
> Perhaps as you are listening to me, you are thinking, "You know, he never talks to me anymore. Whenever I suggest something or ask something, he just kind of shrugs and doesn't comment much at all. I can't get him to interact at all. But I'm afraid to let him take the lead. I'm afraid of what he'll do. I'm afraid of bankruptcy!"

At this point, you are ready to go further into 1 Peter 3:1–6. You can admit that such a wife's fear is real, but you can also show her how holy women of the past, like Sarah, put their hope in God, submitted to their husbands, and did not give way to their fears. You explain how Abraham twice put Sarah in fearful and compromising circumstances (Gen. 12:10–20; 20:1–18). You show how God acted both times to save her from the consequences of his poor leadership. Then you continue:

> When you stand in a morally superior position over your husband, you essentially get between him and God. And God can't get at him. God says, "Stand aside, honey. Let me take care of him." And God will hit him with a four-by-four, and the man will stagger and look into the heavens and ask, "Whaddaya want, God?" A man will take it from God, whereas he won't take it from his wife. And God will deal with him.
>
> It may involve bankruptcy. But you can come back from bankruptcy. You can't come back from divorce. And afterward, your husband will say to you, "Hon, you were right. I'm sorry." And instead of saying, "I told you so," you'll say, "You're my man. We did it once; we can do it again." And you will have "won" your husband.

One way or another, you can show that they are actually reinforcing what the Word teaches by probing and reflecting on their experiences. In a similar manner, you might say to a man who finds it difficult to honor his parents:

> They may have been poor parents. They may have made a lot of mistakes. But they probably did some things right.
>
> Whatever their failures, we owe our parents a great debt. They gave us life. They fed us, clothed us, and put a roof over our heads for years. The human infant is not like an animal infant—able to take care of itself after a few months. Unless someone was watching out for us, and taking care of us, we would have died.
>
> Maybe your dad went to a job he hated and gritted his teeth while some supervisor gave him a bad time. Everything in your dad wanted to stuff it down the boss's throat, but jobs were hard to come by and he was determined to provide for you.
>
> And as we think of the years of that debt, we may be able to speak quietly and respectfully in his presence.

In this way, a husband's folly or a parent's failure does not remain an obstacle to God's truth. A wife can buy yielding, and a son can buy honoring, as actions that will lead to God's blessing.

In order for us to search out how our listeners' experiences are consistent with biblical truth, we ourselves must begin with the deep conviction that God's statements are always true. We must have the spirit of Paul, who wrote, "Let God be true, and every man a liar" (Rom. 3:4; i.e., whatever God says is true, and anyone who says something contrary is wrong). We start with the conviction that no one's life experience invalidates yielding or honoring.

Then, we are motivated by the thought, that while it is accurate to say

"Something is true because it's in the Bible,"

it's even more accurate to say,

"Something is in the Bible because it's true."

There is an "ultimate truth" or "reality in life" that underlies every biblical statement. For example, adultery did not become damaging when
God commanded against it. It wasn't his forbidding it that made it a bad
thing. Instead, it's because God knew adultery would always be harmful
and because he didn't want us to painfully learn that through trial and
error, that he lovingly warned us against it.

Our job is to explain this ultimate truth or reality behind the biblical
words. When we show what God knew that led him to say what he said, we
help the listener to really believe it.

3. A third reason people don't buy something is because something else comes up that is more important to them.

On Sunday our listeners may seem to assent to a particular biblical
truth. But during the week other factors come up that seem more crucial
to their well-being. These other factors outweigh the biblical statement,
and our listeners act according to that pressure rather than according to
God's truth. In such cases, they buy something else *more* than they buy
the biblical statement.

In a vacuum, with all things being equal, they do buy the biblical truth.
But real life is not a vacuum, and all things are not equal. People hold to a
hierarchy of beliefs, a ladder of truths. Some values are higher on the ladder than others. They seem more important, they seem to matter more,
and so people buy them ahead of others.

Suppose, for example, I detest rhubarb pie and essentially buy the statement, "Rhubarb pie is to be avoided." But suppose also that I'm invited to
a friend's house, and as we're waiting for the hostess to bring in the des-
sert, the husband says to me: "Don, you're in luck. My wife has prepared
her secret family recipe, county award-winning rhubarb pie. She doesn't
do this for very many people, because she has to drive two hours to get
decent rhubarb and it takes four to five hours to prepare and bake the pie.
But for you, she's done it."

Now, I may buy the statement, "Rhubarb pie is to be avoided," but I
also buy the statement, "You don't insult the efforts of a loving hostess."
Whichever one of these statements I buy the most is the one I'm going to
act on in that situation. And you can probably guess that I'll choke down a
few swallows before I announce, "I'm too full to eat another bite."

A teenage girl might prayerfully commit herself on Sunday to "dress modestly to the glory of God." But then on Saturday, at the beach, she wears a bathing suit that doesn't fit anybody's definition of modesty and twines herself around some college guy. This doesn't necessarily mean she's a hypocrite. It may simply mean that though she buys modesty, she buys even more having a boyfriend or getting affirmation that her femininity is desirable.

To get her to buy or value God's truth most of all would require bringing up the other values on Sunday, acknowledging their tug on her, and then showing either the superior benefits of acting according to God's truth or the dangerous side effects of acting according to the contrary values. One way or another, the goal is to help her see the biblical truth as more important.

Suppose a woman named Helen is listening to you preach about being honest at the job. Let's imagine that Helen works for an entrepreneur named Sam, who has developed a software program for the medical industry. Hospitals can use the program to track medical supplies, schedule operating rooms, handle payroll, and so on. Once a central hospital adopts the program, most doctors' offices in the community follow suit in order to be compatible with the hospital. Sam's the creative genius behind the program and markets it throughout the state. Helen is his business manager, holding down the fort and supervising two other women in the office.

Helen is a godly woman. Her husband is on the church board. They have a high school daughter and a junior high son, both active in church youth groups. You wish every family in the church could be like this family.

Helen also appreciates Sam as a boss. He pays her well. He lets her take off a few hours to watch her son's soccer game or attend her daughter's after-school theater presentation.

As Helen listens to you preach about being honest at the job, she buys it. She nods agreement at your applications: she doesn't take office supplies home for personal use, she doesn't call in sick unless she's really ill, and she promises accurate delivery dates to clients. On Sunday, in church, she buys the biblical truth.

But then suppose the following Tuesday, about 1:30 PM, she gets a call. It's Sam. Before he can say anything, she blurts, "Sam, where are you? Why aren't you here in the office? Did you forget about your 2:00 PM meeting with Dr. Shiller, the hospital administrator at St. Jude's? You were going to demonstrate your software for him. If St. Jude adopts it, the rest of the doctors in the county will follow suit. Why aren't you here getting ready for the appointment with him?"

"Helen, that's why I'm calling. I'm in a hotel an hour away getting ready to demonstrate the program to the heads of the major teaching hospitals in the country. If they go for it, we'll go national! We may even get a write-up in the *New England Journal of Medicine*."

"But what about Shiller? He's going to be here in a few minutes. What should I tell him?"

"Tell him I'm caught in traffic, and I'll be there any minute."

"Sam, I can't tell him that. By the time you demonstrate the program, answer their questions, and then drive across the city, you won't be here until at least 4:00 PM. I can't tell him you'll be here 'any minute.'"

"Helen, you've got to tell him that. If he finds out I double-booked on him, he'll storm out, and we'll never get him back for a demonstration."

"Sam, I can't lie for you."

"Helen, you tell him that, or I'll get someone at that desk who *can* tell him that" (shouted as the phone is being slammed down).

Helen buys "being honest at the job." But she also buys "having a job." Whichever one she buys the most will determine what she'll do when Shiller shows up at 2:00 PM.

To help listeners buy God's truth above all other factors, we must bring up the competing beliefs or attitudes on Sunday before they face them on Tuesday. During the sermon we must help the listeners feel their full force, and then we must show why acting on the biblical statement is even more desirable. We must bring up in advance the potential conflicts that could arise, visualize them honestly, and walk our people through them so that they can commit to God's truth above all else.

For example, during the sermon you could raise the possibility that a commitment to honesty might come into conflict with a desire to keep one's job. You might say to the Helens in your audience, "Be committed to honesty, even though it might mean losing your job. Trust God's promise: If we are persecuted for righteousness' sake—if we act with integrity and pay a price—we are blessed."

At this point, as they listen to you preach, the Helens are probably thinking, "OK, pastor, you just got me fired. Could you work with that 'blessed' part a bit more? It's a little fuzzy to me."

And so, to help your listeners buy honesty more than keeping a job, you might continue along the following lines:

One way or another, you'll be blessed. God may give you a better job—higher pay, closer to home, better hours. I can't guarantee that, but the Bible says God feeds the ravens and clothes the lilies, and if you need the new job, he'll give it to you.

I can guarantee you a clear conscience. You'll walk out of the office that Tuesday afternoon thinking, "God, something just happened in that office. You're up to something in my life. I'm not sure what, but I just did something that pleased you."

Maybe the blessing will be the impact on your junior high son. Maybe Wednesday morning he'll see you at breakfast in your robe and slippers and get the wrong idea: "Do you guys have a holiday and we have to go to school? No fair!" "No, honey, no holiday. I'm just not going to work today." "What's the matter, Mom? Are you sick?" "No, honey, I'm not sick. To tell you the truth, I got fired yesterday." "You did! What did you do?" "Well, the boss wanted me to say... and I wouldn't." On his way to school, your son excitedly tells his best friend, "My mom got fired because she wouldn't tell a lie." On Sunday, as he shares a hymnbook with you, he looks at the pastor up front, and thinks, "You don't know what happened at our house this week. My mom got fired for telling the truth! This stuff must be real." If getting fired will turn your junior high son into a man of God for the rest of his life, would that be a blessing? You bet it would!

Maybe the blessing is the impact it will have on someone in the office, perhaps even Sam. Maybe, after you tell the truth, and Shiller storms out, you decide to make it easy on Sam by cleaning out your desk and leaving early. As you're putting your personal effects into a cardboard box—family pictures, plants, Far Side cartoons—Sam shows up sooner than expected. "Helen, what are you doing?" "Well, Sam, you said—" "Never mind what I said. Put that stuff back. Put it back! Sit down! Work! You're not going anywhere." Then, as he goes into his office and starts to return a telephone message, he looks back through the door and thinks to himself, "That's one classy lady." A few months later, when Sam is having trouble with his teenagers and he needs to talk to someone who has her head screwed on straight, he may wander out into the office and say, "Hey, Helen, how long has it been since I've taken you to lunch? You like that Italian place around the corner, don't you? How about tomorrow? Good! Maybe my wife will join us." And over lunch Sam is going to work his family situation into the conversation and receive godly counsel.

Maybe the blessing is that God wants you home for the sake of your teenage daughter. He's been trying to get you to quit, but since you haven't, he's getting you fired instead. Your family doesn't need the money as much as your daughter needs you. Have you noticed that her bedroom door is closed every evening, and she's on the phone for hours, talking to her girlfriends? You knock on her door—"Who's there?" "It's me, Mom." "What do you want?" "I got your laundry; can I bring it in?" "OK. Just put it on the bed, Mom. I'll take care of it. Thanks." While you're in the room she cradles the phone to her chest, waiting for you to leave. "Close the door, will you, Mom?" she says. And then you hear her talking again. Your daughter is going through some heavy stuff right now, and she's getting all her advice from non-Christian teenagers. What she really needs is a mother who's home. What she really needs is to help with dinner, so that while she's peeling carrots she can casually drop that oh-so-important question into an everyday conversation. And Mom knows when she's heard a "biggie." She goes to the refrigerator, takes something out—"A couple more carrots, honey"—and answers the question in a matter-of-fact way. And the daughter, still peeling carrots, has gotten the wisdom of a godly mother to help her through life.

One way or another, you'll be blessed.

And every Helen, listening to you preach, is thinking to herself, "I'll take any one of those! Any one of those blessings is better than keeping the job."

In this way—by bringing up the competing beliefs or attitudes within the message itself, by acknowledging their force and attraction, and by showing why God's truth is even more desirable—we help our listeners to buy the biblical value more than anything else.

These are the first two developmental questions, questions that expand or "develop" our biblical outline into a full-fledged sermon:

- What do I need to explain?   *visual*
- Do we buy it?

We turn now to the third question.

WHAT DOES IT LOOK LIKE IN REAL LIFE?   *- Behavior*

Relevance occurs when the listeners "see" how the biblical truth applies to a specific situation. (The word *see* should be highlighted and underlined—with little red hearts drawn around it!)

Unless the listeners get a mental picture of some real-life situation, the biblical truth remains an abstraction. Unless they see a video running in their minds, the biblical concept remains vague and unhelpful. The message has no apparent bearing on their lives until they visualize some person, event, or circumstance in their everyday world.

Our discussion of this third question is not limited to the conclusion of a message. We are not necessarily talking about giving the listeners at the end of the message "three tangible ways you can put this message into practice." Instead, we are talking about a relevancy that pervades the message; all through the message the listeners should constantly "see" the concepts in terms of their everyday lives.

Relevancy is broader than application. Application implies something for the listener to do. Relevancy simply shows how the message connects to life. Apart from any behavior we may eventually urge upon the listener, the whole message should repeatedly picture how the biblical situations or materials are duplicated in contemporary experience.

For example, your introduction to the Mark 4:35–41 sermon (Jesus' stilling the storm)[1] may start out, "Did you ever obey God and have the bottom fall out of everything? Did you ever do exactly what God told you to do and have disaster occur?" At this point there isn't anything for the listener to *do*, but nevertheless you would immediately and relevantly de-

---

1. See pages 38–41.

pict what this might look like in real life—how it would "show up" in everyday situations:

Introduction

> You obey God and move to another city so that you can study at seminary. A few months after the move, however, life seems to fall apart. Your home church is unable to continue its pledged financial support because of an economic downturn; your kids come home from school crying because they are being ostracized and teased by the long-time cliques; your wife has developed undiagnosed allergies in the new community; you receive an F on your first language exam; and you find out that your car has a cracked block. And you pray, "God, why is my life falling apart when all I'm trying to do is obey you?"
>
> You obey God's prompting to honor your mother by taking her into your own home after your dad's death. Everybody seems in agreement; the kids double bunk so that Grandma can have her own room. But after six months the house is in an uproar. Your wife comes to you and says, "It's her or me. Decide which woman you want in this house. She doesn't like the way I cook; she criticizes the way I keep house; she's rearranged my kitchen so that I can't find anything." Your kids are walking on eggshells because Grandma's constantly down on them: "You shouldn't be listening to that devil music. You can't wear that to school—put on something decent." And you're thinking, "God, what are you doing? All I wanted to do was honor my mother, and now my home is a disaster."
>
> A man is convinced God is leading him to marry a certain woman. His parents and church friends confirm what the Spirit has been telling him—that this is God's will. So he obeys. But in the months that follow, his life is in constant and tumultuous upheaval. He sympathizes with the new groom who returned to the minister and said, "When you married me, you said, 'Son, congratulations. You're at the end of all your troubles.' But this last year has been the worst year of my life. You told me I was at the end of all my troubles." "Son," the minister said, "I didn't tell you which end."
>
> Sometimes we obey God, and the bottom falls out of everything.

Throughout the entire message—from the opening paragraphs and all through the progression of concepts—we are constantly asking, "What does this look like in real life? How does it show up in everyday situations? Where do we see it in the events and circumstances of daily life?"

Our goal in speaking is to show how biblical truth bears on contemporary life. Our goal is not simply to give the listener more biblical knowledge. Such knowledge can seem irrelevant.

Suppose I'm teaching Genesis 11–12, Abraham's leaving Ur of the Chaldeans. I describe Ur—a cosmopolitan, commercial, religious city—the center of the ancient Sumerian culture. I talk about its libraries and ziggurats and clay tablets. Because of my study I can probably give more "chamber of commerce" information about Ur than I can about my own hometown. Then, with the latest technology, I trace Abraham's path upon leaving Ur on an auditorium screen—how he follows the Euphrates River valley up toward Haran, staying in Haran until his father Terah's death, and then continuing down the Fertile Crescent into Canaan. (My map, of course, has an arcing green swath for the Fertile Crescent, with white sand for the desert below, showing why Abraham didn't take the shorter path straight across!) Then I trace Abraham's movements down the hilly mountain ridges of Palestine, showing the high places where he built his altars. By the time I'm through, I've "taught" Genesis 11–12. But the listeners are thinking, "The guy's been dead for four thousand years. What do we care?"

The listeners wonder why I've given them all that biblical information. What was my purpose? Was my purpose to simply tell a story of a man crossing great stretches of territory? If so, they'd rather hear about Hannibal crossing the Alps—that one has elephants in it; mine just has camels. Biblical knowledge can seem irrelevant.

Our ultimate goal is not to "teach the Bible" to people. Our ultimate goal is to "teach how what the Bible says fits their life." The reason we're teaching Genesis 11–12 is because God may come to some of our listeners and say the same thing he said to Abraham: "Leave what is comfortable, leave what is familiar, and come with me without knowing what I will put in its place." (Abraham did not know where God was taking him—he was told God would show him the land after he left Ur.)

God may speak such a message to a variety of people:

People are involved in to totality of life; they have problems with spouses, children, parents, lovers, co-workers, themselves, religion, diet, feelings of self-worth and so on... — Don't pass judgment and life will remain worth living...

- a couple he wants to minister cross-culturally;
- a wife struggling over a cross-country move, leaving family, long-time friends, doctors, and neighborhood shops;
- a man wondering whether he should leave IBM, with its secure paycheck, benefits, and retirement, to pioneer his own start-up company;
- a teenager who needs to leave his circle of friends who are a bad influence on him, for the unknowns of "Who will I hang out with? Who will I go to the mall or movies with?";
- a comfortable bachelor, who's afraid to "pop the question";
- a woman who needs to break up with her fiancé, because God is saying, "Fred's a good man, but he's not the one for you; I have someone else in mind." Her response might be, "God, I'm thirty-three years old; Fred is the best thing to come into this small church in the last ten years. If you have someone else in mind, how about bringing him in the front door so that I can take a good look at him before I let go of Fred." But God answers back, "No, let go first, without knowing who I will bring to you."

Even though knowledge alone is irrelevant, it is nevertheless possible to develop a large following from a knowledge-based, information-oriented ministry. Big crowds may come. That's because people get an aesthetic pleasure from "learning something." The success of crossword puzzles or *Reader's Digest* squibs—"Who's the Engineer? (Answer on page 83)"—is because people feel intense satisfaction from "figuring it out." When they've filled in all the blank spaces, they say, "Yeaaah! I got it!" But what have they got? Nothing—just a bunch of white squares with letters in them! Yet they have the mental satisfaction of mastering something new.

The aesthetic attraction of learning something new shows itself in the attitude of the Athenians in Acts 17:19–21:

Then they took him and brought him to a meeting of the Areopagus, where they said to him, "May we know what this new teaching is that you are presenting? You are bringing some strange ideas to our ears, and we want to know what they mean." (All the Athenians and the foreigners who lived there spent their time doing nothing but talking about and listening to the latest ideas.)

But Scripture passes judgment on any preaching that is solely knowledge based, information oriented. That kind of ministry produces a prideful, arrogant people, exactly like the Athenians:

> A group of Epicurean and Stoic philosophers began to dispute with him. Some of them asked, "What is this babbler[2] trying to say?" (Acts 17:18)

> Now about food sacrificed to idols: We know that we all possess knowledge. Knowledge puffs up, but love builds up. (1 Cor. 8:1)

Preaching that is solely knowledge based or information oriented produces a Pharisaism that "knows the law" but is unable to see how deeply it should be changing their lives.

Our ultimate goal in speaking is not knowledge but godly behavior, not information but Christlikeness:

> The goal of this command is love, which comes from a pure heart and a good conscience and a sincere faith. (1 Tim. 1:5)

Our primary intent is not that our listeners learn something but that they use the Scriptures for all the practical ways intended in everyday life:

> All Scripture is God-breathed and is useful for teaching, rebuking, correcting and training in righteousness, so that the man of God may be thoroughly equipped for every good work. (2 Tim. 3:16–17)

Until our listeners "see" how the truths of Scripture apply in the concrete situations of life, their Christianity is shallow, and they are deceived about their spiritual growth:

> But everyone who hears these words of mine and does not put them into practice is like a foolish man who built his house on

---

2. Literally, "this picker-up of seeds." This is a derisive term for one who goes about as a bird picking up seeds from the gutter or a "plagiarizer" who would pass off scraps of learning from hither and yon to make a living; a "chatterer."

sand. The rain came down, the streams rose, and the winds blew
and beat against that house, and it fell with a great crash. (Matt.
7:26–27)

Do not merely listen to the word, and so deceive yourselves. Do
what it says. Anyone who listens to the word but does not do what
it says is like a man who looks at his face in a mirror and, after
looking at himself, goes away and immediately forgets what he
looks like. But the man who looks intently into the perfect law
that gives freedom, and continues to do this, not forgetting what
he has heard, but doing it—he will be blessed in what he does.
(James 1:22–25)

In order for relevance to occur and godliness to form, it is the speaker
who will have to make the applications. The listeners usually will not
make them for themselves. I know this from my own experience when
I'm on vacation and listening to another preacher. At the end of his message—when the music is playing, the congregation is dismissed, and
people are trying to step past me to get to the aisle—if he hasn't given
me some concrete pictures of how the truth bears on my life, I don't stay
seated in my chair, blocking others, appealing to my wife, "Honey, let
me have a few minutes alone. I want to think of how this applies to my
life." No. I rise like the others, turn to my wife, and say, "You want to get
hamburgers or pizza? You get the girls; I'll get the boys. I'll meet you at
the car."

So the next time you as a speaker find yourself saying, "May the Spirit
of God apply this to your hearts," what you're really saying is, "I haven't
the vaguest idea of how it fits; maybe you'll think of something." But they
won't.

We must make the application. Our sermon must be an extended medi-
tation on God's truth, which will result in an understanding not only of
what is said and *why* it is true, but also *where* it is operating or can operate
in our lives—covering all three developmental questions.
So in this third developmental question, our goal is to visualize scenarios that might realistically occur in the listener's life, to picture some
person, event, or circumstance in their everyday world where the biblical
truth would have some bearing.

Person   Event   Circumstances

But how do we come up with these relevant pictures? What skills help us to surface and describe how God's truth shows up in their lives?

There are four steps that will help you discover and present what it looks like in real life.

How is the premise lived out?

1. Think where it would show up in your own life.

Ask yourself, "How have I experienced this? How am I experiencing it? How might I experience it?" (Think in all three tenses; imagine realistic situations in the future as well as actual ones in the past and present.)

For instance, suppose you're talking about the kind of anger that erupts or explodes when we're impatient, irritated, or frustrated. Ask, "When might this kind of anger show up in my life?"

- When you head to the "fifteen items or less," checkout line at the grocery store, only to find yourself behind a cart that has forty-five items in it. And then to further the aggravation, the offending shopper waits until all the items have been scanned and sacked before beginning a lengthy fumbling for coupons and a hunt for dimes and pennies with which to pay.

- When you call some government agency or large corporation and you get an unending, circular series of menu choices that never lead you to a real person.

- When someone cuts you off on the freeway and almost drives you into the guardrail.

- When you come home after work and find bicycles in front of the garage door, despite the many times you've told your children to put them away. You're hungry, your blood sugar is down, and you've had a hard day. You honk loudly and repeatedly, hoping to get someone to come out of the house and move the bikes. But the house is sealed up tight against the weather, and the kids are in front of a noisy TV. Nobody hears you, nobody comes out. Your first impulse is to teach them a lesson by running over the bikes, but you realize you'd then have to buy them new bikes. So you get out of your car, throw the bikes into a corner where it will be difficult for the kids to untangle them, pull the car into the garage, storm into the house, loom over the unsuspecting kids on the floor, and loudly vent, "How many times have I told you to . . ."

- When one of your church board members, in a knee-jerk reaction, throws cold water on one of your suggestions without even trying to understand its advantages.

Wherever it shows up in your life is probably where it also shows up in the lives of your listeners, and you can visualize the situation for them. (You probably wouldn't want to use the last one in a sermon, but you could easily portray an equivalent situation in their lives—e.g., when an in-law pooh-poohs some idea they have, or a coworker ridicules their suggestion at work.)

How is the promise lived out?

2. Run the truth through an expanding grid of the various groups and life circumstances that are in your audience.

Visualize the different kinds of people you'll be talking to—men, women, children. Break these down into subcategories, and rummage around to see if your biblical truth shows up in some situation.

For instance, take the men. What different hats do your men wear? What roles or functions do they have in life? Among other things, they are:

Person / Event / Circumstance

- Husbands
- Fathers
- Workers
- Sons
- Neighbors
- Citizens
- Hobbyists

The more general and vague the word, the higher its level of abstraction, i.e. mammal vs cow

But break these subcategories down further, into sub-subcategories and sub-sub-subcategories. Not all "husbands" or "fathers" are the same. What are the different kinds of "husbands"? How do the men differ in their "fathering"?

- Husbands
  — How long they've been married
    ■ One year
      • A twenty-year-old married one year, first marriage

• A forty-year-old married one year, first marriage
(The wife can still raise the first husband; the
second husband is hopeless!)
▪ Fifteen years
▪ Forty years
— Whether this is the first marriage or a subsequent one for
either spouse
— Whether they had role models for husbanding in their
own fathers

• Fathers
— How many children
— How old the children are
— Whether the children are boys, girls, or both
— Whether he's the biological father or a step-dad

Let's probe the "worker" category above. As you break it down, ask,
"What does someone in each category need to think about or deal with?"
See if your biblical truth strikes fire with one of the scenarios.

• Worker
— Owns the business; the boss
▪ Bottom line; profit
▪ Employees
• Hiring, firing, training
• Morale
• Fringe benefits
▪ Government regulations, OSHA, Worker's Comp
▪ Competition; obsolescence of the product/service
— Works for another; an employee
▪ Dead-end job, no advancement
▪ Boring job, routine
▪ Boss
• Demanding, critical
• Incompetent
• Plays favorites, nepotism
• Harasses, crude, immoral

- Fellow employees
  - Lazy
  - Incompetent
  - Obnoxious
- Safety concerns, health hazards
- Salary, benefits
- Commuting time or distance
- Production pressures; stress; in over one's head
— Retired; on Social Security
  - Still consulting; a different part-time job
  - Struggles over self-worth, purpose in life
  - Adequate pension, retirement funds
  - What now fills up the time
— Unemployed
  - How long between jobs; economic impact on the family
  - Self-image concerns
  - Age discrimination; likelihood of finding another equivalent job
  - Retraining necessary; new schooling

If nothing strikes fire in the "worker" area, you would switch to another—such as their dwelling situations or the different ages of marriage—still asking, "Does my biblical truth 'show up' in any of these circumstances?"

- Dwelling
  — Own their home
    - Property value
    - Neighbors
    - Upkeep
    - Mortgage
    - Taxes, insurance
  — Rent
    - Lack of equity
    - Landlord
      - Unresponsive to needed repairs
      - Rents the apartment above me to a punk rock band

- • Makes restrictive rules regarding what my kids can do
  Swimming, playing on the grass, setting hours
  - • Has a key to my apartment
  - • Raises the rent unexpectedly
  - ▪ Safety (coming from the carport or using the laundry at night)
  - ▪ Neighbors' noise
- — Live with parents
  - ▪ Freedom to come and go without giving account
  - ▪ Privacy; does mom go through my stuff?
  - ▪ Use of the home for parties with my friends
  - ▪ Watching TV with my date without having mom watch with us
  - ▪ Self-image issues, trying to explain to my friends where I live
  - ▪ Sharing in the food costs, having chores
- — Roommates
  - ▪ Meshing lifestyles and personalities
    - • Early morning riser vs. late-nighter
    - • Neatnik vs. slob—clothes on the floor, dishes in the sink
  - ▪ Getting the rent payment together on time
  - ▪ Moral issues, such as having a date spend the night
  - ▪ Borrowing clothes, eating another's food from the fridge

- • Age of Marriage
  - — Newlyweds
    - ▪ Who handles the checkbook
    - ▪ What to spend money on, and how much
      - • Clothes, eating out, club memberships, tithing
    - ▪ In-laws
      - • Unsolicited advice regarding housing, careers, children
      - • Untimely calls, visits; do they have a key to your apartment?
      - • Whose house we go to for Christmas
      - • Whether to accept money from them

- Whose career gets priority when a promotion would mean a move
- When to start a family
- How to save for a house
— Midlife
  - Raising teenagers
  - Handling aging parents
  - Saving for retirement
  - Disillusionments
    - Career ceilings or dead ends
    - Spouse's physical attractiveness lessens
    - Kids turning out bad
— Elderly
  - Health issues; financial concerns
  - Dwindling of social circle as friends die off
  - Remaining independent, as the kids try to take control
  - Loss of spouse

Or suppose you're preaching on the biblical truth, "Blessed are you when you are persecuted for righteousness' sake," and you want to encourage your people to act with integrity even though they may pay a price. How would this "show up" in various lifestyles?

- A businessperson
- A junior high student
- A single career person starting an entry-level job
- A stay-at-home mom with three children
- A seventy-eight-year-old widow whose husband died five years ago

The first three of the above are relatively easy to imagine. Rather than spend time on them, let's take a stab at the last two.

Here's a stay-at-home mom. She has a fourteen-year-old son in the eighth grade, a twelve-year-old daughter in the sixth grade, and a five-year-old child at home. She lives in a nice home and has a loving Christian husband who makes good money at IBM. How would this mom face persecution for acting righteously? Rummage around in her life until you can visualize realistic situations she could identify with.

- She speaks up in a PTA meeting against a proposal to include "alternative lifestyle" units in the sixth-grade curriculum and gets jeered down with charges of bigotry and intolerance.
- She won't let her "all-star" fourteen-year-old son play league soccer games on Sunday during church times. As a result, she not only has to argue with her son, but she also has to deal with the coach's and team's animosity over each Sunday loss.
- She won't send her children for two weeks to her in-laws on their Kansas farm, but she will send them for two weeks with her parents to the beach. That's because her parents are Christians, but her husband's aren't. She doesn't want her teenage son to see the pornography her father-in-law has in the house. In fact, she's not sure she can trust her father-in-law with her twelve-year-old daughter. Her husband supports her decision, but she gets plenty of verbal abuse from her in-laws because of it.
- Her twelve-year-old daughter comes home with an invitation to the birthday party of the most popular girl in the sixth grade. The mom, seeing from the invitation that the location is forty-five minutes away and not being excited about two round-trips, decides to call the hosting mom and offer to stay and help with the party.

The hosting mom responds, "Oh, that's very nice of you to offer, but there would really be nothing for you to do. My friend and I are going to load the girls into our two vans. We're going to see a movie, then go out for pizza, and finally end up back at the house for ice cream, cake, and the opening of presents. All you need to do is pick up your daughter at the end."

Hearing "go to a movie," the Christian mom begins to gently probe. "Oh, what movie were you thinking of taking the girls to?" "Well, our daughter wants to see such-and-such, and we told her she could take her birthday group to it." "Uh—do you know anything about that movie? Some of the things I've read about it—" "Well, my husband and I have seen it. And you know how advanced kids are today. There isn't anything they don't already know." "You know, I'm not sure I'd want my daughter to see that movie. Is it possible that some other—?" "Look, lady, if you don't want your daughter to come to the party, don't come."

Slam goes the phone. She is paying the price for righteousness, from the other mother and eventually from her daughter when she tells her she won't be going to the party.

Or take the seventy-eight-year-old widow. Her husband died five years ago. In the years since, she's remained economically comfortable. How would she face persecution for righteousness' sake? Rummage around in her life; visualize situations, people, and events, until you suddenly see where the truth would fit.

- At her age the ratio of women to men highly favors the men. If she starts to date, her righteous moral standards may not let her compete in certain unseemly ways against the other women, perhaps putting her at a disadvantage in remarrying.
- Suppose she does meet a godly, elderly gentleman. If they just live together without marrying, they keep both their Social Security payments. If they do the righteous thing and marry, our government will persecute them by taking hers away.
- She wants to give $80,000 to your church building program. While that may be fine with you, it may not be fine with her children, who see their inheritance being given away. She may experience considerable hostility from them.
- She lives in Los Angeles. Her granddaughter calls her from Berkeley in Northern California. "Grandma, can I stay with you Friday night? The semester's over, and I'll be going home to Phoenix for the Christmas holidays. But it's a two-day trip—one day from Berkeley to Los Angeles, and a second day from Los Angeles to Phoenix. Can I stay with you Friday?" "Of course you can, honey! It'll be so good to see you again. What time will you arrive?" "Well, my last exam will be over at 11:00 AM, and I don't have much to pack since I'm coming back for the next semester. I should be at your place around 7:00 PM at the latest." "Wonderful. I'll have supper ready for you." "Uh, Grandma, can I bring a friend with me?" "Certainly. What's your friend's name?" "John." "Oh—well, that'll be OK. You can have your mother's room upstairs, and John can sleep on the couch downstairs." "Grandma, John sleeps in the same room with me." "What? Oh, no! No, honey, no! That's not right. You know—" "Never mind, Grandma. We'll get a motel." *Slam.* Rejected because of righteousness.

[handwritten margin notes: Relevance - Application - Illustration]

Run the truth through the different ages, people, and life circumstances that are in your audience. Rummage around in their lives until you can visualize how the truth "shows up" in some specific way. *[handwritten: How is th purpose lived out?]*

3. Develop mental pictures that *apply* the biblical concept, not ones that simply *illustrate* it. *[handwritten: Relevancys sells to questions, Application gives specifics]*

An application pictures a specific situation in your listeners' lives that is equivalent to the one the biblical author is talking about.

An application of courage, for example, might describe a situation in the workplace. Bill is scheduled for a deposition on Tuesday, by lawyers acting on behalf of a woman in his office who's suing his boss for sexual harassment. The lawyers will ask him what he knows about her accusations. Bill knows she has a case; he's witnessed the boss's inappropriate acts and overheard his unseemly comments. If Bill testifies truthfully and "courageously," and the boss finds out about it, Bill will probably lose his job. But even if the boss doesn't find out, if Bill's testimony helps the woman win her case, the resulting settlement will probably bankrupt the company, and Bill will be unemployed. If he doesn't tell the truth, he sins against the woman, to say nothing of running the risk of being caught in perjury. This is an application of courage that perhaps might speak meaningfully to your listeners because it's from their lives.

In contrast, an illustration is a picture or analogy from an area outside our personal lives. An illustration of courage, for example, would be describing the courage of a Civil War general whose horse was shot out from under him, yet he grabbed his sword from the ground and shouted to his men, "Follow me!" To urge our listeners to have a similar courage would probably leave them unmoved, since they can't identify with the situation described—they don't own swords, have never had a horse shot out from under them, and never led mounted cavalry in battle. It's an illustration, not an application.

Stories of Victorian widows, accounts of Indonesian prisoners being persecuted, analogies of geese flying in formation, explanations of how to make a dress—they are all illustrations. They may clarify and they may entertain, but they don't apply—they don't help the listener to see how it shows up in their lives.

For example, suppose you're preaching on 1 Timothy 6:9–10 and your take-home truth is "The love of money can be your downfall."

An illustration would be the story of King Midas, who became miserable because everything he touched turned to gold. Another illustration might be the story of Yusef the Terrible Turk:

It's the 1940s. Yusef comes to America to participate in a heavyweight wrestling tournament. One by one he defeats all his opponents and wins the grand prize of $10,000, a large sum of money for that time.

Two days after winning he's ticketed on a ship to Europe, heading back to his native Turkey. He tells the promoters that he doesn't want his prize in the form of a check; he doesn't trust "paper" and isn't certain the check could be cashed in Turkey. Bundles of dollars or lira would be unwieldy. So he insists on gold coins—a universal medium of exchange, and still available in the United States in those days. He buys a money belt and stuffs the sixty-five pounds of gold coins into the slit of the belt, which he puts around his waist.

The ship's personnel offer to store the gold in the ship's safe, but Yusef is worried about "sticky fingers." He prefers to have the gold on his person at all times, confident that "nobody will mess with Yusef the Terrible Turk."

A few days out to sea, however, an engine malfunction causes the ship to be stranded. Another vessel is sent to transfer all passengers on board. During the transfer, while the boats are swaying on the waves, Yusef tries to jump on board the new vessel. But he misses by a few inches and plunges into the water below. And that's the last anyone ever saw of Yusef the Terrible Turk, as his heavy belt took him straight to the bottom like a stone.

After telling this story, you then solemnly warn your people, "The love of money will be your downfall." And someone in the audience thinks to himself, "I'll remember that the next time I win a wrestling championship and am crossing the Atlantic on a ship wearing a money belt filled with gold."

The story has no bearing on the realities of their lives! Would I tell it in church? Probably. It's an amusing story. But I wouldn't deceive myself into thinking I've been relevant. I've been entertaining, I've been interesting, but I haven't helped my listeners see how the biblical truth fits in their lives. It's only an illustration of the truth.

Instead, I need to apply the take-home truth. I need to picture how the love of money leading to a downfall might "show up" in my listeners' experiences. I need to talk in concrete images:

The Promise lived out ...

- Working eighty hours a week to make money at the expense of your family.
- Extensively gambling, or playing the lottery in hopes of a windfall, but at the expense of the family's economics.
- Incurring large credit card debt in pursuit of a lifestyle.
- Taking "dirty jobs," engaging in unethical practices that pay a lot but corrupt the soul.
- Withholding your tithe and experiencing God's displeasure.
- Arguing over inheritance funds at the expense of family relationships.

Or, suppose you're preaching on Galatians 6:1, "Brothers, if someone is caught in a sin, you who are spiritual should restore him gently," stressing the truth that we are to gently restore those caught in a sin. Suppose, as an example of someone caught in a sin, you imagine a fifteen-year-old girl caught in an unwanted teenage pregnancy, and you want the people to have a soft heart toward such a girl, being ready to restore her.

At this point, an illustration would be to do a word study on the Greek word translated "restore." You might say something like say, "The word *restore* was used in the medical field of setting a bone—restoring it, bringing it back to strength and usefulness so that it could function as intended. It was also used in the fishing industry of mending a net that had gaping holes ripped in it by underwater snags—again, bringing the net back to usefulness so that it could fulfill its original purpose."

All of this is true and might be said to clarify or illustrate the concept, but it wouldn't help to apply it to the teenage girl you've imagined. She's not a broken bone or a ripped net; she's a pregnant teenager. What would it look like to restore her? How would someone see it happening? Such word-study illustrations leave the listeners ignorant of how to genuinely and practically carry out restoration. As a result, a year later, when an actual teenager is seven months pregnant with a child and the

Sunday school superintendent remembers the sermon, he suggests to the pastor that he has thought of a way to "restore" Susie—by asking her to teach the fifth-grade Sunday school class of eleven-year-old girls. "Pastor, that will bring her back to usefulness, where she can function again in the church." The pastor, understandably, has grave misgivings: "Mr. Sunday School Superintendent, I'm not sure having an unmarried pregnant fifteen-year-old teaching eleven-year-olds is what I had in mind." "Oh, what did you have in mind, pastor?" "Uh—uh—I don't know what I had in mind." Because illustrations were used (bones, nets), the girl is not restored, and the church does not grow in godliness. ✠

An application would be to describe an event I witnessed. I was preaching in a large church. The pastor had asked beforehand if I would take a seat in the front row when I was through preaching, since he was going to close the service by taking in new members. As I descended the right steps down the platform and took a seat in the front pew, he came and stood fairly close to where I was sitting and began to call forward the families that were joining the church.

Once they were lined up across the front of the auditorium, he addressed the congregation: "In a moment I'm going to ask you to come up and welcome these folks into our church. Tell them you're glad they're going to be part of us and that you know they're going to enjoy our time together. But before I have you come up, I'm also going to ask you to welcome someone back into our church. Anna, would you come here please."

A young woman seven to eight months pregnant, who had been sitting on the aisle, came forward and stood by him, directly in front of me. There was no husband. The pastor explained that there had been confession, repentance, and restoration to the Lord. And now she was coming before her home church, asking for help in raising the child. She wanted the older women to teach her how to be a good mother. She hoped some of the men would serve as a father figure in the absence of a husband. The pastor concluded, "Now, as you come to welcome these folks into our church, I want you to also welcome Anna back into our church."

As the service dismissed, I watched as individuals came forward and started on the far side of the auditorium, shaking hands and working their way down the line. When they got to Anna in front of me, the line stopped and bunched up. I saw men taking business cards out of their wallets: "Anna, I'm a manufacturer's rep for a pharmaceutical company. If you need any prescriptions, call me. I can probably get you samples and you won't have to pay." I heard women lean toward Anna and whisper, "I have a box of baby clothes up in the attic you can have." *(Furtive glance toward the husband.)* "He thinks we're going to have another baby—but we're not."

Anna was being "restored" to the congregation. Telling this account is an application—it shows the listeners what it looks like in their lives. An illustration brings interest and clarity. An application brings interest, clarity, and *relevance*.

Academic

4. Make your applications detailed and extended, not vague and brief. — Paint the premise — situating in the live

Paint the picture in "full color"—visualize specifics, create conversations, dramatize the actions you want the listeners to do. Rehearse out loud the internal thoughts or reasoning process you want them to go through.

Act it out! Give them a detailed picture.

We have an expression in English: "Do I have to draw you a *picture?*" A person, frustrated at being unable to explain something, throws up his hands and in great exasperation says to another, "Do I have to draw you a picture?" The answer is, "Yes, pastor, you have to draw me a picture."

Nothing happens in our listeners apart from specific pictures. No godliness forms unless the truth is related to concrete situations of life.

Suppose I'm teaching a fifth grade boys Sunday school class, and I come to the end of the lesson. To press home the lesson, I say, "Guys, what does this mean to your everyday lives? It means, 'Be a good Christian.'"

"Uh, Mr. Sunukjian, that's a bit vague. Could you be more specific?"

"Yeah, I see that's kind of broad. OK, it means, 'Respond to those over you.'"

But *respond* is not a picture word. And when you're in the fifth grade, everybody is "over you."

So I try again. "It means, 'Obey your parents.'" *Parents* is a picture word, but *obey* is not. But they're willing to let it go at that: "Thanks, Mr. Sunukjian. That's good. We've never heard that before."

But I must not be content with such vagueness and brevity. I must visualize in extended detail some situations in their lives, so that they can see what the godliness would actually look like in various concrete moments.

For example:

> Guys, it means when your mom gives you sixty-five cents and tells
> you, "Use this at school to buy milk to go with your sack lunch,"
> and you work your way up to the front of the canteen line, and the
> lady behind the counter asks you what you want—it means you
> use the sixty-five cents to buy milk and not junk food.

Now the boys have a picture, and some small godliness can form in
their lives as they anticipate pleasing God in some concrete situation.

Similarly, suppose our introduction to the Mark 4:35–41 sermon
(Jesus' stilling the storm)[3] describes the resulting uproar in a home when
a widowed mother moves in with her son and his family, giving this
as an example of our "obeying God and having the bottom fall out of
everything:"

> You obey God's prompting to "honor your mother" by taking her into
> your own home after your dad's death. Everybody seems in agree-
> ment; the kids double bunk so that Grandma can have her own room.
> But after six months the house is in an uproar. Your wife comes to you
> and says, "It's her or me. Decide which woman you want in this house.
> She doesn't like the way I cook; she criticizes the way I keep house;
> she's rearranged my kitchen so that I can't find anything." Your kids are
> walking on eggshells because Grandma's constantly down on them:
> "You shouldn't be listening to that devil music. You can't wear that to
> school—put on something decent." And you're thinking, "God, what
> are you doing? All I wanted to do was honor my mother, and now my
> home is a disaster."

FCF

In addition to this detailed and extended picture of the *problem* in the
introduction, we must be sure to give an equally vivid and specific picture

---

3. See pages 38–41, 76, 106–7.

THT

of the *solution* later in the message. Too often we're concrete and extended in presenting the problem but then vague and brief in applying the solution. We can't assume the listener will know how to carry out the biblical truth—"resist Satan's efforts and trust God's power"—unless we describe what that would look like. A brief exhortation to "resist Satan's efforts to use your mother to disrupt your home" might leave him wondering whether he should hold up a silver cross against his mother and shout, "Down, you devil-woman!" Instead, we must help him specifically visualize what it would look like to "resist Satan" in this situation. We might say something like:

Maybe you get up early in the morning before anyone else in the house is awake. You make yourself a cup of coffee, and you sit in a comfortable chair in the darkness. And you pray. You pray, "God, my mother is a godly woman, but she's of another generation. Lord, help her to see that my kids are good kids—that they love you and are living for you. And Lord, help them not to agitate her or provoke her unnecessarily. Help them to accommodate her as much as they can while they're in her presence. Lord, my mother's also used to being in charge in her own home and kitchen. But she's got to yield to my wife here. Help her to see that. And Lord, help my wife to cut her some slack and not take it too personally. Father, don't let Satan get into our home and disrupt it. Keep him out. Keep him away. I pray for your strong protecting power against him." You resist Satan, and you trust God's power.

By presenting our truth through extended, detailed pictures, we follow the biblical model. For example, in 1 Kings 17 we find an extensive picture. Elijah, in a time of famine, hides from Ahab by a brook. Scavenger ravens—birds that seldom approach humans or share their food even with other ravens—bring him bread and meat. When the brook dries up, God sends Elijah to an even more unlikely source of help—a destitute widow in the heart of Sidon, Jezebel's home territory and the center of

Baal worship. From this lengthy biblical picture we form our take-home truth: "God is able to miraculously provide for his own in hard times and hostile places."

Our resulting sermon should not conclude with simply vague exhortations to our listeners to "trust God to do the same in your lives—to miraculously provide for you in hard times and hostile places." Instead, it should visualize several specific hard times and hostile places that our various listeners might experience, and suggest concrete ways that God might miraculously provide. Relevancy is in the details.

Since God uses extended biblical pictures again and again to present the truth to us, we should use equally extended pictures to carry it forward into our world.

As we ask these three developmental questions—What do I need to explain? Do we buy it? What does it look like in real life?—we discover what we need to say about each statement in our outline to make our message clear, convincing, and relevant to the listener.

occurs when the listener "see" how the biblical truth applies to a specific situation.

it all begins with surrender...

Select Effective Answers

IN THE PREVIOUS CHAPTER WE looked at the questions we ask regarding the concepts of a message:

1. What do I need to explain?
2. Do we buy it?
3. What does it look like in real life?

In this chapter we want to consider some of the answers we all-too-frequently offer—the dubious supporting or amplifying materials we select to make a point clear, convincing, or relevant.

Certain supporting materials have been used in sermons for centuries. But whether these materials are still helpful or effective in our contemporary culture is open to question. As we thoughtfully examine some of them, we may sense they're not quite as valuable as we imagined they would be. While they may serve to fill up the preaching time, it's doubtful they are spiritually powerful or penetrating as far as the listener is concerned.

Specifically, I suspect that the following are relatively ineffective ways to explain a concept, convince the listeners that it's true, or help them apply it to their lives:

- Dictionary definitions
- Statistics
- Quotations
- Parallel passages
- Biblical illustrations

DICTIONARY DEFINITIONS ✓

I suspect that when a speaker says, "According to Webster," most listeners become glassy-eyed. They know they're going to hear some abstract, unknown word defined by other abstract, unknown words. They know their understanding of the word is not going to be advanced.

You're almost always better off to put any definition into your own words. Better yet, give a picture—a situation, a scenario—that effectively "defines" what you mean. For example, instead of saying, "Patience is the will or ability to wait or endure without complaint," say, "Patience is reading *The Little Ladybug* a fourth time to your two-year-old on the toilet-training seat; patience is waiting another four seconds before honking at the car in front of you when the light turns green; patience is smiling and not fidgeting while the clerk calls for a 'price check' on some item the person ahead of you in line is buying."

STATISTICS ✓

Contemporary listeners are probably unaffected by statistics. Since we hear them all the time, they slide off us like water off a duck's back. Further, we are too aware that while "statistics don't lie, liars use statistics."[1] In other words, we've come to suspect that almost any statistic has an agenda behind it.[2]

Though we hear statistics in every election and read them daily in the newspaper, they probably aren't what sway us. That's why smart candidates prefer, and good magazine articles start with, a picture—an extended example of one person or one event that dramatizes the issue—something the listener can visualize and identify with.

QUOTATIONS ✓

There are only two reasons to use a quote—because the language is sparkling, or because the speaker is an authority in the field. If neither of

---

1. At a seminar I attended, the front of the speaker's T-shirt said, "88% of statistics are made up on the spot." The back of the T-shirt added, "Including this one."
2. I read in the paper recently, "A new survey reports that 79 percent of moms want flowers for Mother's Day." Guess who did the survey. Yep—FTD.com.

these applies to your potential quote, you'll probably be more effective if you say it in your own words.

For a quote to have sparkling language, it would have to be fairly short, almost a one-liner.[3] The exception might be an extended humor column, or a magazine article that covered several paragraphs.

But even these latter examples would be difficult to present effectively. They were originally written for the eye, not for the ear. They were designed to be read, not to be heard. A speaker would need exceptional out-loud reading skills in order to sustain a long quote, somewhat akin to the professional expertise of a network commentator "reading" the evening news.

It's also true that quoting something because of the authority or credibility of the speaker is seldom necessary. The speaker may be an authority to you, but chances are he isn't for your listeners. You may know who Spurgeon is, but to most contemporary listeners he'll sound like a fish. Chrysostom may be an important figure in church history for you, but he sounds like a flower to most people in your audience.

The wonderful truth is that a congregation almost always accepts their pastor as the authority in spiritual matters. God has spoken to them through their pastor, their pastor's words have blessed and changed their lives, and they know their pastor loves them. "If my pastor says it, I trust he knows what he's talking about. And I don't know those other guys he's quoting."[4]

PARALLEL PASSAGES

Sometimes after sufficiently explaining the primary passage that they're preaching from, speakers will turn to other parallel biblical passages and explain them also. Their concordance study, or the parenthesis at the end of a paragraph in a book they've read, gave them a list of verses that addressed the same topic. So they have the congregation turn to multiple verses in the Bible that essentially make the same point. At best, this is treading water.

---

3. Something like, "As Winston Churchill said, 'A fanatic is someone who won't change his mind and can't change the subject.'"

4. An example of legitimately quoting to gain authority might be if the pastor, while teaching on God's covenant sign with Israel, makes the statement, "There are no medical advantages to circumcision." Given the overwhelming American use of this procedure and the presumption that there must be some good medical reason for its widespread use, the pastor might add some credibility to his statement by quoting "Dr. So-and-So, Chief of Pediatrics at UCLA Medical Center, author of *Modern Pediatrics*, a textbook used by more medical schools than any other, who says on page . . ."

At worst, it's a lazy man's way of filling time. In neither case does it advance the message. It only stresses or wearies the listeners by asking them to flip from book to book to book in the Bible simply to see the same point.

Such unnecessary cross-referencing sounds something like this: "I want you to see that not only does Paul make the point in Romans, but Peter also makes it in his first epistle. Please turn to . . . (*followed by a three-minute explanation of the new verse in Peter*). James also teaches this in . . . (*another three-minute explanation of the same concept*). Finally, John . . . (*a fourth presentation of the same biblical concept*)."

The listener probably has one of two reactions:

- "Pastor, I didn't buy it when Paul said it in Romans, so I'm not going buy it when Peter says it, or James, or John. Rather than repeatedly explaining the same thing, you would probably accomplish more by probing and dealing with my objections."
- "Pastor, I bought it when you explained it from Romans. I don't need to have it explained again from other verses. Instead, I need for you to help me see how it shows up in my life."

Besides being unnecessary, such cross-referencing occasionally can obstruct accurate preaching. By bringing in data from other passages, you run the danger of importing details or coming up with interpretational viewpoints that your original author did not intend. This can happen, for example, if you borrow details from parallel accounts in the Gospels. For example, Luke's theological use of the feeding of the five thousand is different from Matthew's. Matthew records the account to show "how we can accomplish the seemingly impossible tasks God gives us" (p. 81). But Luke brings up the miracle within an extended context where he's answering the question, "Who is Jesus?"[5]

The Holy Spirit did not keep Luke ignorant of details that Matthew included, nor vice versa, but rather led each author to select (and omit) the particular details that would establish their specific individual truths. If you bring in details from Luke that Matthew purposefully omitted, you run the danger of gravitating toward Luke's truth while preaching Matthew's account.

---

5. Luke "bookends" his account of the feeding (Luke 9:10–17) with the identical question that was circulating among the common people (9:7–9 and 9:18–19). The same question—"Who is Jesus?"—is put to Peter (9:20) and is eventually answered by the Voice from heaven (9:28–36).

Now, obviously there are times when it's perfectly valid to turn from your primary passage to another place in Scripture:

- When your primary biblical author himself refers to the other passage, as when the New Testament account alludes to some Old Testament context. For example, when Jesus asks—"Haven't you read what David did when he and his companions were hungry? He entered the house of God, and he and his companions ate the consecrated bread—which was not lawful for them to do, but only for the priests. Or haven't you read in the Law that on the Sabbath the priests in the temple desecrate the day and yet are innocent?" (Matt. 12:3–5)—the chances are your listeners haven't read these things, and you would need to show them the Old Testament contexts that Jesus is referring to.

- When you sense your listeners would doubt your interpretation of a particularly difficult passage (e.g., a passage dealing with divorce and remarriage or what it means to be "filled with the Spirit"), and you wish to bolster your interpretation. Such areas are few. On most topics, congregations have confidence that their pastor is teaching them correctly.

- When you wish to create a cumulative effect—multiplying passages to show how prevalent or important a concept is, that it is stressed again and again in Scripture. In such cases, put the references on a screen; don't task the listeners with turning to them. And read them with a minimum of comment; don't give lengthy explanations of them, since your main reason for citing them is not for their meaning but for their weight of number.

Aside from these exceptions your overriding assumption ought to be that each biblical author was sufficiently clear when he wrote to his original readers, and that you also ought to be able to make his meaning sufficiently clear to your listeners, without comparison to other passages—a comparison *his* original readers could not have made.[6]

---

6. The church of Corinth could not compare their letter with the letter written to the church at Philippi, since Philippians had not yet been written. In fact, it was several hundred years before the canon was formed and the collected documents became available even in a limited way (given the difficulty of obtaining vellum or parchment copies).

BIBLICAL ILLUSTRATIONS

The time to teach a biblical story is when it is the primary passage for your message, not when it is a secondary illustration of another passage. In other words, you should preach the story Joseph and his brothers as part of a series through Genesis and not as an illustration of Romans 8:28 (i.e., that all things work together for good).

Biblical illustrations are seldom as helpful or as effective as contemporary pictures from the everyday lives of your listeners and rarely should be used. This is true for a number of reasons.

First, biblical events and situations are usually far removed from the experiences of our listeners and tend to strike them as "from a foreign culture and from another age, when maybe God did such things." Few of your listeners, hearing of Joseph, for example, expect to be sold to Egyptian merchants, to be seduced by their boss's wife, to interpret dreams for convicts in prisons, or to become chief-of-staff to their country's leader. Such experiences are difficult for your listeners to identify with; they're not true to life today.

Second, speakers sometimes too quickly assume that a biblical story fits or illustrates another passage, and they end up connecting the passages in ways contrary to the theological intent of the original authors. The story of Joseph does not really fit the teaching of Romans 8:28. The point of Genesis 50:20 is that God used the brothers' evil intentions to bring about good circumstances in Joseph's life. But that's not the point of Romans 8:28.

The point of Romans 8:28–30 is that God will work in your sufferings and weaknesses to produce the good character of Christlikeness. Romans 8:28 isn't teaching that no matter what happens in your life, God will bring good circumstances out it, but rather that the "good" he's working in all situations is to conform you to the likeness of his Son.

Third, using a biblical illustration can deceive you into thinking you've *applied* the truth, when all you've really done is *repeated* it. Instead of properly moving from the biblical passage to the timeless truth to contemporary application, you've moved from the biblical passage to the timeless truth and then back to another biblical passage.

For example, suppose you're preaching Colossians 3:5–6, and your point is, "Greed brings God's wrath." If you then tell the story of 1 Kings

21—how Ahab's greed for Naboth's land brought God's wrath—you haven't yet applied the biblical truth; you've simply repeated it. You haven't advanced the message; you've gone backward:

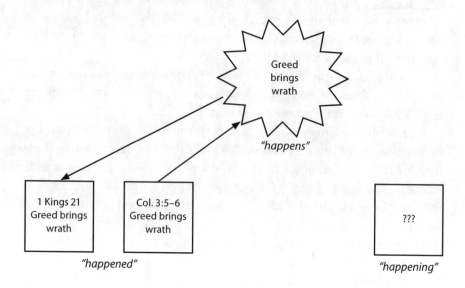

The best time to teach biblical narratives is when they are the primary passage for your message—when they are the *source* of the truth, rather than an *illustration* of it. As a primary passage, they can lead you to *eternal truth;* as an illustration, they can only give you an *ancient example.*

Our discussion brings us back to the fact that a contemporary picture is generally the best way to make a point clear, convincing, or relevant to your listeners. A visualized situation from daily experience is the most effective way to handle any of the developmental questions—to *explain* a concept, to show people that it's *true,* or to help them see what it *looks like* in their lives.

At this point in the process of preparing our message, we've developed three kinds of materials: a biblical flow of thought, a take-home truth, and the contemporary relevance.

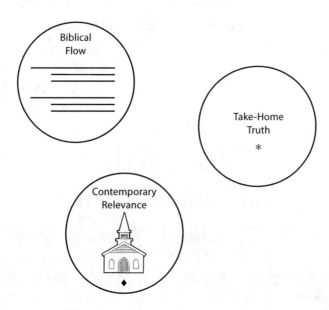

We're just about <u>ready to meld these three together into our final ser-mon outline.</u> But before we do, we want to return briefly to the take-home truth and sharpen it into its final sermon form. We want to state it as briefly, attractively, and memorably as possible.

Context - RW Background
Clarity - questions about passage
Content - author's thoughts
Cover - RW for us
     (what, why, how)
     (implicit topic, question, answer)
Concrete - The change the Holy Spirit intends

–7–

Sharpen the Take-Home Truth

The change the Holy Spirit intends
= Sharpen the premise

BEFORE WE BRING EVERYTHING together in the final sermon outline, we want to sharpen the take-home truth into its final sermon form. We've already formed it at a timeless, theological truth level (chap. 4). But now we want to phrase it as succinctly and as memorably as possible.

The reason we come back to it at this stage in the process is because often, as we're gathering the materials for the developmental questions (chaps. 5 and 6), some catchy way of saying it will occur to us.

For example, as I was working on the take-home truth of Exodus 13:17–22, "God leads us on a path of his choosing in order to get us safely to our promised destination," I noticed the locations of Goshen and Canaan on a map and the relatively straight-line trade route that connected them. My mind was somewhat absently ruminating, "The Israelites are at point A, Goshen; they want to get to point B, Canaan. There's a straight line between these two points, but instead of taking this short, direct route, God zigs and zags them through the desert before they finally get there."

Suddenly the phrases that were running through my head reminded me of the geometric axiom—"The shortest distance between two points is a straight line"—and I thought, "This axiom is not true in this case; if Israel is going to avoid war and get to Canaan at all, the shortest distance for them will have to be a zigzag. If they take the short, straight route, they'll never make it." And the final form of the take-home truth popped into my head—"The shortest distance between two points is a zigzag."

The self-contradictory nature of this statement, and its off-kilter resemblance to the axiom we learned in high school geometry, makes it more likely to stick in the listeners' minds and enable them to recall the truth of the message.

Our goal at this stage in preparation is to make the take-home truth simple and crisp so that the listener can easily grasp it. Notice how the language of the take-home truth of 2 Corinthians 12:7–10 becomes increasingly timeless and contemporary as you move from its passage form, to its truth form, to its sermon form:

> To keep me from becoming conceited because of these surpassingly great revelations, there was given me a thorn in my flesh, a messenger of Satan, to torment me. Three times I pleaded with the Lord to take it away from me. But he said to me, "My grace is sufficient for you, for my power is made perfect in weakness." Therefore I will boast all the more gladly about my weaknesses, so that Christ's power may rest on me. That is why, for Christ's sake, I delight in weaknesses, in insults, in hardships, in persecutions, in difficulties. For when I am weak, then I am strong.

PASSAGE FORM

The reason Paul ceased his earnest prayer for the thorn's removal,
and began instead to value it,
was because he learned the thorn was keeping him from exalting himself
and was making him strong for God.

TRUTH FORM

Instead of persistently asking God to remove our limitations,
we should instead value them
as things that are keeping us humble
and making us effective for God.

Message Blurb...

SERMON FORM — *Todays phrase*

The change by Holy Spirit in truth

The thing you most pray God would remove from your life is perhaps the thing you most want to keep.

Application

Timely:

Concre

In the previous example, the final sermon form, for brevity and memory's sake, concentrates on the first two lines—*what* is the correct response to a thorn—and drops the last two lines—*why* that response is correct. The sermon as a whole would, of course, fully develop the latter points, and the phrasing of the truth form would certainly occur in the message. But since the take-home truth is what you want them to remember even if they forget everything else, its final sermon form might choose to highlight *what* they should do, even above *why* they should do it. *(Application: &*

Honing the take-home truth into its final sermon form sometimes *fill,* takes several stabs until the language crystallizes into something sharp and clean and clear. For example, here's the outline flow for Psalm 90:

I. Our existence, contrary to God's, is brief and temporary (vv. 1–6).

II. Our brief existence is full of trouble and sorrow because of our sin (vv. 7–11).

III. Focusing on the brevity of life will awaken us to wise, sinless living (v. 12).

IV. As we live wisely and sinlessly, we can hope for God's blessing (vv. 13–17).
    A. We can ask for future joy in proportion to our past sorrow (vv. 13–15).
    B. We can ask God to work on our behalf (v. 16a).
    C. We can ask God to impress our children with his greatness (v. 16b).
    D. We can ask God to prosper whatever we set out to do (v. 17).

Either of the following sentences would capture the essence of the message in timeless truth form:

Numbering our days will lead us to the wisdom of repentance and holiness, so that we may enjoy God and experience his power.

If I can number my days, I will turn from the sin that brings trouble and sorrow, and toward the obedience that brings blessing.

In the above example, while each of these is accurate and helpful and would undoubtedly be stated somewhere in the message, neither seems phrased in any memorable fashion. Here are the stabs I took at coming up with something shorter and more striking, along with my evaluation of each attempt:

- *To plan on death is to enrich life.*
  (That's not too bad. Let me try another.)
- *You make your life better*
  by planning on your death.
  (Nope. That's no better than the first one.)
- *Your life becomes richer when*
  your death becomes realer.
  (I know there's no such word as "realer," but I can probably work with that. There's something about the parallelism of the lines and language that sound good. And the repeated "r" sound of "rich" and "real" may have some possibilities.)
- *When your death becomes real,*
  your life becomes rich.
  (See, I knew I could work with "realer." This looks pretty good. No, wait. There's a problem. This is passive—it suggests, "If you should ever be so lucky as to have your death become a reality to you." But the biblical truth is active—"Teach me to take the initiative and number my days." I need to phrase it actively.)
- *The more real you can make your death,*
  the more rich you will make your life.
  (Ah, that's good! It's active, it's parallel, and it's balanced. I like it. I'll try a couple more, but this looks like one I could go with.)
- *The more real your death is,*
  the more rich your life will become.
  (No, that's no improvement over the one above.)

- *If you will plan on your death,*
  you will enrich your life.

     (No, I don't like this one any better either. I'm going with the good one above.)

So I settled on what I thought was a good way of saying it:

>   The more real you can make your death,
>   the more rich you will make your life.

Then sometime later I was talking with someone about it, and the person said, "Oh I know another good way you can put it: 'Count your days, to make your days count.'" And I thought, "Where were you when I was working on the message?"

Let's take one more example, Psalm 100, to see how a careful study of the passage, along with a clear outline, can lead to a powerful take-home truth:

>   Shout for joy to the LORD, all the earth.
>   Worship the LORD with gladness;
>   come before him with joyful songs.
>   Know that the LORD is God.
>   It is he who made us, and we are his;
>   we are his people, the sheep of his pasture.
>
>
>   Enter his gates with thanksgiving
>   and his courts with praise;
>   give thanks to him and praise his name.
>   For the LORD is good and his love endures forever;
>   his faithfulness continues through all generations.

The above spacing and indentations highlight the psalm's two major movements and the poetic parallelism of its individual lines.

Both movements begin with imperatives, with an invitation to "shout" and "enter." In the first movement, we are told to come with "joy," "gladness," and "joyful songs." The reason is because we know the true "God"—

Yahweh (LORD). We have been created by him and brought into intimate relationship with him. "Be *glad* because you belong to the true *God*."

In the second movement, we are told to enter with "thanksgiving," "praise," and "thanks." The reason is because this one true Yahweh God is "good to us." His love for us endures throughout the years; his faithfulness to us continues from one generation to the next. "Give *thanks* because the LORD is *good*."

Working with these twin concepts—be glad because you know the true God and be thankful because this God is good to you—here are some of the stabs I made at honing a final take-home sentence for the sermon:

- *Come with joy, gladness—he is God.*
  Come with thanksgiving, praise—he is good.

- *Come with gladness and gratitude*
  for he is God and he is good.

- *Come with a glad heart for he is God.*
  Come with a grateful heart for he is good.

- *Come with a glad and grateful heart,*
  for your God is good.

The last sentence seemed to be the most succinct and had a phrasing that commended itself.

Many times the sermon form of the take-home sentence will differ little from the truth form. We don't often end up with something that could be etched in stone on a building, but we do our best to present God's good revelation in the most exact, compelling, and memorable way possible.

Introduction

A — State the point
    Show in the Biblical text (the biblical
                                author is saying
                                This — only the
                                pertinent

B — Image (helping them to see)
    — to direct, to inform

C — Objections

A — state the point
    Then — add a transition for the next point.

Context - RW Background
Clarity - Questions the passage raises
Content - Authors thoughts (main ideas) Answe
Cover - RW for us   RR
        ↳ what, why, how
Conarts - ↳ implied topic, question answer
        To change to Holy Spirit intends

— 8 —

Shape the Sermon (Part 1)
Structural Patterns

Truth

WE'RE NOW READY TO BRING together all the parts of the process—the biblical flow of thought, the take-home truth, and the contemporary relevance—into a final sermon outline.

Truth (Topic)
outline

I. Timeless theology
A. Passage specific
B Contemporary
   Application

1.

2. what is the l
question the bi
author is addre
with this flow
thought?
And what an
is he giving t
that question

= Topic + Assertion =
...turning the question
into an incomplete
Sentence + answer
= THT

Take-Home
Truth
*

3.

In developing your final sermon outline, there are two major questions you must decide: what is the largest question that is being answered through this flow of thought? what is the answer of this question?   longer

- Where in the biblical flow of thought will you place the take-home truth (*)? = Central truth (the reason: write this passage...)
- Where in the biblical flow of thought will you place the contemporary relevance (♦)? (application of the take-home truth) Cover

142

[handwritten margin notes: answer/assertion ... Time When, ... Manner in which, ... Reason why, ... Means by which]

We'll take up the first of these questions in this chapter—talking about structural patterns. We'll talk about the second—relevancy patterns—in *[186]* the next chapter.

The decision of where to place your take-home truth—whether in the introduction, or later in the body of the message—commits you to either a *deductive* or *inductive* structural pattern.

We'll first describe each of these patterns, then give some examples, and then talk about when you might use each.

DESCRIPTION OF THE TWO PATTERNS

[handwritten: Proposition]

In a deductive pattern, the complete take-home truth (*)—both the topic/question ("what you're talking about") and the assertion/answer ("what you're saying about it")—is stated somewhere in the introduction of the message, before you turn to the biblical passage. Early on, the listeners hear the single sentence you want them to take home from the message as a whole.

Visually, a deductive pattern looks like this:

[handwritten: Anchor and Magnet clause]

In outline form, a deductive pattern unfolds as follows:

Introduction
1.
2.
3. Take-home truth [*]—the full topic/assertion or question/answer statement

[handwritten: What... Why...]

   I.   Main point

   II.   Main point

   III.   Main point

In an inductive pattern, only the topic or question ("what you're talking about") appears in the introduction. The complete take-home truth (*) emerges later in the body of the message, whenever the assertion or answer ("what you're saying about it") appears in the biblical flow of thought. Visually, an inductive pattern looks like this:

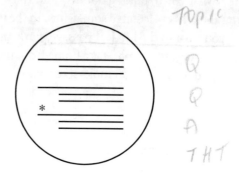

In outline form, an inductive pattern unfolds as follows:

   Introduction
      1.
      2.
      3. Topic/question

   I.   Main point

   II.   Main point

   III.   Main point—assertion/answer [*] becomes apparent

EXAMPLES OF DEDUCTIVE AND INDUCTIVE PATTERNS

Here are several outlines to illustrate each structural pattern, along with brief observations concerning the advantage and drawback of each pattern.[1]

Deductive Patterns

what you're talking about
what you're saying about what you're talking about.

Example 1

Suppose you're preaching a message on the purposes of a church, taken from Acts 2:42–47:

1st generation disciples

> They devoted themselves to the apostles' teaching and to the fellowship, to the breaking of bread and to prayer. Everyone was filled with awe, and many wonders and miraculous signs were done by the apostles. All the believers were together and had everything in common. Selling their possessions and goods, they gave to anyone as he had need. Every day they continued to meet together in the temple courts. They broke bread in their homes and ate together with glad and sincere hearts, praising God and enjoying the favor of all the people. And the Lord added to their number daily those who were being saved.

Public   *private*   *blessed they were...*

A deductive sermon structure would be outlined as follows:

Introduction
1. In order to be the church God wants us to be, we need to know the goals or purposes of a church.
2. Today we're going to look at the activities of the early church in order to see what God intends a church to do.
3. We're going to see that the purposes of a church are to instruct, fellowship, worship, and evangelize [*].
4. Please turn to Acts 2:42–47.

---

1. In each outline, the introduction will be given rather fully, while the body of the message may be somewhat bare-bones. The reason for this extra attention to the introduction is because several factors crucial to oral clarity (discussed in chaps. 11–12) occur in the introduction, and we'll need this more detailed development as we use these same outlines in these later chapters.

I. The purpose of a church is to instruct.   *List =*

II. The purpose of a church is to fellowship.   *THT Summary*

III. The purpose of a church is to worship.

IV. The purpose of a church is to evangelize.

In the above example, since the sermon's main points comprise a list, the take-home truth turns out to be a summary of all the major points.

Example 2   *Deductive*

THT = Dominant idea of the message

Here's an example where the take-home truth is not a summary of the points but rather the dominant idea of the message. The Scripture is Matthew 7:7–11:

mental   *physical*   *Spiritual*

"Ask and it will be given to you; seek and you will find; knock and the door will be opened to you. For everyone who asks receives; he who seeks finds; and to him who knocks, the door will be opened.

"Which of you, if his son asks for bread, will give him a stone? Or if he asks for a fish, will give him a snake? If you, then, though you are evil, know how to give good gifts to your children, how much more will your Father in heaven give good gifts to those who ask him!"

Introduction
1. Our Lord encourages us to pray, to ask God for things, and to expect him to give them to us. (Quote Matt. 7:7–8.)
2. Someone says, "I've tried that; it doesn't work. I asked; God didn't give it to me. I don't buy it."
3. For the sake of that person, and for the sake of all of us who would like to be encouraged in our praying, let's turn to Matthew 7:7–11 and see what Jesus is saying. (Read Matt. 7:7–11.)
4. In these verses Jesus is telling us, "Ask, and if it's a good thing, God will give it to you" [*].

the Answer   *Take home truth ...*   *What your talking about / what your saying about / what your talking about.*

✓ 5. In order to be encouraged in our praying, let's see who this is a promise to, and what it's a promise of.

implied

again — Who is this a promise to?

I. (This is a promise for genuine children who are trying to please the Father.)[2]

Detail — A. First of all, this is a promise for those who are genuine children of God.

Insight — 1. Jesus refers to "your Father in heaven." *(illustration) p 120*

Application — 2. If you have been "born again" through faith in Christ, this promise is for you. *Relevance*

Detail B. But more specifically, this is a promise for those children who are trying to please their Father.

Insight 1. This promise occurs toward the end of a lengthy sermon in which Jesus has been describing the behaviors that please the Father.

Application 2. If your desire is to obey God and please him in whatever way you can, this promise is for you.

again — What is this a promise of?

II. This is a promise that God knows how to give you good gifts even more than you know how to give your children good gifts.

Detail A. You know how to give good gifts to your children—bread, fish.

Insight B. You know how to do this, despite being "evil"—i.e., despite having human imperfections and limitations.

Application C. God, having no imperfections or limitations, knows even more what good gifts to give you.

again — III. Come, therefore, with all the spontaneity of a child, asking for what you want and expecting that if it is good for you to have it, your Father will say yes.

---

2. The parentheses indicate that this particular sentence will not be spoken orally at this point but instead will form itself in the listener's mind after the subpoints have been presented. See appendix A, guideline 5, for proper outlining.

Since most sermons, as in the previous example, are not a list of points, the deductive take-home truth usually expresses the dominant thrust of the message as a whole.

Example 3 *Deductive*

Finally, here's an example of a deductive structure in a topical message that brings together several Scriptures on the subject of "honoring your father and mother."

THT providing the topical answer

Introduction

1. Today I want to talk about the fifth commandment—"Honor your father and mother."
2. Some of you are thinking, "Oh good, I hope the kids are listening."
3. This commandment, however, was not primarily addressed to children but to a nation of adults gathered at the base of Mount Sinai.
4. We tend to think of the commandment in terms of children because of Paul's words in Ephesians 6:1–3.
   a. Paul tells children to "obey your parents," and cites this commandment.
   b. But Paul's words do not limit "honor" to "obedience." Rather, what Paul is saying is, "When you are a child, this is how 'honor' shows up—through 'obedience.'"
5. *Honor* is a broad, encompassing word, meaning "attach weight to," "hold in high regard," "publicly esteem."
6. This overall meaning, however, shows itself in different specific ways, depending on how old we are.
   a. When we are children, living under our parents' roof, we honor them by obeying them.
   b. But a man "leaves father and mother," a woman transfers her allegiance from her father to her husband, and honor no longer shows itself through obedience.
7. What does honor look like at the other end of life—when our parents are aged—which is what God most of all had in mind when he gave the command to adults at Sinai?

Question

8. The answer is: When our parents are aged, to honor them is to support them financially [*].

The Answer

9. Let's look at a couple of Scriptures that will show that this is primarily what God had in mind, and then let's consider some specific steps we might take to follow through on it.

I. The Scriptures teach that we are to honor our parents in their sunset years by making sure they are taken care of financially. [Each of the following subpoints would probably take ten minutes to develop.]
   A. Financially supporting our parents in their old age takes precedence over giving to the Lord's work (Matt. 15:1–6).
   B. Financially supporting our parents in their old age reveals, more than anything else, our own genuine godliness (1 Tim. 5:3–8).

II. There are three specific actions that will enable us to follow through on this command. [Each of the following subpoints would probably take five minutes to explain and apply.]
   A. Be committed in your own mind, and agree with your spouse or siblings, that you will do whatever is necessary to take care of your parents in their old age.
   B. Tell your parents of your commitment to their financial well-being.
   C. Increase your monthly giving to the Lord so that your lifestyle adjusts to a level where hundreds of dollars each month could be transferred to your parents if necessary.

The advantage of the deductive pattern is that the take-home truth emerges early and clearly. It's easy for the listener to pick it out at the start of the message. The wording of the introduction usually highlights it as the speaker presents it in crisp, distinct, emphatic language.

The disadvantage of the deductive pattern is that you "give away all the cookies at the start." A listener, hearing the take-home truth in the introduction, might conceivably say, "Got it! I'm out of here. Gonna beat the crowd to the restaurant, or catch the game in the first quarter!" Of course no one actually gets up and walks out after the first few minutes of an introduction, but the potential drawback of the deductive pattern is that there's no longer any suspense, or tension, or movement toward the climax of the message.

The advantage of the deductive pattern is clarity; the challenge is sustaining interest. We'll look at how to meet this challenge in a moment.[3]

Inductive Patterns

[handwritten: topical / dominant]

[handwritten: Anchor or Magnet clause]

In an inductive pattern, the listener hears the topic or question in the introduction but doesn't get the assertion or answer until later in the body of the message.[4]

[handwritten: List = THT Summary (The Specific truth / answer is the last point.]

Example 1

[handwritten: Inductive]

Suppose you're preaching a topical message in order to encourage people to join a small-group ministry. You might set up an inductive structure something like this:

Introduction

1. God's spiritual input into our lives takes place at three levels.
   a. In large gatherings, we celebrate, worship, and hear his Word.
   b. In midsize gatherings, we enjoy Christian friendship and mutual interests.
   c. In small gatherings, we have the potential for the deepest levels of personal interaction.
2. Though this third level, the small gathering, is sometimes missing in our churches today, it was prominent in the early church as the believers met in each others' homes during the week (Acts 2:46; 20:20).
3. What specifically does God add to our lives at this third level that doesn't occur at the other two levels? What happens in small groups that brings excitement and spiritual growth as nothing else can [= topic/question]?

[handwritten left margin: Question / a) What you / talking about…]

[handwritten left margin: Principal]

I. It's in small groups that we become devoted to one another (Rom. 12:10).

[handwritten: 2nd most important]

[handwritten: – Detail / = Insight / – Application]

---

3. See pages 156–59 for this discussion.
4. "Later" could be either at one of the Roman numeral main points or in the conclusion. Whereas the deductive pattern reveals the take-home truth *before* addressing the biblical content, the inductive pattern uses the movements or concepts in the passage to *build toward* the full statement of the take-home truth. *[handwritten: = induce]*

II.   It's in small groups that we instruct one another (Rom. 15:14).

III. It's in small groups that we encourage one another (1 Thess. 5:11) [*].

The central truth—"We should gather in small groups for the mutual devotion, instruction, and encouragement that can bless our lives"—would emerge as soon as the speaker gives the third Roman numeral. Though the speaker may continue for another ten minutes in the message, the listener has mentally put together the complete take-home truth as soon as the last element in the list is mentioned.

In the above example, since the main points are a list, the take-home truth would be a summary of the main points.

Example 2

Our outline of Mark 4:35–41 is an example of an inductive pattern building to a central truth that is the dominant idea of the message, rather than a summary of the points.

Introduction

1. Sometimes we obey God and the bottom falls out of everything.

2. We despair and wonder, "God, why is this happening, and what do you want me to do?" [The second half of the question is the key topic/question—"What should we do when obeying God leads to difficulty?"]

3. Today we'll see the disciples in a similar situation and learn why such things happen and what our response should be.

4. Please turn to Mark 4:35–41.

I.   The disciples obey Jesus and find themselves in a life-threatening storm that fills them with despair (4:35–38).

II. The reason such things happen may be that Satan is attempting to prevent God's purposes.

Answer

III. When obedience leads to difficulty, resist Satan's efforts and trust God's power [*].

Example 3   *Induction*

2nd
Point

Here's an inductive structure where the take-home truth occurs in the second of three major points.[5] The passage is James 4:13–16:

THT = found in the middle

(Now listen, you who say, "Today or tomorrow we will go to this or that city, spend a year there, carry on business and make money." Why, you do not even know what will happen tomorrow. What is your life? You are a mist that appears for a little while and then vanishes. Instead, you ought to say, "If it is the Lord's will, we will live and do this or that." As it is, you boast and brag. All such boasting is evil.

Introduction

1. My most vivid memory of JFK's assassination was watching the evening footage on TV that had been filmed earlier that day—the motorcade through Dallas, Kennedy smiling and waving in the open car—and thinking to myself, "You have no idea that in a few minutes you will die."

2. The local newspaper this week reports several instances where people unexpectedly came to the end of their lives. (Read excerpts.)

3. None of us expects this to happen to us, but neither did they.

4. Because we don't really know what's ahead, Scripture says there's a certain way we ought not to plan and a certain way we should plan [= topic/question].

Phrased as an
implied question

---

5. Points II and III in the following outline would each take only four to five minutes to present, while the introduction might take seven to eight, and point I would require fifteen. The Roman numerals do not need to be identical in the amount of space or time given to them. The movements, or hunks, in a sermon's development are guided by the logical progression of the author's concepts and by the developmental questions necessary for a particular audience, and not by some imposed notions of symmetry or proportionality.

5. You're probably making plans.
   a. Plans for your summer vacation
   b. Plans for school in the fall
   c. Plans for marriage
   d. Plans for your company or your career
   e. Plans for your retirement

6. As you think about all these things in the future, there's a certain way, the Bible says, that you ought not to plan, and a certain way you should plan [= topic/question].[6]

7. Please turn to James 4 to see God's wisdom on these things.

I. We ought not to plan with any sense of finality or certainty, as though we control the future (4:13–16).

A. James describes a group of businessmen who are planning with a sense of certainty to enter a new market for a specific period of time in order to make a profit (4:13).

B. Don't misunderstand; the Bible is not against our making plans.

   1. The Bible encourages planning and speaks of its benefits (Prov. 6:6–9; 21:5).

   2. The issue is not *whether* we should plan but *how*.

C. Planning with a sense of finality or certainty is arrogant and evil (4:16).

   1. It's arrogant.
      a. You don't know what will happen tomorrow (4:14a).
         i. Many things could interrupt or change your plans to go to work or school tomorrow.
         ii. Many things could interrupt or change your plans for next week and next month.
         iii. Many things could interrupt or change your plans for your business or career in the next year.

---

6. While points 4 and 6 of the introduction are written as statements, they really imply a question—how should we plan. The topic/question doesn't necessarily have to be punctuated with a question mark.

        iv. Many unexpected turns have occurred in your
            life in the last five years, and another unexpected
            turn could be coming in three months.
    b. You don't know whether you will even be alive to-
      morrow (4:14b).
        i. Strike a match, and watch the smoke evapo-
          rate—that's how impermanent your life is.
        ii. Of all the people who are going to die by this
          coming Wednesday, few are now expecting it to
          happen.
  2. It's evil, for you are living as a practical atheist, as if there
    is no God.

[handwritten margin note: Transition — insight]

[handwritten note: What I'm talking about; what I'm saying about it...]

[handwritten margin note: principle]

[handwritten margin note: THT] ✓ II. We should plan with the conscious thought, "Here's what I'll do,
    Lord, if it's what you have in mind" [*].
    A. If the Lord wills, we'll be alive tomorrow (4:15a).
    B. If the Lord wills, we'll carry out our plans tomorrow (4:15b).

[handwritten margin note: principle]

III. Planning with this recognition of God's sovereign control will
    keep us conscious of his goodness and love.
    A. If something goes differently from what we expected, it means
      God had something better in mind for us.
    B. We will live peacefully under his tender care.

Conclusion
    1. Look at the events on your calendar, and say, "Lord, here's
      what I'm planning if it's what you have in mind."
    2. Make your plans in pencil, and know that God has the
      eraser. And he also has a pen, to write what *he* wants in
      ink.

The advantage of the inductive pattern is that it more easily sustains
the tension or suspense to the end of the message. The listener has to keep
listening since the answer, or take-home truth, is still ahead.

The challenge of the inductive pattern is that it requires greater attention to *oral clarity* so that the listeners will not lose their train of thought

as the sermon progresses toward the take-home truth. We'll look at how to meet this challenge in chapters 11, 12, and 15.

WHEN TO USE A DEDUCTIVE OR INDUCTIVE PATTERN

Most messages can be structured either deductively or inductively. You can choose.

For example, the message on the "purposes of a church" (p. 145) could be structured <u>inductively</u> instead of deductively, simply by <u>setting up an</u> <u>implied question</u> in the introduction instead of the take-home truth:

> Introduction
>
> 1. In order to be the church God wants us to be, we need to know the goals or purposes of a church.
> 2. Today we're going to look at the activities of the early church in order to see what God intends a church to be doing.
> 3. We're going to discover that there are four primary purposes of a church [= topic/question].
> 4. Please turn to Acts 2:42–47.
>
> I.   The purpose of a church is to instruct.
>
> II. The purpose of a church is to fellowship.
>
> III. The purpose of a church is to worship.
>
> IV. The purpose of a church is to evangelize [* = where the summary take-home truth becomes complete].

Similarly, the topical message on small groups (p. 150) could have been presented <u>deductively</u> instead of inductively, <u>by changing the introduc-</u> <u>tion's question into a statement of the truth:</u>

> Introduction
> 1. God's spiritual input into our lives takes place at three levels.

    a. In large gatherings, we celebrate, worship, and hear his Word.

    b. In midsize gatherings, we enjoy Christian friendship and mutual interests.

    c. In small gatherings, we have the potential for the deepest levels of personal interaction.

2. Though this third level, the small gathering, is sometimes missing in our churches today, it was prominent in the early church as the believers met in each other's homes during the week (Acts 2:46; 20:20).

3. The reason for this prominence is because some spiritual growth and excitement happens best in small groups.

4. We should gather in small groups for the mutual devotion, instruction, and encouragement that can bless our lives [*].

  I.   It's in small groups that we become devoted to one another (Rom. 12:10).

  II.   It's in small groups that we instruct one another (Rom. 15:14).

  III.   It's in small groups that we encourage one another (1 Thess. 5:11).

When to Use the Deductive Pattern

A deductive pattern might be preferable when the listeners have some questions of their own about the take-home truth. Though you as the speaker are not asking a question, your statement of the central truth raises questions in the minds of the listeners. And their questions will be along the lines of the developmental questions:

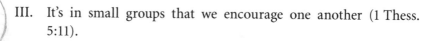

"I just heard your central truth, but I have no idea what you're talking about. Could you *explain* what you mean?"

"I just heard your central truth, but I don't buy it for a minute. Can you *prove* what you just said, or show me how it's true?"

"I just heard your central truth, but I don't know how to *do* it. Can you give some examples or situations so that I can know what it would look like in my life?"

The previous message on honoring your father and mother[7] was structured deductively because when the listeners hear the central truth in the introduction—"When our parents are aged, to honor them is to support them financially"—they would immediately have lots of internal questions: *Deductive = meant to answer internal questions*

- "Where in the world did you get that idea? I've been reading the Bible for years, and I never heard that before. 'Honor' means 'money'? You preachers find 'money' everywhere! I don't buy it."
- "Does this mean I have to bring them into my home to live with me? Explain what you mean by 'support financially.'"
- "How much money are we talking about? I can barely make it now, just with my own family and kids. I've got to think about college for the kids and my own retirement. Where am I going to get more money to take care of my parents? How can it possibly show up in my life?"
- "What about my brothers and sisters? Don't they have some responsibility?"
- "What if I send money to my mom or dad, and they use it foolishly—for booze or bingo—instead of for the necessities they need?"
- "It's their own fault that things are tight for them. If they hadn't been so foolish or wasteful in their planning for retirement, they wouldn't be in such trouble. Why should I have to pay for their mistakes?"
- "How old is 'aged'? If my dad comes to me at age fifty-five and says, 'Son, it's your turn,' can I say, 'Dad, can you hang in there 'til sixty-five?'"

Deductively!

Even though the message gives away the take-home truth at the start, the listeners are not emotionally thinking, "Got it! I'm out of here!" Instead, they're thinking, "Whoa, wait a minute! I've got some questions, and I hope you're going to answer them in the rest of the message." In other words, the

7. See pages 148–49.

Deductive Tension

tension or suspense is sustained, not by the speaker's topic/question raised inductively in the introduction, but by the internal questions that form in the listeners' minds as they hear the deductive central truth.

Note how this introduction to a sermon on Matthew 7:7–11 assumes that the listener will have questions about the deductively stated central truth:

Introduction

Central truth

1. Our Lord encourages us to pray, to ask God for things and to expect him to give them to us. (Quote Matt. 7:7–8.)
2. Someone says, "I've tried that; it doesn't work. I asked; God didn't give it to me. I don't buy it."
3. For the sake of that person, and for the sake of all of us who would like to be encouraged in our praying, let's turn to Matthew 7:7–11 and see what Jesus is saying. (Read Matt. 7:7–11.)

Central truth

4. In these verses Jesus is telling us, "Ask, and if it's a good thing, God will give it to you" [*].
5. In order to be encouraged in our praying, let's see who this is a promise to, and what it's a promise of.

Even though the listeners hear the central truth in points 1 and 4 of the introduction, their basic attitude toward it has already been identified in point 2—they don't buy it.

Or they may want some additional explanation. They may be thinking, "Does having my prayer answered hinge on the definition of 'a good thing'? Are you going to tell me the reason I didn't get what I asked for was because it wasn't 'good'? It certainly seemed 'good' to me. Explain what you mean by 'a good thing.'" Their interest in listening further is to see if the preacher can help them resolve their tension or uncertainties about the stated truth.

Often the questions the listeners have are exactly the ones you intend to deal with as you move through the biblical flow of thought and the *Tension* developmental issues. In fact, in a deductive pattern, you often raise these questions on behalf of the listener in the introduction, using them to preview coming "hunks" in the message. Notice how this occurs in point 9 of the introduction to "honoring your father and mother":

9. Let's look at a couple of Scriptures that will show that this is primarily what God had in mind, and then let's consider some specific steps we might take to follow through on it.[8]

The message answers the tension — the preacher suggests a better way.

Essentially the speaker is saying through this preview, "I'm first going to help you buy the fact that the Bible teaches this, and then I'm going to help you see how it can show up in your life."

Something similar takes place in point 5 of the Matthew 7:7–11 sermon introduction.[9] The speaker's preview suggests that a better explanation of the statement will help the listeners buy it and live according to it.[10]

5. In order to be encouraged in our praying, let's see who this is a promise to, and what it's a promise of.

When to Use the Inductive Pattern

An inductive pattern is probably best when your main points are a list. There's no advantage in having an introduction give away the four purposes of a church or the three reasons to be in small groups (see pages 145 and 150). The listener's interest is better sustained by unfolding them one at a time.

An inductive pattern should also be used when the listeners would probably have no major objections or questions to the take-home truth. In the message on James 4:13–16,[11] if the listeners heard the central truth in the introduction—"We should plan with the conscious thought, 'Here's what I'll do, Lord, if it's what You have in mind'"—they would probably shrug and say, "Yeah, sure, I guess so," and the rest of the message might seem anticlimactic.

The message on Mark 4:35–41[12] could probably go either way. We've developed it inductively, but had we deductively given away the content of points II and III in the introduction, it probably would have worked

---

8. See pages 148–49.
9. See pages 146–47.
10. We'll talk about how and when to use these introductory previews in chapter 12.
11. See pages 152–54.
12. See pages 151–52.

as well. The listeners, hearing those deductive statements early on, would probably have questions such as:

- "Does Satan really exist? If he does, does he have the power to cause the disasters you mentioned in your opening examples?"
- "How do you know it's Satan causing the difficulties and not human foolishness?"
- "'Resist Satan'? How in the world do I do that? What would that look like?"

Since most biblical passages are themselves inductive, with the author reasoning toward a conclusion or unfolding a story to a climax, we might approach each sermon with a slight bent toward inductive and then switch to deductive on the occasions that the previously mentioned factors would favor it.[13]

---

13. Luke 18:1–8 seems to be the only deductive parable we have. And even there, the deductive statement at the start—"Jesus told his disciples a parable to show them that they should always pray and not give up"—is Luke's summary rather than Jesus' original opening.

9

Shape the Sermon (Part 2)
Relevancy Patterns

Passage Outline —> truth Outline
— what the author said
— what the author says about what he said

(19)

ONCE YOU'VE DECIDED WHERE you will place your central truth—deductively in the introduction, or inductively later in the message—you're ready *Applied*
for the second question in shaping your final sermon outline: Where in the *THT*
biblical flow of thought will you place the contemporary relevancy (♦)?

I'll describe and illustrate three effective relevancy patterns—relevancy
at the end, relevancy interspersed, and relevancy wrapped—and suggest
when to use each.

In order to easily compare these different patterns, we'll work with one
common biblical passage for all three[1]—Acts 6:1–7:

> In those days when the number of disciples was increasing, the *situation*
> Grecian Jews among them complained against the Hebraic Jews— *stress*
> because their widows were being overlooked in the daily distribu-
> tion of food. So the Twelve gathered all the disciples together and — *search*
> said, "It would not be right for us to neglect the ministry of the
> word of God in order to wait on tables. Brothers, choose seven — *solution*
> men from among you who are known to be full of the Spirit and
> wisdom. We will turn this responsibility over to them and will
> give our attention to prayer and the ministry of the word."
>
> This proposal pleased the whole group. They chose Stephen,
> a man full of faith and of the Holy Spirit; also Philip, Procorus,

---

1. This is not to say that every biblical passage can be handled just as effectively in any of the
three patterns. For reasons we'll discuss in this chapter, some passages and sermons gravitate
toward certain patterns. But in order to compare apples to apples in our discussion of the three
patterns, we'll take one passage and foist it onto each pattern.

Nicanor, Timon, Parmenas, and Nicolas from Antioch, a convert to Judaism. They presented these men to the apostles, who prayed and laid their hands on them.

⌐ So the word of God spread. The number of disciples in Jerusalem   ⌐*NEW* increased rapidly, and a large number of priests became obedient   *SITU* to the faith. ⌐

Luke frames this account with an inclusio, or "bookend" comment: the number of disciples was increasing before this event (v. 1) and continued to increase after this event (v. 7). This means we are to understand this event within the context of rapid church growth.

This rapidly growing Jerusalem church experiences a problem created by language difficulties. Some elderly Greek-speaking Jewish women are being neglected or slighted during the daily distribution of food handled by the Aramaic-speaking apostles. These are women from the Greek-speaking Diaspora who find themselves in Jerusalem, depleted in funds, and, because of their language barrier, unable to articulate their needs or follow instructions so as to get the assistance they need.[2] The new growing Jerusalem church is simply swamped with needy people showing up in the daily food lines, and those who can't speak up get left out.

Greek-speaking men come to the rescue of these elderly widows. As a result of their complaint, the apostles propose a solution to the whole community of disciples: rather than let this burgeoning task draw the apostles away from their primary ministry, the group should pick seven men of proven godliness and wisdom and turn the distribution responsibility over to them.

The proposal meets with approval, and seven men, all of whom have Greek names, are chosen. As these men carry out their responsibility, and as the apostles devote themselves to prayer and preaching, the needs of the widows are met and the church continues to grow.

Putting this into a passage outline, we might identify the following three "hunks," along with their subordinate units:[3]

---

2. These may be women who intended only a brief pilgrim visit to Jerusalem for the Feast of Pentecost (Acts 2) but, in extending their stay to learn more about the new movement of Christianity, have depleted the financial resources they brought with them. Or, before their husbands died, they may have immigrated to Jerusalem to die in the Holy City and have now outlived both their husbands and their financial reserves.

3. Note again how the passage outline anchors you to the biblical author's flow of thought and that its hunks or movements do not necessarily have to be proportionate in length or biblical material.

Passage Ooth' [handwritten]

Passage Oot'liv → truth Ootliv → Sermon Outliv [handwritten]

I. The Jerusalem church is a growing church (6:1a). *Situation* [handwritten]

II. This growing church has a problem with widows' food (6:1b). *stress* [handwritten]

III. The church solves the problem through designated lay leadership *Search* (6:2–7). *solution* [handwritten]
    A. The apostles propose the solution (6:2–4).
    B. The people accept the solution (6:5–6).
    C. The problem is solved (6:7).
        1. The needs are met.
        2. The growth continues.

new Situation [handwritten]

Now let's see how this biblical flow of thought might become a final sermon outline, using each of the three relevancy patterns. In some cases we'll also combine these relevancy patterns with the two structural patterns (deductive and inductive). *the Connection to a modern audience...* [handwritten]

RELEVANCY AT THE END

- Application / THT [handwritten]

Description and Examples

Placing the relevancy at the end means that, after a brief introduction, you unfold the entire biblical account before you draw out its relevancy to a modern audience. You explain the whole passage, without interruption, before you make contemporary application at the end of the message.

In outline form, a deductive, relevancy-at-the-end sermon would look something like the following:

    Introduction
        1.
        2.
        3.
        4. A deductive statement of the timeless take-home truth
           [*]

    I. A deductive statement of the passage's take-home truth
        A. A statement covering the first passage unit

      B. A statement covering the second passage unit

      C. A statement covering the third passage unit

  II.   Repeating the deductive statement of the <u>timeless take-home</u> truth [*]

Relevancy — A. An application of the take-home truth to one situation [♦]

Relevancy — B. An application of the take-home truth to another situation [♦]

Relevancy — C. An application of the take-home truth to a third situation [♦]

Relevancy — D. An application of the take-home truth to a fourth situation [♦]

Visually, the relevancy-at-the-end pattern, combined with a deductive structure, looks like this:

A sermon outline on Acts 6:1–7 using the deductive, relevancy-at-the-end combination might take this form:

Introduction

Situation   1. We would all like to be part of a growing church like . . . (name some churches).

        2. We think this would solve our problems.

           a. We would have enough teens to have an effective youth program.

           b. We would have enough money to hire additional staff and fund new ministries.

        3. But problems arise even within growing churches, sometimes even because of the growth itself.

        a. Growing churches have problems of insufficient parking.
        b. Growing churches have problems of inadequate nurseries.
    4. When problems arise in a growing church, the way to solve them is through designated lay leadership [* = deductive statement of the timeless take-home truth].
    5. This is how the early church solves its problem created by growth in Acts 6:1–7.

I. The Jerusalem church solves its problem created by growth through designated lay leadership [* = deductive statement of the passage's take-home truth].
    A. The Jerusalem church is a growing church.
    B. The church has a problem with widows' food.
    C. The church solves the problem through designated lay leadership.
        1. The apostles propose the solution.
        2. The people accept the solution.
        3. The problem is solved.

II. We can solve our problems of growth through designated lay leadership [* = repeating the deductive statement of the timeless take-home truth].
    A. We can solve our parking problem through two teams of men [♦].
        1. Our problem is caused by an inefficient configuration of parking spots on our lot.
        2. We can solve this problem through designated task forces—one group of "engineers" to reconfigure the striping of our parking lot and another group to play "traffic cop" the first few weeks until we learn the new traffic flow. Fred Smith will be in the foyer after the service to sign you up for one of these task forces.
    B. We can solve our problem of inadequate nursery facilities by having Helen coordinate the planning of the new room with new moms [♦].

1. The board has authorized removing the wall between rooms 101 and 102 in our educational building in order to provide more space for our expanding nursery.

2. Any new moms who want to help design and furnish the enlarged room—choosing attractive color schemes, modern cribs, and appropriate toys—please let Helen know on the tear-off tab where it says, "Helen, here's my phone number; call me."

In outline form, an inductive, relevancy-at-the-end sermon would unfold as follows:

Introduction
1.
2.
3.
4. An inductive raising of the topic/question

I. (The unsaid statement of the passage's take-home truth, toward which the subpoints are inductively heading)
   A. A statement covering the first passage unit
   B. A statement covering the second passage unit
   C. A statement covering the third passage unit

II. A statement of the timeless take-home truth [*]
   A. An application of the take-home truth to one situation [♦]
   B. An application of the take-home truth to another situation [♦]
   C. An application of the take-home truth to a third situation [♦]
   D. An application of the take-home truth to a fourth situation [♦]

A sermon outline on Acts 6:1–7, using the inductive, relevancy-at-the-end combination might take this form:

Introduction
1. We would all like to be part of a growing church like . . . (name some churches).
2. We think this would solve our problems.
    a. We would have enough teens to have an effective youth program.
    b. We would have enough money to hire additional staff and fund new ministries.
3. But problems arise even within growing churches, sometimes even because of the growth itself.
    a. Growing churches have problems of insufficient parking.
    b. Growing churches have problems of inadequate nurseries.
4. When problems arise in a growing church, how should we solve them [inductive raising of the topic/question]?
5. For the answer, let's turn to Acts 6:1–7 to see how the early church solves a problem that comes from growth.

I. (The Jerusalem church solves its problem created by growth through designated lay leadership [unsaid statement of the passage's take-home truth, toward which the subpoints are inductively heading].)[4]
    A. The Jerusalem church is a growing church.
    B. The church has a problem with widows' food.
    C. The church solves the problem through designated lay leadership.
        1. The apostles propose the solution.
        2. The people accept the solution.
        3. The problem is solved.

II. We can solve our problems of growth through designated lay leadership [* = statement of the timeless take-home truth].
    A. We will solve our parking problem through two teams of men [♦].

---

4. The parentheses indicate that this particular sentence will not be spoken orally at this point but instead will form itself in the listener's mind after the subpoints have been presented. See appendix A, guideline 5, for proper outlining.

1. Our problem is caused by an inefficient configuration of parking spots on our lot.

2. We will solve this problem through designated task forces—one group of "engineers" to reconfigure the striping of our parking lot and another group to play "traffic cop" the first month until we learn the new traffic flow. Fred Smith will be in the foyer after the service to sign you up for one of these task forces.

B. We will solve our problem of inadequate nursery facilities by having Helen coordinate the planning of the new room with new moms [♦].

1. The board has authorized removing the wall between rooms 101 and 102 in our educational building in order to provide more space for our expanding nursery.

2. Any new moms who want to help design and furnish the enlarged room—choosing attractive color schemes, modern cribs, and appropriate toys—please let Helen know on the tear-off tab where it says, "Helen, here's my phone number; call me."

New Situation

If we were to use an inductive pattern, combined with relevancy at the end, the visual image would be:

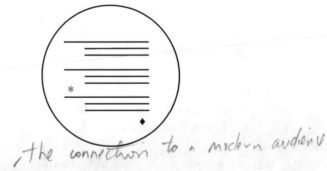

, the connection to a modern audience

When to Use the Relevancy-at-the-End Pattern

When might you use a relevancy-at-the-end pattern, combining it with either a deductive or inductive structure? You might gravitate toward this pattern when only your passage's take-home truth lends itself to contemporary application, and not its individual hunks.   *Search*

For example, in a sermon on Genesis 29:1–14, note that only the overall central truth seems suitable for application and not the individual sub-points of the passage flow: *p. 163*

Introduction

Situation

1. In the musical *Fiddler on the Roof*, Tevye's daughters sing to the village matchmaker to "make me a perfect match."

2. Many a single person has a similar request of God: "Are you a matchmaker? Do you have someone specifically, perfectly suited for me?"

3. Today we're going to see that God's answer to that question is yes. God is a matchmaker. If God is calling you to marriage, then his plan for you is very specific, and he will, without fail, lead you to the one he has for you. He will control the timing and sequence of events and bring you to the perfect match he intends for you [* = deductive statement of the timeless take-home truth].[5]

Solution

4. God does not call everyone to marriage. He fashions a life for some that is full, meaningful, and productive apart from marriage.

5. But if God has called you to marriage, we're going to see from the life of Jacob that his plan for you is very specific and that he will, without fail, lead you to the one he has for you.

stress

6. Jacob, forty years old and unmarried, is being sent away by his parents, both to escape Esau's wrath and hopefully to find a wife among their relatives in a distant country. Sick over what he's leaving and fearful of the unknowns ahead (it's been sixty years since his family has had contact with the relatives; Jacob is uncertain of how to find their country, and unsure of whether his relatives even still live

---

5. Though this take-home truth emerges inductively in 29:14, the sermon is structured deductively for a couple of reasons: (1) it would be difficult to sustain an inductive question, "What will God do for those he has called to marriage?" over such a long passage; and (2) the deductive structure will work because the take-home truth probably raises some form of the second developmental question in the listener's mind—"Oh, pastor, I hope you can convince me that's true" (cf. pp. 156–59).

in that same area), Jacob has a dream on his last night in the Promised Land. In the dream God promises him that he will someday return to the land, married, and with sons and daughters.

7. The dream tells Jacob that God is calling him to marriage and that in the days ahead God will control the timing and sequence of events to make it happen.

8. We pick up the story in Genesis 29.

Search

I. God controls the timing and sequence of events to lead Jacob to Rachel [* = deductive statement of the passage's take-home truth].

A. God leads Jacob to the right geographical area—the "land of the eastern peoples" (29:1).

B. God leads Jacob to three shepherds, who are from the settlement of Haran, the place he is seeking (29:2–4).

C. God reveals through the shepherds that Jacob's relatives are still in the area, and are financially able to take him in (29:5–6).

D. God causes Jacob to be impressed with Rachel and enables him to impress her in return (29:7–10).

1. Jacob is impressed both by the girl and by the condition of the sheep she tends.

2. Jacob impresses Rachel by lifting a heavy stone and watering her sheep.

E. God leads Jacob to release his pent-up emotion, as he unburdens himself to Rachel, telling her of the anxious events of the past months (29:11–12).

F. God causes Laban, Rachel's father, to echo the words of Adam to Eve, indicating that Jacob will form the most intimate union with his family (29:13–14).

Solution

II. If God has called you to marriage, he will, without fail, lead you to the one he has for you [* = repeating the deductive statement of the timeless take-home truth].

A. If you are married, this means "God has joined you together," and you should not "separate" [♦].

B. If you are unmarried, you can expect God to control the timing and sequence of events to bring you together.
 1. It might occur in a college class [♦].
 2. It might occur while you're at a distant convention or training seminar [♦].
 3. It might happen when a visitor comes to church [♦].
C. Because God is your matchmaker, you can date without pressure and marry without fear [♦].

You would probably choose a relevancy-at-the-end pattern for this message, since only the overall take-home truth carries across to the contemporary world and any attempts, like the following, to apply the smaller hunks in the story would seem to be stretching and close to silly:

- God led Jacob to the right geographical area; God will give you a job transfer to Chicago.
- God led Jacob to three shepherds by a well who were able to point out Rachel to him; God will lead you to three workers by the office drinking fountain who will introduce you to a pretty girl in the office.
- God enabled Jacob to impress Rachel; God will make you "Salesperson of the Year" in order to draw the attention of that pretty girl.

A responsible approach to the passage would shun such attempts to find modern equivalents of the smaller units and would apply only the large take-home truth through a relevancy-at-the-end pattern.

Caution: Avoid Abusing the Pattern

The relevancy-at-the-end pattern is commonly abused, especially when speakers approach narrative sections of the Bible. Speakers will unfold the entire biblical account, but then, instead of applying the one central truth of the passage, they'll make several miscellaneous and unrelated applications drawn from different verses in the passage.

Speakers fall into this abuse when they fail to have one timeless take-home truth that covers the whole passage. Seeing the narrative only as *story*, rather than as *theology* designed to reveal one central truth, they

instead seek many smaller truths from individual phrases in the biblical
account.

For example, here's how Mark 4:35–41[6] (Jesus stilling the storm) might
be commonly abused:

> Introduction
> 1. We often wish we could control the weather for a perfect
>   church picnic or an outdoor wedding.
> 2. Mark Twain once commented, "Everybody talks about
>   the weather, but nobody does anything about it."
> 3. Today we're going to see a time when Jesus controlled the
>   weather, to the amazement of his followers.
> 4. And we'll see some practical lessons we can draw from
>   this incident for our daily lives. [The listeners are dubious
>   that one of the lessons will be how they can control the
>   weather.]
> 5. Please turn to Mark 4:35–41.
>
> I. Jesus controls the weather.[7]
>   A. Jesus directs his disciples to leave the crowd and go to the
>   other side of the lake (4:35–36).
>   B. During the crossing, a storm nearly swamps the boat (4:37).
>   C. Jesus has been calmly sleeping during the storm, unconcerned
>   about the urgency (4:38a).
>   D. After unsuccessfully bailing water, the disciples finally appeal
>   to Jesus (4:38b).
>   E. Jesus works a miracle, showing he has the power to control
>   the weather (4:39–41).
>
> II. I see four practical lessons we can learn for our daily lives.[8]
>   A. If we are going to follow Jesus, sometimes we have to "leave
>   the crowd behind" (4:36).

---

6. Cf. the following against the outlines on pp. 38–41.
7. Note the lack of a single sentence that states the truth or theology of the sermon in a nutshell.
   In the speaker's mind, there's no timeless point to the story as a whole, so the speaker simply
   tells the story and then applies lots of little points.
8. Here come the miscellaneous and unrelated applications drawn from different verses in the
   passage.

1. Some of you businessmen need to stop doing business the way the world does business and leave the crowd behind.
2. Some of you teenagers are going with the wrong group; you need to leave the crowd behind.

B. Ministry is fatiguing, and we should take advantage of opportunities to keep ourselves well rested (4:38).
    1. Don't burn out for God.
    2. God is not panicked by urgency; he's always in control.
C. We should go to Jesus when difficulties first appear, rather than struggling unsuccessfully in our own strength until they seem hopeless (4:37).
D. We should have no fear, for Jesus can control the storms of life (4:39).

Some listeners are impressed with such preaching. The speaker usually tells the biblical story with flair, creativity, and accuracy. And the applications may strike the listeners as insightful—"Wow, our pastor is a real Bible student. I never would have seen that in the passage. But there it is—'leaving the crowd behind.'"[9]

Other listeners, however, may rightfully question whether this was the biblical author's intended meaning. And they may judge the disconnected applications as somewhat arbitrary, fanciful, and perhaps even contrary to other biblical passages.[10] ② *time less take-home truth*

③ In the relevancy-at-the-end pattern, the contemporary applications must not be miscellaneous and unrelated observations taken from different verses in the passage. Instead, they must be similar applications of the one, same central truth, as it might pertain to various individuals or situations among the listeners. The speaker is asking, "What does this single take-home truth look like in the life of . . . a teenager, a stay-at-home mom, a retiree, or a single person in an entry-level job?"

---

9. While some contemporary listeners may be impressed, I suspect the original author, Mark, would groan, "I didn't see it either (and I wrote it!), because it isn't there!"
10. Discerning listeners might wonder, for example, why the drowsy disciples in Gethsemane didn't simply answer Jesus' query as to why they were sleeping with, "Ministry is fatiguing, and we're trying to keep ourselves well rested."

The connection to a modern audience. Relevancy of the 1st u... occurs after the explanation of the Uni...

RELEVANCY INTERSPERSED

Interspersing the relevancy means that, after a brief introduction, you unfold one part or segment of the biblical passage and apply that unit before moving on to the next part or segment. Then you add the second unit's explanation and application to the previous point.

In this pattern, the relevancy is progressively unfolded, moving in tandem with the passage units. As noted earlier, the applications are not miscellaneous or disconnected points spun off in different directions. Instead, the same applications are threaded through the message, and grow as the biblical content advances. The speaker returns to a previous application and adds something to it.

This interspersed pattern is appropriate when each of your passage's parts has some unfolding contemporary relevance.

In outline form, an inductive, relevancy-interspersed sermon would unfold as follows:

    Introduction
      1.
      2.   *who, what, where, when, why; how?*
      3.
      4. An inductive raising of the topic/question

  I. A statement covering the first unit of the truth outline
     A. A statement covering the first unit of the passage outline
     B. A statement relating the contemporary relevancy of the first unit [♦]

  II. A statement covering the second unit of the truth outline
     A. A statement covering the second unit of the passage outline
     B. A statement relating the contemporary relevancy of the second unit [♦]

  III. A statement covering the third unit of the truth outline, forming the take-home truth [*]
     A. A statement covering the third unit of the passage outline

B. A statement relating the contemporary <u>relevancy</u> of the third
    unit [◆]

Visually, the relevancy-interspersed pattern, combined with an inductive structure,[11] looks like this:

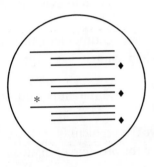

An inductive, relevancy-interspersed sermon on Acts 6:1–7 might progressively unfold as follows:

Introduction
1. We would all like to be part of a growing church like . . .
    (name some churches).
2. We think this would solve our problems.
    a. We would have enough teens to have an effective
        youth program.
    b. We would have enough money to hire additional staff
        and fund new ministries.
3. But problems arise even within growing churches, some-
    times even because of the growth itself.
    a. Growing churches have problems of insufficient
        parking.
    b. Growing churches have problems of inadequate
        nurseries.
4. When problems arise in a growing church, how should
    we solve them [inductive raising of the topic/question]?

---

11. The interspersed pattern will usually be used with the inductive structure since both the bibli-
    cal points and the applications are cumulatively building toward a climax. See pages 189–91,
    however, for an example of a deductive, interspersed sermon.

5. For the answer, let's turn to Acts 6:1–7 to see how the early church solves a problem that comes from growth.

I.   The Jerusalem church, like ours, is a growing church [first unit].
    A. The Jerusalem church is a growing church (6:1a).
    B. We are a growing church—visuals, charts, statistics [♦].

II. Growing churches sometimes have problems [second unit].
    A. The Jerusalem church has a problem with widows' food. (6:1b).
    B. Our problems are different [♦ adding the next concept to the unfolding].
        1. We have the problem of inefficient parking.
        2. We have the problem of inadequate nursery facilities.

III. The solution to problems of growth is through designated lay leadership [* = third unit, forming the take-home truth].
    A. The Jerusalem church solves its problem through designated lay leadership (6:2–7).
        1. The apostles propose the solution.
        2. The people accept the solution.
        3. The problem is solved.
    B. We can solve our problems of growth through designated lay leadership [♦ returning to the same applications mentioned previously].
        1. We can solve our parking problem through two teams of men.
        2. We can solve our nursery problem by having Helen coordinate meetings with new moms. *The connection to a modern audience*

RELEVANCY WRAPPED

In the wrap pattern, your introduction probes at length the relevancy of the first passage unit, even before the passage is mentioned. In other words, the contemporary relevancy of the first unit is front-ended. (This differs from the interspersed pattern, where the relevancy of the first unit occurs after the explanation of the unit.)

After the explanation of the second unit in the passage, the speaker returns to the same contemporary situations mentioned in the introduction to complete the application.

I use the term *wrap* because the flow of thought sounds like the application has been wrapped around the biblical units:[12]

> Contemporary relevance of first unit (introduction)
> Explanation of first unit
> Explanation of second unit
> Contemporary relevance of second unit

The wrap pattern works especially well in narrative literature, where your introduction can raise contemporary situations that are analogous to the situation in the first passage unit. Whereas an interspersed development in the body of the message has a "we're like them" feel to it—

> Here's what was going on in the biblical world.
> The same thing is going on in our lives.
> Here's how they dealt with it.
> We're going to deal with it the same way.

—the wrap pattern comes to the listener with a "they're like us" feel:

> Here's what's going on in our lives.
> The same thing was going on in the biblical world.
> Here's how they dealt with it.
> We're going to deal with it the same way.

If there are only two biblical units (as above), the wrap pattern has similarities to the relevancy-at-the-end pattern, since once you start unfolding the biblical account, you explain the whole passage (the two middle units) without interruption before you return to complete your applications.

If there are more than two biblical units, the wrap pattern then continues in an interspersed form.

---

12. The shaded areas indicate the relevancy sections wrapping around the biblical units.

Here's what's going on in our lives.
The same thing was going on in the biblical world. *Interspersed*
This is why it was happening to them.
It's also why it's happening to us.
Here's how they dealt with it.
We're going to deal with it the same way.

Visually, the wrap pattern, combined with an inductive structure looks like this:

Wrapped to interspersed format = Relevancy wrapped

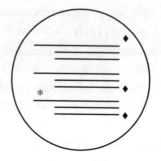

A sermon outline on Acts 6:1–7, wrapping the relevancy of the first *two* biblical units[13] into the introduction, might look like the following:

Introduction

Relevancy

1. We are a growing church—visuals, charts, statistics
    [♦ of first unit].
2. But some problems have arisen due to our growth
    [♦ of second unit].
    a. Our parking is inefficient.
    b. Our nursery is inadequate.

Explanation

3. To discover how to solve these problems, let's turn to Acts
    6:1–7 to see how the early church solved its problem due
    to growth.

---

13. Generally in the wrap pattern, only the first unit's relevancy is probed in the introduction. But
    occasionally, as in this example from Acts 6:1–7, the first two units might be handled together
    at the start.

I.   The Jerusalem church is a growing church (6:1a).[14]

 II. This growing church has a problem with widows' food (6:1b).

III. The solution to problems of growth is through designated lay leadership [*].

A. The Jerusalem church solves its problem through designated lay leadership (6:2–7).

B. We can solve our problems through designated lay leadership [♦ of third unit].

1. We can solve our parking problem through two teams of men.

2. We can solve our nursery problem by having Helen coordinate meetings with new moms.

 Our earlier example of a sermon on Mark 4:35–41 is a wrap pattern that eventually continues as an interspersed pattern:

Introduction

1. Sometimes we obey God, and the bottom falls out of everything [♦ first unit].

a. You move to a new city to begin a new job—one year later your wife has developed allergies, your kids hate their new school, and the company has folded.

b. You honor your widowed mom by bringing her into your own home—after six months the house is in

---

14. In the wrap pattern, the first movement or outline point in the body of the message is stated historically, from the passage outline, since the timeless truth statement and its application have already been developed in the introduction. In other words, since the listener has already heard the shaded parts below, the only thing left to say in the body of the message is the passage statement:

   Timeless truth statement of the first passage unit
   Historical statement of the first passage unit
   Application of the first passage unit

   Notice that this also occurs in the next outline from Mark 4:35–41—the first hunk in the body of the message is stated historically, since its timeless truth statement ("So obey God and the bottom falls out of everything") and its applications (new j mom, marriage) have already been given in the introduction.

> chaos due to your mother's constant criticizing of your wife and scolding of your kids.
>
> c.   You marry—the first year is a disaster.

2. We despair, and wonder, "God, why is this happening, and what do you want me to do?"

3. Today we'll see the disciples in a similar situation and learn why such things happen and what our response should be.

4. Please turn to Mark 4:35–41.

I. The disciples obey Jesus and find themselves in a life-threatening storm that fills them with despair (4:35–38).

II. The reason such things happen may be that Satan is attempting to prevent God's purposes.

A. The storm is Satan's attempt to prevent the growth of the kingdom.

1. Jesus has been teaching that his kingdom will grow large and include Gentiles, due to his disciples' preaching and their ability to handle demonic opposition (3:13–4:34).

2. They are now crossing to Gentile territory, where Jesus will rescue a man from Satan's kingdom and send him as a witness to Gentiles (5:1–20).

3. The storm is a demonic attempt to prevent the growth of the kingdom.

   a.   Whenever Mark records Jesus "rebuking," it's always of demonic activity.

   b.   The command to the wind to "Be still," is the same command to the demon in Mark 1:25.

B. Our difficulties may be Satan's attempt to prevent what God wants to do through us [♦ second unit].

1. Your difficulties in the new city may be Satan's attempt to . . .

2. Your problems with your mother may be Satan's attempt to . . .

3. The turmoil in your marriage may be Satan's attempt to . . .

Here's how they dealt with it

III.   We should resist Satan's efforts and trust God's power [*].

planation

   A.   Jesus rebukes the demonic activity behind the storm and encourages the disciples to trust God's power (4:39–41).

   B.   We should resist Satan's efforts, and trust God's power [♦ third unit].

       1.   You might resist Satan's efforts in the new city by . . .
       2.   You could resist Satan's activity in your home by . . .
       3.   You can resist Satan's disruption of your marriage by . . .

Relevance

We've going to deal with it in the same way.

By using various combinations of these structural (deduction and induction) and relevancy (at the end, interspersed, and wrapped) patterns, you can shape a variety of sermon structures that will appeal to your creativity and sustain your listeners' interest from week to week.

In the next chapter, we'll address one final area in shaping the sermon—not so much how to create a pattern or structure for our sermon, but rather how to handle an unfamiliar pattern or structure in the biblical passage itself.

10

Shape the Sermon (Part 3)

Chiastic Passages

WE'VE LOOKED AT THE TWO major questions you have to decide as you structure your final sermon outline:

1. Where in the biblical flow of thought will you place the take-home truth (*)?
2. Where in the biblical flow of thought will you place the contemporary relevance (♦)?

But there's a third issue we need to consider: How do you shape your final sermon when the biblical passage is *chiastic*—that is, when the original biblical passage repeats previous themes in inverted order? Because of our exclusive training in linear patterns, we're usually unprepared to spot or handle this ancient literary form.

In our contemporary world almost everything we write is in a linear pattern. We start at the beginning and stop at the end.

I.

II.

III.

But in biblical literature, the authors often wrote in a chiastic pattern. They started at the beginning, reached the end, then reversed their thought, and stopped at the beginning.[1]

I.

II.

III.

II.

I.

Since chiastic patterns are so foreign to our contemporary world, we tend not to spot them easily as we read or study biblical material. In fact, our initial reaction when we encounter a chiastic passage is often, "Why doesn't this guy learn how to outline! He's unorganized. His material is confusing."[2]

Because of the repetitive nature of chiastic passages, as well as the frequency with which chiasm appears in the Scriptures, we need to understand this literary pattern and consider how to preach it to a contemporary audience.

UNDERSTANDING CHIASTIC PASSAGES

The word *chiasm* derives from a Greek verb meaning "to mark with two lines crossing like an X" (the Greek letter chi). If two statements expressing the same thought, only in reverse order, are placed one under the other, and then lines are drawn connecting the corresponding elements, the lines will resemble an X:

---

1. As a literary pattern, the chiastic structure had several advantages: (1) it allowed the author to flag the core element in his take-home truth by placing it at the center point where the content begins to reverse itself, (2) it gave the reader a sense of unity and completeness as the material came full circle, and (3) its balance and repetition expedited teaching, and aided the memory during liturgy.
2. This may explain why you so seldom hear a sermon on a whole psalm. Speakers, not recognizing a psalm's chiastic structure during their study, throw up their hands in frustration at trying to outline it in a linear fashion, and settle instead for preaching only a part of the psalm.

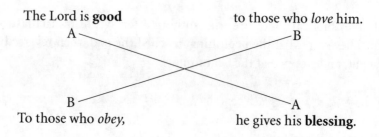

In the example above, the two lines express essentially the same thought, but the corresponding phrases have been reversed in the second line. In the first line, the phrase "The Lord is good" appears at the start of the sentence; in the second line, the corresponding phrase, "he gives his blessing" is at the end of the sentence.

While the "crossing X" gives rise to the term *chiasm*, the pattern itself is more commonly expressed through an ABBA arrangement, so that the corresponding elements can be more easily visualized and so that longer chiastic structures can be represented.

    A   The Lord is good
        B   To those who love him
        B   To those who obey
    A   He gives his blessing

A chiastic pattern can extend over many verses and even whole chapters and books.[3]

James 4:13–16

    A   Arrogantly planning your future is evil (4:13)
        B   You do not know what you will do (4:14a)
            C   Or whether you will live (4:14b)
                D   It's up to the Lord (4:15a)
            C   Whether you will live (4:15b)
        B   And what you will do (4:15c)
    A   Arrogantly planning your future is evil (4:16)

---

3. For a single chiastic structure covering the combined books of 1 and 2 Samuel, see David A. Dorsey, *The Literary Structure of the Old Testament* (Grand Rapids: Baker, 1999), 135.

Psalm 3

> A   They say, "God will not deliver him" (3:1–2)
>
> > B   You are a warrior on my behalf (3:3)
> >
> > > C   I cry to you for help (3:4)
> > >
> > > > D   You make me safe and unafraid (3:5–6)
> > >
> > > C   I cry to you for help (3:7a)
> >
> > B   You are a warrior on my behalf (3:7b)
>
> A   I know, "From the Lord comes deliverance" (3:8)

The first hint that your passage might be chiastic will probably come as you struggle with the repetitive elements while trying to form your initial passage outline. Hopefully this struggle will lead you to ask yourself, "Do I have a chiastic passage?" And if you determine that you do, then back away from your desk, stand up, and do a little jig! You've just discovered your take-home truth.

In a chiastic structure, the point of the V is the take-home truth. The innermost thought in the arrangement is the one the author is stressing; it's the dominant concept around which the rest of the material revolves.

In James 4:13–16 above, for example, the take-home truth is, "*It's up to the Lord* whether we live and do anything, and any thought to the contrary is foolish arrogance."

The central truth of Psalm 3 is, "*We can experience peace and safety* in the midst of pressures and attacks from all sides if we ask God for help and are confident of his ability to deliver us."

PREACHING CHIASTIC PASSAGES

While a chiastic structure aids the preacher in discovering the central truth, it nevertheless presents a challenge for preaching the flow of thought. Modern listeners undoubtedly would be puzzled if the last ten minutes of a sermon essentially said the same thing as the first ten minutes.

There are several possible approaches for preaching chiastic passages.

If the chiastic structure occurs briefly within a few verses, such as James 4:13–16 above, you probably could preach the passage without ever burdening your listeners with a discussion of "chiasm." You could easily construct a linear outline for your final sermon.[4]

---

4. See the "linear" sermon outline of James 4:13–16 on pages 152–54.

Sometimes the chiastic structure, while returning to a previous theme, has a sufficiently different nuance on that theme so that, again, a linear outline will work. For example, Psalm 92 has the following chiastic structure:

> A   Proclaim the Lord's love and faithfulness (92:1–3)
>> B   The righteous rejoice over the works of the Lord (92:4–5)
>>> C   The senseless do not know the wicked will be destroyed (92:6–8)
>>>> D   All evildoers, God's enemies, will perish (92:9)[5]
>>> C   The elect will witness their enemies being destroyed (92:10–11)
>> B   The righteous flourish forever in the presence of the Lord (92:12–14)
> A   Proclaim the Lord's justice and holiness (92:15)

Even though the chiastic sections match, there's a progression of thought through the psalm: God's love and faithfulness expressed through his works become more specifically defined as the psalm unfolds—he destroys all his enemies. This means the psalmist will ultimately be victorious over his particular enemies and will flourish forever in the house of his God. A simple linear outline could handle this progressive flow:

I.   Proclaim the Lord's love and faithfulness (92:1–3).

II. Because you know something that gives you joy, something the senseless fool does not know—that all evildoers will perish (92:4–9).
  A. You have joy because you know God's deeds and thoughts (92:4–5).
  B. The senseless fool does not have this knowledge (92:6).
  C. The truth is: The wicked will be destroyed; all God's enemies will perish (92:7–9).

III. But God has chosen you for victory and joy (92:10–14).

---

5. The psalmist indicates his point of the V in verse 9 by making it the only Hebrew poetic triplet in the midst of parallel doublets.

A. The exalted horn symbolizes victory and strength (92:10a).
B. The fine oils and flourishing trees symbolize joy and festivity following victory (92:10b–14).
 1. Your joy will overflow (92:10b).
 2. You will see the defeat of your enemies (92:11).
 3. You will flourish forever in the Lord's presence (92:12–14).

IV. Proclaim the Lord's justice and holiness (92:15).

In a longer and more intricate chiastic passage, however, you might have to educate your listeners about chiasm, and then combine the corresponding elements into a familiar linear outline for preaching.

For example, Malachi pronounces judgment on Israel through an extended, repeated chiasm: God is angry with them because, instead of giving him the honor he is due, they have shown profound disrespect for him in their worship (Mal. 1:6–14):

A Honor (v. 6)
"A son honors his father, and a servant his master. If I am a father, where is the honor due me? If I am a master, where is the respect due me?" says the LORD Almighty. "It is you, O priests, who show contempt for my name. But you ask, 'How have we shown contempt for your name?'"

B Disrespect (vv. 7–8)
"You place defiled food on my altar. But you ask, 'How have we defiled you?' By saying that the LORD's table is contemptible. When you bring blind animals for sacrifice, is that not wrong? When you sacrifice crippled or diseased animals, is that not wrong? Try offering them to your governor! Would he be pleased with you? Would he accept you?" says the LORD Almighty.

C Anger (v. 9)
"Now implore God to be gracious to us. With such offerings from your hands, will he accept you?"—says the LORD Almighty.

B   Disrespect (v. 10)

"Oh, that one of you would shut the temple doors, so that you would not light useless fires on my altar! I am not pleased with you," says the LORD Almighty, "and I will accept no offering from your hands."

A   Honor (v. 11)

"My name will be great among the nations, from the rising to the setting of the sun. In every place incense and pure offerings will be brought to my name, because my name will be great among the nations," says the LORD Almighty.

B   Disrespect (vv. 12–13a)

"But you profane it by saying of the Lord's table, 'It is defiled,' and of its food, 'It is contemptible.' And you say, 'What a burden!' and you sniff at it contemptuously," says the LORD Almighty. "When you bring injured, crippled or diseased animals and offer them as sacrifices, . . ."

C   Anger (vv. 13b–14a)

". . . should I accept them from your hands?" says the LORD. "Cursed is the cheat . . ."

B   Disrespect (v. 14b)

". . . who has an acceptable male in his flock and vows to give it, but then sacrifices a blemished animal to the Lord."

A   Honor (v. 14c)

"For I am a great king," says the LORD Almighty, "and my name is to be feared among the nations."

You might show this chiastic structure to your listeners in some visually abbreviated way:

A Honor
  B Disrespect
    C Anger
  B Disrespect
A Honor
  B Disrespect
    C Anger
  B Disrespect
A Honor

And then you would explain that you want to unfold the material in a pattern more familiar to them by examining all the A elements first, then the B ones, and then conclude with the C units.

The final sermon outline could look something like this (using the deductive and interspersed patterns):

Introduction
1. When we pray and ask God for help, we would like to sense that he hears us and will act on our behalf.
2. If he listens and does not act, we become frustrated, edgy, and full of questions: "Why don't you act? Why don't you do what I ask?"
3. A group of people once asked God those same questions: "Why don't you give us the weather and rain that will make our crops grow? Why don't you enable our towns to defend themselves and our nation to become independent? Why is your face toward us stern and unsmiling? You say you love us and chose us. So why don't you act?"
4. God's answer to them was, "It is because you do not really honor or respect me; your actions and thoughts reveal an inner contempt for me."
5. His answer stunned them. Yet that may be his same answer to us—"I do not answer your prayers because at the core of your life I am not important to you; your spirit toward me is one of profound disrespect" [* = deductive take-home truth].

     6.   We need to consider carefully what God is saying. Please turn to Malachi 1:6–14.

     7.   As we read, we will have a vague sense that some things are being repeated. [Briefly explain chiasm and visually present the structural pattern.]

     8.   Since in our culture we're more used to a linear pattern, I'm going to group the common themes and consider them together.

I.   We ought to hold God in the highest honor.

   A. Israel should honor God.

     1.   A son honors his father (1:6).

     2.   A servant respects his master (1:6).

     3.   In every part of the world there are those who honor God (1:11).

     4.   He is a great King (1:14).

   B. We should hold God in the highest honor.

II.   But instead we often treat him with disrespect.

   A. Israel's actions revealed an inner contempt for God.

     1.   They sacrificed defective, inferior animals (1:7–8).

     2.   They sacrificed injured "road-kill" (1:12–13a).

     3.   They broke their vows (1:14a).

     4.   Their entire worship was a sham (1:10).

   B. Sometimes our actions reveal a profound disrespect of God.

     1.   We give him the leftover of our money.

     2.   We fail to give him the best hours of our time.

     3.   We have poor follow-through on our service.

     4.   We come to worship late, rushed, groggy.

III.   Such disrespect brings the displeasure of God.

   A. God was angry with Israel.

     1.   The individual cheater was cursed (1:14).

     2.   The nation's prayers went unanswered (1:9).

   B. God will no longer be implored, or favorable to us.

Conclusion
1. God has loved us with an everlasting love.
2. Such love should lead us to adore and honor him above all else in life.
3. You honor him when, having given him your best, you still wish you could do more.

Through these last three chapters we've determined the flow of our final sermon outline, combining two structural patterns (deductive and inductive) with three relevancy patterns (at the end, interspersed, and wrapped), along with suggestions on how to handle chiastic passages. Now we're ready to create an introduction that will engage the listeners in the message and draw them into God's truth.

As you start to think about your introduction, you've already made some preliminary decisions regarding it. You've already decided, for example, whether your introduction will deductively reveal the take-home truth or whether it will inductively raise the topic/question. You've also decided, if you're using the relevancy-wrapped pattern, that your opening paragraphs will probe some contemporary situation that is similar to the first biblical unit.

But these preliminary decisions need to be placed within an introduction's precise sequence or flow of thought. That sequence is the subject of our next two chapters.

– 11 –

Create the Introduction (Part 1)
Engage, Focus, and Set the Stage

THE GOAL OF THE INTRODUCTION is to engage the listeners, focus the message, and transition to the biblical passage.

The introduction can be visualized as a funnel, capturing the listeners at the widest edges of their interest, directing them with clarity and a sense of need to the biblical passage, and taking them into the first hunk of the message.

P P P P P P P
P P P P P P
P P P P P P P
. ?
 	
┌ ─ ─ │ ─ ─ ┐
└ ─ ─ │ ─ ─ ┘
 	
I.
  II.
    III.
 	
Chap./V.
 	
I. First hunk of the message
	Engage the listeners' interest, using as many paragraphs as necessary to create a need for, or curiosity about, the message.
	
	Focus the message on either the take-home truth (deductive) or the topic/question (inductive).
	
	Set the stage biblically (i.e., context, background, setting).
	
	Preview the coming hunks, the direction the message will take.
	
	Announce the passage and wait for them to find it.

Because each of these steps is vital to either relevancy or clarity, and because the sequence in which they occur is critical to an orderly flow,[1] we'll look at each of these in considerable detail. We'll address the first three in this chapter, and the last two in the next one.

ENGAGE THE LISTENERS' INTEREST

The first step in the introduction—engaging the listeners' interest—is usually the longest. Depending on the message, it could take anywhere from two to ten minutes. The goal is for the listener to end up wanting to hear the rest of the message, either because of some need that was created or some curiosity that was stirred.

Usually the introduction starts with the listeners rather than with the passage. Since the Bible is God speaking to them, it helps to start with whatever it is in their lives that God wishes to address through this message.

Anything that engages the listeners and makes them want to hear the rest of the message is probably a good introduction—relating a personal story, referring to a recent event, making a startling statement, exploring a contemporary issue, probing a common need, promising some benefit, addressing some contradiction, offering to resolve some biblical difficulty—the list is almost endless.

Here are a few examples, some of which combine several methods.[2]

Relating a Personal Story and Referring to Recent Events (James 4:13–16)

Nell and I were living in the city of Dallas the day John F. Kennedy was shot.[3] I was in graduate school at the time.

I have three vivid memories from that day.

First, I remember where I was when I first heard the news. They say that's very common for people—to remember exactly where

---

1. Once in a while you might preview the coming hunks before you set the stage biblically, but not often. And, occasionally, a particular message might not require one of these two steps.
2. The examples in this chapter are written in the oral style in which they would be preached— short sentences, occasional sentence fragments, repetition for clarity. We'll talk about the differences between an oral style and a literary style in chapter 14.
3. See pages 152–54 for the full sermon outline.

they were when they heard something momentous. I was outside the school library, talking with a friend, when another student came up to tell us the news.

My second memory—I remember the route Kennedy's motorcade was on when the shooting occurred. I went that same route every day on my way to my part-time job with the freight lines. I knew the curve of the road. I knew the rise of the grassy knoll. I knew the Texas School Depository Building overlooking the street.

My most vivid memory, though, is the third one. I remember the evening of the shooting. I was watching the footage on TV that had been filmed just eight hours earlier that day: the motorcade through the streets of Dallas; Kennedy in the open car, smiling, waving, pointing, laughing—not knowing that in the next few minutes his life would end. And as I looked at the man on the screen, just eight hours earlier—smiling, alive—I found myself thinking, "You have no idea that in a few minutes you will die."

In our paper this week—a thirty-four-year-old man, down at the beach, splashing in three feet of water with a friend. Suddenly a rip-tide takes him out beyond his depth, and despite mouth-to-mouth resuscitation, he's pronounced dead within an hour.

A man and wife in their fifties, on a motorcycle, in the approach lanes to enter the toll road. A driver in a car ahead, suddenly not wanting to go onto the toll road, makes a U-turn, not seeing the motorcycle behind. The husband suffers moderate injuries, but the wife's injuries are fatal; she dies three days later.

This morning's paper—"They were simply kids"—two seventeen-year-old boys. Committed Christians, best friends. They went to dinner with the parents of one of the boys at his favorite restaurant—Japanese food. The boys leave in a separate car to stop off at the Golden Spoon, get some videos, in order to hang out at the other boy's home. But somewhere in between stops, their car veers into oncoming traffic. The driver of an oncoming SUV tries desperately to avoid a collision but can't. Both boys die at the scene. Sheriff's investigators can't say why the car went out of control. They rule out drugs or alcohol; perhaps mechanical failure.

Common to all of these is the sheer unexpectedness of such things happening. The people involved had no idea it was coming—Kennedy, the man splashing in three feet of water, the man and wife on a motorcycle, the two boys and their families. It was the farthest thing from their minds. They didn't expect it to happen.

None of us, as we sit here, expect anything like this to happen to us. Neither did they. But the honest truth is, we don't really know what will happen the rest of today . . . or tomorrow . . . or this week . . . or this summer.

Making a Startling Statement (Exod. 20:12)

This morning I want to talk about the fifth commandment—"Honor your father and your mother."[4] Some of you are thinking, "Oh good, I hope the kids are listening."

But that commandment wasn't given to kids. It was given to a nation of adults gathered at the base of Mount Sinai.

Exploring a Contemporary Issue (Capital Punishment)

Five years ago a man named Timothy McVeigh pressed the button on a bomb, a bomb that crushed a nine-story federal building in Oklahoma City. He killed nineteen children who were in a day care in the building. He killed another 147 people who were working or visiting in the building. That was five years ago.

Three months from now, on May 16, he will be put to death by chemical injection.

One woman who's glad McVeigh is going to die is Janie Cloverdale, a sixty-three-year-old grandmother. Her two grandsons, Elijah and Aaron, ages two and five, were killed in the day care that day. She says, "I've got questions about the death penalty, but not in this case."

But other people do have questions about the death penalty, even in Oklahoma City, where it happened. A local group known as the Oklahoma Coalition Against the Death Penalty has seen attendance at their monthly meetings grow from five people a month to nearly

---

4. See pages 148–50 for the full sermon outline.

seventy people in the last few months. They're all in favor of life im-
prisonment for McVeigh, instead of the death penalty. . . .

Probing a Common Need and Promising Some Benefit (Gen. 29:1–14)

One of the all-time great musicals is *Fiddler on the Roof*, the story
of Tevye, a Jewish milkman living in Russia.[5] He's caught between
"tradition" and the changes happening around him. In one of the
songs in the musical, his three daughters sing to Yenta, the village
"matchmaker"—a woman who scouted out all the eligible bachelors
and available women, kept a record in a book, and was in business to
"match" them, or bring them together. And the girls sing:

> Matchmaker, matchmaker, make me a match,
> Find me a find, catch me a catch.
> Matchmaker, matchmaker, look through your book
> and make me a perfect match.

"Make me a perfect match." That's not only a line in a musical;
that's also a prayer that many a single person breathes out to God:

> God, are you a matchmaker? Do you have a book?
> And if you do, do you have someone in mind for me?
> Someone perfectly suited to me?
> God, are you a matchmaker?

This morning we're going to see that the answer to that question
is yes. This morning we're going to see that if God has called you to
marriage . . .

---

5. See pages 169–71 for the full sermon outline.

Addressing Some Contradiction and Probing a Common Need (Exod. 13:17–22)

Early in geometry we learned that "the shortest distance between two points is a straight line."[6] That means, if I'm at point A and I want to get to point B, the shortest distance between these two points is a straight line.

Now that may be true in geometry, but as you and I think about what God is doing in our lives, we wonder if God doesn't think that "the shortest distance between two points is a zigzag." And by that I mean, we're at point A, and we sense that God intends to take us to point B—that's his will for our life, that's the dream, that's the vision, that's what the Spirit of God has affirmed to our heart. And as far as we're concerned, the shortest distance between where we are and where we believe God is taking us is a straight line. But if God is taking us there, he must think the shortest distance is a zigzag.

For example, you may have just started an entry-level job at a particular company. As you think about your future with the company, you sense that someday God may have you in that corner office on the second floor—the one with the windows and the gold nameplate on the door. Something in your heart says, "That's where I'm going to end up someday, that's the position I'm eventually going to have in this company." And in your mind, the shortest distance between your entry-level job and the second-floor office is a straight line. It goes something like this:

- You get assigned to some project that's central to what the company does. You do well.
- As a result, the next time you're put in charge of a different task force, working on another major project. You finish the project on time and under budget.
- This good track record brings you to the attention of the "decision-makers" in the company. They label you as a "comer," "someone to watch," someone who's "on the fast track for promotion."

---

6. See appendix C for the full outline and manuscript of this message.

- The higher-ups start moving you around to different positions so that you can gain experience with the whole operation.
- And then, when that corner office becomes vacant, you're the natural choice for it.

That's the route you visualize—a nice straight line.

But if God is taking you there, he's on a strange path. Because instead of being assigned to something central to what the company does, you got assigned to something peripheral to the company's operations. Instead of coming to the attention of the "decision-makers," you're stuck in some side cubicle, and nobody knows you work for the company.

Offering to Resolve Some Biblical Difficulty (Matt. 7:7–11)

Our Lord encourages us to pray, to ask God for things, and to expect that he will give them to us.[7] He says:

> Ask and it will be given to you; seek and you will find; knock and the door will be opened to you.

And then he repeats himself for emphasis:

> For everyone who ask receives; he who seeks finds; and to him who knocks, the door will be opened.

Someone says, "Naah, I don't think so. I asked; God didn't give it to me. I prayed; I didn't get it. I don't think that's true. I don't buy it."

For the sake of that person, and for the sake of all of us who want to be encouraged in our praying, let's turn to these words of Jesus and see what he's saying.

* * *

A seminary student once started a sermon in class by asking the audience to turn to 2 Kings 2:23–24. I could sense the students inter-

---

7. See pages 146–47 for the full sermon outline

nally frowning, "This is probably not a good introduction; it should start with us, rather than with the passage." But they dutifully turned to the passage and followed him while he read:

> From there Elisha went up to Bethel. As he was walking along the road, some youths came out of the town and jeered at him. "Go on up, you baldhead!" they said. "Go on up, you baldhead!" He turned around, looked at them and called down a curse on them in the name of the LORD. Then two bears came out of the woods and mauled forty-two of the youths.

When he finished reading, he asked the class, "Does it bother you that this is in your Bible? Are you embarrassed by this? What kind of God is this—a crotchety old prophet can't take a little teasing, and so forty-two youths die? Are you bothered by this? Today I want to show you that this tells us something profound about our God, something we desperately need to hear."

Needless to say, all the seminary students wanted to hear more, hoping the speaker would help them reconcile their view of God with the apparent carnage of this passage.

FOCUS THE MESSAGE

Once you've engaged the listeners so that they're interested in the message and wanting to hear more, their next concern is, "OK, where are you going with this message? What's it about? What am I supposed to get from it?"

At this point, therefore, you need to focus the message for them—either deductively give them your take-home truth, or inductively raise your topic/question. Either of these will bring the listener to a sharp and concise feeling of "Oh, OK, I know what we're after."

Let's return to some of the previous examples, carrying them forward, to see how the focus is provided. I'll abbreviate the engaging material and then provide the full wording for the focus. We'll begin with some deductive examples and then go to inductive ones.

Deductively Focus on the Take-Home Truth

Genesis 29:1–14

One of the all-time great musicals is *Fiddler on the Roof,* the story of Tevye, a Jewish milkman living in Russia.[8] He's caught between "tradition" and the changes happening around him. In one of the songs in the musical, his three daughters sing: "Make me a perfect match." That's not only a line in a musical; that's also a prayer that many a single person breathes out to God:

> God, are you a matchmaker? Do you have a book?
> And if you do, do you have someone in mind for me?
> Someone perfectly suited to me?
> God, are you a matchmaker?

This morning we're going to see that the answer to that question is yes. We're going to see that [**Focus: take-home truth**] if God is calling you to marriage, then his plan for you is very specific, and he will, without fail, lead you to the one he has for you. If God is calling you to marriage, he will control the timing and the sequence of events and bring you to the perfect match he intends for you. So you can date without pressure or anxiety, and you can marry without doubt, without fear.

Now I need to be clear in what I'm saying. God does not call everyone to marry. It's not his intention that everyone marry. God fashions life for some so that their relationships are full and meaningful apart from marriage, their days are busy and productive, and they appreciate the freedom and richness of life God has given them.

Some of you may sense that this may be the life God has marked out for you, and if that's the case, you are joyful and content.

But there are others of you who sense that God is calling you to marriage. It hasn't happened yet. And maybe it won't happen in the next few months—you're not in a relationship that's moving toward that. But as best you can know, God has put this desire in you. And

---

8. See pages 169–71 for the full sermon outline.

you often find yourself asking him, "God, do you have someone specific in mind for me?"

This morning, we're going to see from the life of Jacob that [**Focus: take-home truth**] his plan for you is very specific, and he will, without fail, lead you to the one he has for you. We're going to see that if God is calling you to marriage, he will control the timing and sequence of events and bring you without fail to the perfect match he intends for you. You can date without pressure and marry without fear.

In order to see this, we're going to turn to a time in Jacob's life when he's in his forties and unmarried. We know he's unmarried and in his forties because the Bible tells us his twin brother Esau, the same age as him, had married . . .

Exodus 13:17–22

Early in geometry we learned that "the shortest distance between two points is a straight line."[9] That means, if I'm at point A and I want to get to point B, the shortest distance between these two points is a straight line.

Now that may be true in geometry, but as you and I think about what God is doing in our lives, we wonder if God doesn't think that "the shortest distance between two points is a zigzag." And by that I mean, we're at point A . . .

For example, you may have just started an entry-level job at a particular company . . .

Maybe you've started a business, and your business is at point A. But as you think about the growth of your business, the Spirit of God gives you a mental picture of point B—a certain volume, a certain size of your company . . .

For you, point A may be "single" and point B is "married" . . . But if God is taking you there, he's on a very erratic path, because romantic possibilities are coming and going, and coming and going, mostly going.

[**Focus: take-home truth**] Today I want us to see that sometimes, with God, the shortest distance between two points is a zigzag . . .

---

9. See appendix C for the full outline and manuscript of this message.

Matthew 7:7–11

[Engage] Our Lord encourages us to pray, to ask God for things, and to expect that he will give them to us.[10] He says:

> Ask and it will be given to you; seek and you will find; knock and the door will be opened to you.

And then he repeats himself for emphasis:

> For everyone who ask receives; he who seeks finds; and to him who knocks, the door will be opened.

Someone says, "Naah, I don't think so. I asked; God didn't give it to me. I prayed; I didn't get it. I don't think that's true. I don't buy it."

For the sake of that person, and for the sake of all of us who want to be encouraged in our praying, let's turn to these words of Jesus and see what he's saying.

(Turn to Matthew 7:7–11 and read the passage.)

In these verses Jesus is saying [**Focus: take-home truth**], "Ask, and if it is good, God will say yes. Ask, and if it is good for you to have it, God will give it to you. Come like children, who spontaneously, effervescently, ask for what they want, trusting their father's wisdom. You too have a Father in heaven who loves you and is wise. Ask. If it is good, God will say yes."

Inductive Focus on the Topic/Question

James 4:13–16

[Engage] Nell and I were living in the city of Dallas the day John F. Kennedy was shot.[11] I was in graduate school at the time.

I have three vivid memories from that day. . . .

My most vivid memory, though, is the third one. I remember the evening of the shooting. I was watching the footage on TV that had been filmed just eight hours earlier that day: the motorcade through the streets of Dallas; Kennedy in the open car, smiling, waving,

---

10. See pages 146–47 for the full sermon outline.
11. See pages 152–54 for the full sermon outline.

pointing, laughing—not knowing that in the next few minutes his life would end. And as I looked at the man on the screen, just eight hours earlier—smiling, alive—I found myself thinking, "You have no idea that in a few minutes you will die."

In our paper this week . . .

None of us, as we sit here, expect anything like this to happen to us. Neither did they. But the honest truth is, we don't really know what will happen the rest of today . . . or tomorrow . . . or this week . . . or this summer.

And because this is true—that we don't really know what's ahead—the Scripture says [**Focus: question**] it ought to affect how we plan, how we set out on the days that are ahead. The fact that we don't know what's coming, the Bible says, ought to affect our thoughts about the future—not to make us morbidly preoccupied with fears of looming disasters, not to fill us with gloom or anxiety. But instead, in very practical ways, it ought to affect how we schedule things on our calendar.

[**Focus: question**] Because we don't know what's coming, there's a certain way we ought not to plan and a certain way we should plan. Because we don't know for sure what's ahead, there's something we should avoid in our planning and something we should include in our planning.[12]

What plans are you making? [**Focus: question**] There's a certain way you ought to make them, the Bible says.

Are you making plans for your vacation this summer? Planning what day you will leave?

Are you making plans for school in the fall? What school you will attend?

Are you making plans for marriage? How long you will be engaged? What date the wedding will be? Where it will be held?

Are you making plans for your company or your career? The goals you will focus on?

Are you making plans for your retirement? How many more years you will work? What funds you will have available?

---

12. Though the focus sentences are grammatically written as declaratives, and do not have a question mark for punctuation, the listener is still internally and emotionally left with an inductive topic/question: "How *should* I plan? What *should* I avoid; what *should* I include?"

As you think about all these things that are in the future [**Focus: question**] there's a certain way, the Bible says, that you ought not to plan and a certain way you should plan. There's something you should avoid in your planning and something you should include in your planning.

Capital Punishment

[**Engage**] Five years ago a man named Timothy McVeigh pressed the button on a bomb, a bomb that crushed a nine-story federal building in Oklahoma City . . .

One woman who's glad McVeigh is going to die is Janie Cloverdale, a sixty-three-year-old grandmother. Her two grandsons, Elijah and Aaron, ages two and five, were killed in the day-care center that day. She says, "I've got questions about the death penalty, but not in this case."

But other people do have questions about the death penalty, even in Oklahoma City, where it happened . . .

Two years ago, we heard a lot about another case, a woman who was converted in a Texas prison. Her name was Karla Faye Tucker . . .

Many Christian leaders, who usually were in favor of the death penalty, began to plead for special consideration in her case . . .

America is divided on the death penalty, on capital punishment. Is it justice or vengeance? Does the Bible teach it? Did Jesus and the New Testament change it? Should Christians be for it or against it?

This morning [**Focus: question**] I want us to look as best we can at what the Bible says. What does the Word of God say about capital punishment? And then, in light of that biblical teaching, what might be some good steps for America to take? What might be some changes our country could consider?

Mark 4:35–41

[**Engage**] Did you ever obey God and have the bottom fall out of everything?[13] Did you ever do exactly what God said, only to find yourself facing disaster?

---

13. See pages 151–52 for the full sermon outline.

> For example, you move to a new city to begin a new job . . .
> You decide to honor your widowed mom by bringing her into your own home . . .
> You marry . . .
> When these things happen, we despair, and wonder [**Focus: question**], "God, why is this happening to me? All I wanted to do is obey you, and my life is a disaster. Why is this happening, and what do you want me to do?"
> Today we're going to look at the disciples in a similar situation— they obey Jesus, and find themselves in the worst disaster of their lives—and we'll see [**Focus: question**] why these things happen to us and what God wants us to do.

By focusing the introduction on either the deductive take-home truth or the inductive topic/question, you converge the previous engaging paragraphs to a crisp and concise point, so that the listeners are clear on what they're supposed to get from the sermon that day.

SET THE STAGE BIBLICALLY

Setting the stage biblically is sometimes known as giving the background, or providing the context, or developing the setting. All of these phrases are appropriate; what's not appropriate is *when* speakers usually do it. Speakers usually give the background at the wrong spot in a message—they give it after the introduction is over and the listeners have turned to the passage for the day. Instead, they should give it before the chapter and verse is ever announced.

Once the listeners have heard the introduction and have turned to the announced passage, they're mentally ready to read that passage. But if the speaker instead says something like, "Before we begin, let me give you a little background," he breaks their natural expectation and flow of thought and perhaps slightly irritates them.

For example, suppose you hear the following sermon:

[Engage] Many of you in this room are still relatively "young" in terms of church leadership. And by that, I simply mean that when you get together with other leaders in your ministry, chances are you're one of the younger members of the group. If you're on a church staff, most of the others are probably older than you. If you're a pastor, many of the men on the board are old enough to be your father.

And one of your legitimate concerns is, "How can I have credibility with these older men? How can I act so that they don't dismiss me because of my youth? What can I do so that they take me seriously and listen to what I have to say rather than treat me as a runny-nosed kid, still wet behind the ears?"

[Focus: question] How can a younger man have the respect of older men? How can he have credibility with them?

The answer to that question [Announce the passage] is found in 1 Timothy 5:1. Would you turn there please, to see how younger men can have credibility with older men?

[Background] The apostle Paul is writing to Timothy, who is pastoring a church in the city of Ephesus. Paul had started the church some ten years earlier on one of his missionary journeys. Most of the leaders in the church had been won to the Lord by the apostle . . .

The listeners, having heard, "Please turn to 1 Timothy 5:1," would naturally turn to the passage and probably start reading it silently to themselves in order to discover the answer to the question the speaker raised. They also would expect the speaker to immediately start developing the answer from the verse they're reading.

But if the speaker instead reverses the progression of thought, giving background information that logically and historically precedes the verse they've been told to look at, their expectation is frustrated as the natural flow of thought is broken.

Notice how the flow is smoother and easier if the background is put before the preview and the announcing/reading of the passage.

[Engage] Many of you in this room are still relatively young in terms of church leadership. And by that, I simply mean that when you get together with other leaders in your ministry, chances are, you're one of the younger members of the group. If you're on a church staff, most of the others are probably older than you. If you're a pastor, many of the men on the board are old enough to be your father.

And one of your legitimate concerns is, "How can I have credibility with these older men? How can I act so that they don't dismiss me because of my youth? What can I do so that they take me seriously and listen to what I have to say rather than treat me as a runny-nosed kid, still wet behind the ears?"

[**Focus: question**] How can a younger man have the respect of older men? How can he have credibility with them?

[**Background; set the stage biblically**] This is a question younger men have always faced. In the early days of the Christian church, there was a young man who found himself pastoring a church that had been started by the apostle Paul. Most of the leaders of the church had been won to the Lord by the apostle. The young pastor, already somewhat shy and retiring in personality, was having difficulty leading the older men as he felt he should. And he expressed his concerns to his older friend, the apostle.

And Paul wrote back to him: "My dear young friend [**Preview the coming hunks of the message**], if you can avoid acting a certain way and instead always conduct yourself in another way, you'll have credibility with the older men. If you will steer clear of this and concentrate on this, you'll have their respect."

In order for us to see what we should avoid and what we should do in order to have credibility with older men, let's turn to the apostle's words to his young friend. [**Announce the passage**] They're found in 1 Timothy 5.

First, there's something we should avoid—we should avoid rebuking an older man harshly. Look at what Paul says in verse 1 . . .

In this more natural sequence, setting the stage biblically functions as the proper transition from the first two contemporary steps (i.e., engaging and focusing) to the latter two textual ones (i.e., previewing the coming hunks of the message and announcing the passage). Thus the flow becomes a natural "funnel" that increasingly takes the listener to the text.

In summary, as a general rule the background/setting/context should be given in the introduction and not after the listeners have turned to the passage. Since its content is preparatory to the passage, it should be given prior to announcing the passage.[14] Setting the stage biblically is simply giving the listeners whatever brief, summary information they need to intelligently come to the passage.[15] Once they're at the passage, you and they should stay with the passage and not go backward into the prior context or setting.

When you set the stage biblically, be sure to do so without telling the listeners specifically where in the Bible you're going to take them (i.e., do not yet give the passage for the day). They may figure out the general section of Scripture you're going to eventually land in,[16] but lacking instructions to turn to a specific chapter and verse, they will stay attentive to you while you give the necessary background.[17]

Notice how the following examples set the stage biblically but refrain from specifically announcing the passage.

Genesis 29:1–14

In this example, setting the stage biblically takes longer than usual, since the listeners need to know the reason Jacob is fleeing his home and the promise God has given him—that he will someday return, married, with sons and daughters.[18]

---

14. When we talk about setting the stage biblically in the introduction, we're talking about giving background or context information that is *preliminary* to the passage—information the listener needs in order to approach the passage as a whole. Once you begin to expound the parts of the passage, other cultural or historical details will come up which require explanation. Speakers sometimes use similar language—"Let me tell you the historical background to this verse"—to refer to these details. These more specific details are rightfully treated during the exposition proper since they are *part* of the passage, and not *prior* to it.

15. We have a tendency to give more background than is necessary. Our comments should be limited to only those matters that are essential in order to understand the passage in view. A Father's Day sermon from Ephesians 6:4, for example, probably doesn't need any background at all. Listeners are perfectly capable of understanding the verse without being informed of the previous argument of Ephesians or even the fact that Ephesians 6:4 is part of the three reciprocal couplets Paul develops in the "table-talk," or "household," section of 5:22–6:9.

16. In the 1 Timothy 5:1 example above, when the listeners hear the words, "in the early days of the Christian church" and "the apostle Paul," they would rightly assume you're going to be in one of the Epistles. But since they don't yet know which one, they'll remain attentive as you continue to unfold the rest of the introduction.

17. In many of our churches, announcing the chapter and verse is like ringing Pavlov's bell—the listeners immediately start turning in their Bibles to find it, not paying attention to anything the speaker may still be saying. As long as the speaker doesn't say the magic words, "Please turn to . . . ," even if the passage appears in the bulletin or has been read earlier in the service, they'll refrain from turning to it and will instead continue to look up and listen.

18. See pages 169–71 for the full sermon outline.

[**Engage**] One of the all-time great musicals is *Fiddler on the Roof,* the story of Tevye, a Jewish milkman living in Russia. He's caught between "tradition" and the changes happening around him. In one of the songs in the musical, his three daughters sing "Matchmaker, matchmaker . . ."

"Make me a perfect match." That's not only a line in a musical; that's also a prayer that many a single person breathes out to God:

> God, are you a matchmaker? Do you have a book?
> And if you do, do you have someone in mind for me?
> Someone perfectly suited to me?
> God, are you a matchmaker?

This morning we're going to see that the answer to that question is yes. We're going to see that [**Focus: take-home truth**] if God is calling you to marriage, then his plan for you is very specific, and he will, without fail, lead you to the one he has for you. If God is calling you to marriage, he will control the timing and the sequence of events and bring you to the perfect match he intends for you. So you can date without pressure or anxiety, and you can marry without doubt, without fear.

Now I need to be clear in what I'm saying. God does not call everyone to marry. It's not his intention that everyone marry. God fashions life for some so that their relationships are full and meaningful apart from marriage, their days are busy and productive, and they appreciate the freedom and richness of life God has given them.

Some of you may sense that this may be the life God has marked out for you, and if that's the case, you are joyful and content.

But there are others of you who sense that God is calling you to marriage. It hasn't happened yet. And maybe it won't happen in the next few months—you're not in a relationship that's moving toward that. But as best you can know, God has put this desire in you. And you often find yourself asking him, "God, do you have someone specific in mind for me?"

This morning, we're going to see from the life of Jacob that [**Focus: take-home truth**] his plan for you is very specific, and he will, without fail, lead you to the one he has for you. We're going to see that if God is calling you to marriage, he will control the timing and sequence of events and bring you without fail to the perfect match he intends for you. You can date without pressure and marry without fear.

[Set the stage biblically] In order to see this, we're going to turn to a time in Jacob's life when he's in his forties and unmarried. We know he's unmarried and in his forties because the Bible tells us his twin brother, Esau—the same age as him—had married some pagan Hittite women at age forty and that these marriages had brought grief to Isaac and Rebekah, his parents.

And so the parents, partly to keep Jacob from a similar marriage to the pagans around them, but mostly to get him out of harm's way—because Esau was vowing to kill him for how he had tricked him out of the family blessing—the parents tell Jacob to leave quickly for a distant land. They tell Jacob to find a community called Haran, where their relatives were last known to live; to see if he can locate a man there named Laban—that's his mother's brother, his uncle. If he can find this man, Laban, and his family, perhaps he can stay with them. Maybe he can find a wife there and begin to raise a family. And then someday, maybe, if things ever settle down, he can come back to his own land. But right now he must leave quickly, before Esau has a chance to kill him.

Jacob hurriedly throws a few things into a bag and heads out.

His second night out, on the border between his country and the next, as he's leaving the land that is central to God's promises, maybe never to see it again, he's fearful of what's ahead:

> He doesn't know where he's going; he doesn't know where Haran is.
>> He has only a vague idea of the country he's heading for.
>> He's afraid he could veer off a few degrees in any direction and totally miss it.
> If he does manage to find Haran, he doesn't know if their relatives are still there.
>> It's been sixty years since they had any contact with them.

They could have moved or died. He could get there and find that they are gone.

If they are there, he doesn't know if they will welcome him or instead see him as a burden, another mouth to feed. Would they resent him or be glad to see him? How long could he stay with them?

As for a wife, who knows if there's anyone there that he would want to marry or who would want to share the uncertainties of his life?

There he is on his second night out. He's homesick for what he's leaving and fearful of what's ahead—"God, is my life going anywhere? Are you part of it? Do you have any plans for me?" As he finds a place to sleep before crossing the border, God comes to him in a dream and gives him a promise, a promise that includes marriage. God says, "Jacob, I'm going to be with you in the days ahead, and I'm going to bring you back to this land. And when I do, your sons and daughters will multiply to become a great nation."

The last part is the promise of marriage—"your sons and daughters." "Part of my plan for you," God says, "is that you will marry and have children, and your sons and daughters will become a great nation."

The dream tells Jacob that God is calling him to marriage and that in the days ahead God will control his movements and God will control the timing and sequence of events to make it happen.[19] God will lead him without fail to the one he has for him.

[**Announce the passage**] It's at this point that we pick up the story in Genesis 29. Please turn there in your Bibles.

---

19. Note that the same language or phrasing that was used in the engage section—"called to marriage" and "God will control the timing and sequence of events"—is also used in the background section. This consistent use of similar wording is essential if the listener is to hear the connection between the two sections and see how the background is contributing to the theme of the message. We'll return to this—the necessity of consistent key language threaded through the message—in chapter 15 when we talk about oral clarity.

Exodus 13:17–22

The sermon from Exodus 13 is an example of the introduction setting up a wrap pattern.[20] It's also one of the few instances where the preview of coming hunks comes before setting the stage biblically.[21]

[Engage] Early in geometry we learned that "the shortest distance between two points is a straight line." That means if I'm at point A and I want to get to point B, the shortest distance between these two points is a straight line.

Now that may be true in geometry, but as you and I think about what God is doing in our lives, we wonder if God doesn't think that the shortest distance between two points is a zigzag. And by that I mean, we're at point A . . .

For example, you may have just started an entry-level job at a particular company . . .

Maybe you've started a business, and your business is at point A. But as you think about the growth of your business, the Spirit of God gives you a mental picture of point B—a certain volume, a certain size of your company . . .

For you, point A may be "single" and point B is "married". . . But if God is taking you there, he's on a very erratic path, because romantic possibilities are coming and going, and coming and going, mostly going.

[Focus: take-home truth] Today I want us to see that sometimes, with God, the shortest distance between two points is a zigzag.

[Preview of coming hunks] I want us to see that God sometimes deliberately takes us on a zigzag path. Knowingly, intentionally, purposefully, he takes our lives on an alternate route. I want us to see why he does this—what's his reason, what's his purpose, what's he trying to accomplish? And then, finally, how does he keep us encouraged? How does he sustain us on the way? In the midst of the zigs and zags, when we don't seem to be making any progress, how does God keep us moving expectantly and joyfully toward the goal?

[Setting the stage biblically] In order to see that God deliberately takes us on a zigzag route, we're going to turn to a time in Israel's

20. See pages 176–81 for the wrap pattern.
21. See appendix C for the full outline and manuscript of this message.

history when he deliberately takes them on a zigzag path. Israel is at point A. They know what point B is. And they know for sure that God's going to take them there. Yet God purposely, deliberately takes them in the opposite direction.

Point A for them is the land of Goshen in Egypt, where they've been slaves for four hundred years. Pharaoh has just capitulated. The ten plagues have decimated Egypt. Wailing and mourning echo through the land because of the death of the firstborn. Pharaoh gives up. "Get out! Leave! Go!" he says to Moses.

Israel rendezvous in the land of Goshen, point A. Point B is Canaan, Palestine, the Promised Land. There's no question that's their destiny. That's where Abraham, Isaac, and Jacob are buried. That's the goal. That's where God is going to take them.

Now the shortest distance between point A, Goshen, and point B, Canaan, is a relatively straight line—an international trade route that goes from Goshen, along the Mediterranean seacoast, through Philistine territory, and into Canaan. Israel can get from point A to point B in eight to ten days following that international highway—a straight line.

But instead, God takes them in the opposite direction. [**Announce the passage**] Let's turn to Exodus 13:17, where we'll see God deliberately taking Israel on a zigzag path. Exodus 13:17.

James 2:1–13

Notice the extensive wrap pattern through the introduction of this next example—a vivid, detailed picturing of what the first movement in the text would look like in a contemporary church.[22] The focus is inductive, on a topic/question. The stage is set, using the same consistent key language of "first-time visitors to the church" and "which one would you go to" to show that James's readers are faced with the same topic/question. Once this background is developed, the passage is announced.

[**Engage**] Let's suppose we have in the audience this morning some first-time visitors to the church. Let's imagine two different families who have come.

---

22. See appendix C for the full outline and manuscript of this message.

If you were outside when the first family drove up, you would have looked at their car kind of enviously—expensive, new, shiny. "Somebody's doing OK to be able to afford that."

The car of the second family was right behind them. This car— well, you kind of heard it even before you saw it. You know—that noise that tells you "this engine isn't long for this world." And when you looked at the car, it was old, rusty, paint splotchy and faded, sides dented, back trunk held down with rope, windows rolled down because the air-conditioning is broken. "Mmm, things must be tough for them. Low-paying job. Probably hardly making it."

Both cars park, and the two families walk from the parking lot to the door. You're getting your bulletin at the same time they are, and you notice a difference in how the two families are dressed.

The first family—hey, the latest styles, well-tailored, coordinated outfits, matching accessories. I mean, we're talking Nordstrom's all the way. The parents both look like they work out—fit, trim. It's obvious the woman's been to the hairdresser—styled, frosted. Attractive makeup. Their kids—a daughter in college, a son in high school—are well dressed, poised, confident.

The second family is getting their bulletins behinds them. The man is in faded corduroys, ill-fitting shirt. Shoes scuffed, slanting to the sides because the heels are worn away, shoelaces dragging. The woman is wearing a housedress. Purse doesn't match. Hair needs work. Their kids—overweight, self-conscious, uncomfortable.

As they're getting their bulletins, you suddenly realize you recognize someone in that first family.

Maybe the man is the head of an engineering firm or a software company that you'd like to work for or maybe sell something to. It'd be good to establish a contact with him for business reasons.

Or maybe you recognize the wife as a professor at the university, someone who hires research assistants, and your daughter is applying for one of the jobs in her department.

Or maybe you recognize their son—you've seen his picture in the paper—he's the all-state quarterback for the local team. Hmm, be kind of nice if he were part of the youth group.

Or maybe the daughter is beautiful, and your twenty-five-year-old son standing next to you is one of the leaders of the college group.

You're sure he'd love to tell her about the group's activities and maybe see that she gets to the college class and has a good time.

The second family? They're nobody you've ever seen before. You're not even sure they live in your bedroom community; maybe they're from one of the apartments in a nearby city.

Both families finally have their bulletins and walk into the back of the auditorium. One steps to the right, the other to the left. Both families kind of stop and hesitate because they're not sure where they should sit. This is their first time, and they're trying to get the lay of the land and figure out where they should go.

By now you also have come into the back of the auditorium, and you see both families, one on each side. Both of them hesitating, trying to make up their minds and decide what they should do. And it occurs to you that you could offer some help . . . to one of them.

[**Focus: question**] Which family do you go to? Which one do you walk toward? Which family do you give attention to?

You'd be tempted to go to the first family. "Hi, my name is Don Sunukjian. Can I help you? We don't save seats here, so you can sit anywhere you want. My wife and I normally sit in this section—you can get a good view of the screen, and afterward you can get to the donuts and coffee more quickly. Why don't you join us?"

You'd be tempted to go to that first family, because—you never know—it might lead to a sale, or maybe a job for your daughter, or a date for your son. You'd be drawn to the first family—they're attractive, and they might be able to do something for you. You might benefit in some way.

Two families come into church. [**Focus: question**] Which one would you go to?

[**Set the stage biblically**] That's the same question James poses in a letter he writes to some Christian friends of his—friends he hasn't seen for fifteen years. He used to be their pastor when they attended his church in Jerusalem, before they had left the city. Actually they had fled the city. For a period of time it had become too dangerous to be a Christian in Jerusalem.

One of the church members, Stephen, had been falsely charged and executed. The authorities were planning similar trumped-up charges against other Christians too. And so, many families had fled for safety's sake to other cities and countries, in order to start life over.

But in their new cities, they were viewed with suspicion. They were immigrants, refugees, strangers. Life was tough. The obstacles they faced seemed insurmountable.

They couldn't find jobs. They had trouble getting permits to set up businesses. Even if they managed to open their doors, they found themselves boycotted by the community or trashed by local hooligans. At the local markets, their wives were being cheated and hassled. At school, their children were being tormented. The citizens of the towns hated them because they were Jews, and the Jews of the towns hated them because they were Christians. They found themselves isolated and harassed by a hostile society.

On Sundays they gathered in their small church, a fragile minority, looking for comfort from each other in a menacing environment.

And their former pastor writes to them. He knows how vulnerable they are and the temptations that come because of that. And so, as he writes, he imagines a Sunday when two first-time visitors might come to their church. Two different men from the community, checking them out, each one maybe interested in attending the church a bit. One of the first-time visitors is obviously wealthy. They recognize him as an influential man in the community. The other visitor is the opposite; he is poor, and nobody knows him. And James raises the question for his friends [**Focus: question**], "Which one would you go to? Which one would you pay attention to?"

Let's look at how James describes these two visitors, and at the answer he gives to his question. [**Announce the passage**] Please turn to James 2.

One of the visitors, James says, is obviously wealthy and influential in the community. Notice how James puts it in verse 2: "A man comes into your meeting wearing a gold ring and fine clothes." . . .

In all of these examples, the background came from material that was prior to the passage; it concerned information that preceded the verses you were going to look at. But sometimes the background is actually in the first phrase of your primary biblical passage; exegetically the first few words of your chosen verses look "backward" into the previous chapter or verses. When this is the case, these words also should be treated as background in the introduction rather than as an unconnected series of comments in the body of the message after the passage has been announced.

Take Romans 12:1 as an example:

> Therefore, I urge you, brothers, in view of God's mercy, to offer your bodies as living sacrifices, holy and pleasing to God—this is your spiritual act of worship.

The first phrase—"Therefore, I urge you, brothers, in view of God's mercy"—is really Paul looking "back" over all the mercies he's mentioned in chapters 1–11: God's free gift of salvation, the presence of the Holy Spirit, the ultimate glory that awaits us, and God's faithfulness to fulfill all his promises. He's summarizing the previous material that he's developed.

Notice, in the abbreviated message that follows, how the flow becomes awkward and disconnected when this first phrase is handled in the body of the message rather than as background in the introduction.

[Engage] There are many things we can do that would please God—study his Word, pray, encourage other believers, support his work financially. But there is one thing, more than anything else, that would delight his heart. There's one thing we can do that would please him the most.

Let's turn to Romans 12, verses 1–2, where we will learn what this is—**[Focus: question]** what God wants us to offer him more than anything else. Paul writes:

> Therefore, I urge you, brothers, in view of God's mercy, to offer your bodies as living sacrifices, holy and pleasing to God—this is your spiritual act of worship.

Paul first says, "therefore." Whenever you see a "therefore," you should ask what it's "there for."[23] Paul is thinking of all the things

---

23. Sorry, I couldn't resist the hoary pun.

> God has done for us, all the blessings of the previous chapters—our salvation, our enjoyment of the Spirit, our anticipation of heaven, our confidence in a faithful God.
>
> Now he wants to "urge" his listeners. He's begging them, pleading with them—it's a strong word, "I urge you."
>
> Notice that he calls them "brothers." He knows they're saved. He appeals to them as family members . . .

At this point the listener has totally lost track of what the message is supposed to be about—"what we can offer God that will please him more than anything else." The speaker's comments on the first phrase of the text have broken the flow of thought between the focused topic/question of the introduction and the answer that is yet to appear in the text.

In contrast, notice how smoothly the thought flows when the first phrase is handled in the introduction as background, setting the stage. The speaker explains the phrase even before announcing the passage and then simply reads through it in the body of the message on the way to the question's answer.

> [**Engage and set the stage biblically**] God has done so much for us. He has been full of mercy toward us. [**Explain the first phrase of the text in advance, expanding on the specific mercies mentioned.**] Out of his love and mercy he has freely saved us, given us his Spirit, promised us eternity, and assured us that he will be faithful to accomplish it all.
>
> [**Focus: question**] How should we respond to God for all his mercy? What should we offer him in return for all he's done for us?
>
> Paul gives the answer in one of his letters. After reminding a group of Christians at length of God's great mercy[24] to them, he urges them to make the only appropriate response.
>
> Let's turn to Romans 12:1 to see how we should respond to God's mercy.
>
> Paul writes [**read through the opening phrase without comment**]:

---

24. Notice again how the consistent key word *mercy* threads through the whole introduction, enabling the listener to hear the connection between the sections.

> Therefore, I urge you, brothers, in view of God's mercy, to offer your bodies as living sacrifices, holy and pleasing to God—this is your spiritual act of worship.
>
> How should we respond in light of all that God has done for us? We should respond to God's mercy, Paul says, by offering our bodies as a living sacrifice . . .

Hebrews 12:1 is another example of where you might use the first phrase to set the stage biblically in the introduction rather than break the flow of thought in the body of the message:

> Therefore, since we are surrounded by such a great cloud of witnesses, let us throw off everything that hinders and the sin that so easily entangles, and let us run with perseverance the race marked out for us.

Since the first phrase looks backward to chapter 11, you might handle it in a preparatory manner; before you focus on the new message of chapter 12.

In Ephesians 4:1, both the first and last phrases look backward. The first phrase, "a prisoner for the Lord," connects with 3:1, and the last phrase, "the calling you have received," summarizes chapters 1–3: "As a prisoner for the Lord, then, I urge you to live a life worthy of the calling you have received."

You would probably handle these first and last phrases in your introduction and then simply read through verse 1 to get your first Roman numeral from verses 2–3. Here's a condensed version of what setting the stage might sound like.

> Paul, in prison because of his commitment to the Gentiles, writes to his Gentile friends to urge them to live worthy of the calling they've received. And this morning as we turn in our Bibles to Ephesians 4, we'll discover what this worthy life looks like. Please turn to Ephesians 4.
>
> The first thing we discover is that we live worthy of our calling when we live with others in humility and peace. Let's read Ephesians

> 4:1–3 . . . [Read through the previously explained verse to get to the main point in verses 2–3.]
>
> Notice that a worthy life is one that is "completely humble and gentle" . . .

The goal is to provide an easy and clear flow of thought for the listeners—from *engaging* them in some contemporary need or curiosity, to *focusing* them on either a take-home truth to be received or a question to be answered, to *setting the stage* by connecting the theme to the biblical world.

The next steps are *previewing* what the large hunks or movements of your message will be, so that the listener can anticipate the unfolding progression of thought; and then, finally, *announcing* the chapter and verse. We'll look at these last two steps in the next chapter.

12

Create the Introduction (Part 2)
Preview the Hunks and Announce the Passage

A GOOD INTRODUCTION *engages* the listeners' interest, *focuses* them on either the take-home truth or the topic/question that will be answered, *sets the stage* biblically for the passage that will be looked at, and then, when it would help the listeners to more clearly track with the message, it *previews* the coming hunks or movements that will organize the body of the message before *announcing* the passage.

PREVIEW THE COMING HUNKS

A preview, or overview, lets the listeners know how the message will unfold. It says to the listeners, "Here's a map of how to listen to me."

Sometimes a preview is so essential that if the speaker omits it, the listeners will have difficulty connecting the first movement or hunk in the body of the message with whatever was said in the introduction.

Notice, for example, how the listeners lose the train of thought in the following abbreviated message.

[**Engage**] We all struggle with low times in our spiritual lives—times when our sin has distanced us from God, times of spiritual coldness, prolonged times when we are out of fellowship with him.

During these low times, our potential for sinning against others and harming them is great. We can damage our ministries, wound our friends, and bring sorrow to our families.

[**Focus: question**] How can we gain spiritual renewal? How can we get back into fellowship?

> **[Announce the passage]** Second Chronicles 28–29 gives us the answer. Please turn there in your Bibles.
>
> **[First movement]** In 2 Chronicles 28 a wicked king named Ahaz is on the throne in Judah. His sixteen-year reign is a time of unprecedented debauchery and idolatry, as he leads the nation into the lewd fertility rites and unspeakable human sacrifices of the Canaanite religion:
>
> > He walked in the ways of the kings of Israel and also made cast idols for worshiping the Baals. He burned sacrifices in the Valley of Ben Hinnom and sacrificed his sons in the fire, following the detestable ways of the nations the LORD had driven out before the Israelites. He offered sacrifices and burned incense at the high places, on the hilltops and under every spreading tree. (2 Chron. 28:2–4)
>
> As a result of this evil, God allows the Arameans to defeat Ahaz in battle and take many of his people as prisoners to Damascus. God also lets him suffer heavy casualties at the hands of the northern king of Israel (2 Chron. 28:5–8). Other ancient enemies—Edomites and Philistines—also attack and inflict damages (vv. 17–18). Ahaz attempts to buy the protection of the king of Assyria, but the Assyrian king keeps the money and does nothing to help him (vv. 20–21).
>
> In desperation, Ahaz begins to worship the foreign gods of his captors, thinking, "If those gods helped my enemies, maybe they'll help me if I also worship them" . . .

At this point, the listeners have lost track of what the sermon was to be about. Though they may understand the meaning of the speaker's words, they see no connection between them and the question he raised in the introduction—"How can we gain spiritual renewal?" The speaker does not seem to be answering the question. The listeners, therefore, lapse into an unthinking, blank passivity, because they can't figure out the message's flow.

But if the speaker gives a preview of the coming hunks, the listeners will be clear on the connection and will actively and intelligently follow the unfolding thought. The preview would sound something like the following.

[Engage] We all struggle with low times in our spiritual lives—times when our sin has distanced us from God, times of spiritual coldness, prolonged times when we are out of fellowship with him.

During these low times, our potential for sinning against others and harming them is great. We can damage our ministries, wound our friends, and bring sorrow to our families.

[Focus: question] How can we gain spiritual renewal? How can we get back into fellowship?

[Preview] Let's look at a period in Israel's history when they were in a low time spiritually and were being harmed by it, and let's see how they gained spiritual renewal. Let's look at how an evil king's idolatry brought them under the judgment of God, and let's see what it took to bring them back into fellowship.

[Announce the passage] Please turn to 2 Chronicles 28–29 in your Bibles.

[First movement] In 2 Chronicles 28 Israel is in a low time spiritually,[1] suffering the consequences of sin. A wicked king named Ahaz is on the throne in Judah. His sixteen-year reign is a time of unprecedented debauchery and idolatry, as he leads the nation into the lewd fertility rites and unspeakable human sacrifices of the Canaanite religion.

The preview lets the listeners know that before the speaker answers the focus question, he's first going to develop a biblical situation that corresponds to his opening introduction. And the listener's mental processing is clear: "OK, you've talked about our low times and raised the question of how we get out of them. But I understand you're first going to show me some biblical people in a low time, and then you're going to use their experience to answer your question. Good—I'm tracking with you."[2]

---

1. Note the consistent use of the key phrase "low time spiritually" to connect the sections of the introduction.

2. The full sermon outline might be as follows (an inductive structure, using a relevancy-wrapped pattern that eventually continues as an interspersed; the listener forms the point II take-home truth as subunits II.A and II.B are joined together):

    Introduction
    1. We all struggle with low times in our spiritual lives.
        a. Example/application
        b. Example/application

In order to understand this critical area of previewing, let's probe two important questions: "When do I need to give a preview of the coming hunks or main points?" and "If I do need to give a preview, how do I phrase it?"

When Do I Need a Preview?

Whether a preview is necessary or not depends on the overall structure of the message (i.e., whether the focus is deductive or inductive) and on whether the main points (i.e., the Roman numerals) of the sermon are a list or a progression. The chart below summarizes these decisions as to when a preview is needed, and the following pages provide examples and explanations.

DETERMINING WHETHER A PREVIEW IS NEEDED

If the overall structure/focus is ...	and the main points are ...	a preview is ...	Pages
1. deductive	a list	unnecessary	225
2. deductive	a progression	necessary	225–29
3. inductive, single question	a list	unnecessary	229
4. inductive, single question	a progression	necessary	229–31
5. inductive, single question	answer + second question	unnecessary	231
6. inductive, multiple questions	answers to each question	unnecessary	231–33
7. inductive, multiple questions	answers to some questions	necessary	233–34

   2. These low times can harm us, our families, our ministries.
   3. How can we get out of them? How can we gain spiritual renewal?
   4. Let's look at a time in Israel's history when they are in a low time and being harmed by it, and see how they gained spiritual renewal.
   I. The southern kingdom of Judah is in a low time, experiencing the harmful consequences of disobedience (2 Chron. 28).
      A. King Ahaz has led the nation in idolatrous worship.
      B. As a result, God has allowed other nations to punish Judah.
   II. (In low times we gain spiritual renewal through consecration and worship.)
      A. We gain spiritual renewal through consecration.
         1. Judah gained spiritual renewal through consecration (2 Chron. 29:1–24).
         2. We gain spiritual renewal by consecrating ourselves.
            a. Example/application
            b. Example/application
      B. We gain spiritual renewal through worship.
         1. Judah gained spiritual renewal through worship (2 Chron. 29:25–36).
         2. We gain spiritual renewal through worship.
            a. Example/application
            b. Example/application

1. If the overall sermon structure/focus is deductive (i.e., the take-home truth has been given in the introduction), and the main points are a list, no separate preview is necessary because the take-home truth has already summarized the main points.

In the following sermon, since the deductive take-home truth summarizes the list of Roman numerals, no separate preview is necessary; the take-home truth serves the purpose of revealing the message flow.

> Introduction
>   1. If we're going to be the church God wants us to be, we need to know his purposes for us.
>   2. Today we're going to see that God's purposes for a church are to worship, instruct, fellowship, and evangelize. [* = deductive take-home truth]
>   3. Please turn to Acts 2:42–47.
>
> I. The first purpose of a church is to worship.
>
> II. The second purpose of a church is to instruct.
>
> III. The third purpose of a church is to fellowship.
>
> IV. The fourth purpose of a church is to evangelize.

Your main points are a list when:

- There is some sense of counting or enumeration ("first," "second," etc.).
- Every main point has the same key language or phrasing as the take-home truth (e.g., "purposes for a church").
- The sequence of the main points is logically interchangeable. (While the sequence above follows the order in the passage, there's no logical reason why the original author couldn't have reversed or interchanged some of the items. In other words, the concepts could be developed just as clearly in any sequence.)

2. If the overall sermon structure/focus is deductive, and the main

points are a progression (i.e., a sequence of logically connected thoughts leading to or supporting the take-home truth), you need to preview the coming sequence.

The main points will be a progression when they carry forward some unalterable sequence, in either a narrative story or a reasoning chain of thought. The preview is necessary in order for the listener to see how the main points relate to the take-home truth.

In the following sermon on Matthew 7:7–11, the main points are a logical progression, with the take-home truth occurring in point II. Since this take-home truth is deductively stated in the introduction but does not immediately show up in the first major point, the necessary preview tells the listener to expect a preliminary concept before the full explanation of the take-home truth.

Introduction

1. Our Lord encourages us to pray, to ask God for things, and to expect him to give them to us. (Quote Matt. 7:7–8.)

2. Someone says, "I've tried that; it doesn't work. I asked; God didn't give it to me. I don't buy it."

3. For the sake of that person, and for the sake of all of us who would like to be encouraged in our praying, let's turn to Matthew 7:7–11 and see what Jesus is saying. (Read Matt. 7:7–11.)

4. In these verses Jesus is telling us, "Ask, and if it's a good thing, God will give it to you" [* = deductive take-home truth].

5. In order to be encouraged in our praying, let's see who this is a promise to, and what it's a promise of. [**Preview, letting the listener know there will be a preliminary point I before explaining the take-home truth in point II.**]

Who is this a promise to?

I. (This is a promise for genuine children who are trying to please the Father.)[3]

---

3. The parentheses indicate that this particular sentence will not be spoken orally at this point but instead will form itself in the listener's mind after all the subpoints have been presented. See appendix A, guideline 5, for proper outlining.

   A. First of all, this is a promise for those who are genuine children of God.

      1. Jesus refers to "your Father in heaven."

      2. If you have been "born again" through faith in Christ, this promise is for you.

   B. But more specifically, this is a promise for those children who are trying to please their Father.

      1. This promise occurs toward the end of a lengthy sermon in which Jesus has been describing the behaviors that please the Father.

      2. If your desire is to obey God and please him in whatever way you can, this promise is for you.

What is this a promise of?

  II. This is a promise that God knows how to give you good gifts even more than you know how to give your children good gifts.

   A. You know how to give good gifts to your children—bread, fish.

   B. You know how to do this, despite being "evil"—i.e., despite having human imperfections and limitations.

   C. God, having no imperfections or limitations, knows even more what good gifts to give you.

  III. Come, therefore, with all the spontaneity of a child, asking for what you want and expecting that if it is good for you to have it, your Father will say yes.

In this sermon on Exodus 13:17–22,[4] the take-home truth is deductively stated in the introduction and then biblically demonstrated in point I. But since there is an additional progression of Roman numerals after point I, the preview lets the listener know the message will not stop at point I.

   Introduction

      1. Early in geometry we learned, "The shortest distance between two points is a straight line."

---

4. See appendix C for the full outline and manuscript of this message.

    2. But sometimes, as we look at what God is doing in our lives, we wonder if he doesn't think that the shortest distance between two points is a zigzag.

    3. We find ourselves at some point A, and though we believe God intends to take us to a point B, we seem instead to be headed in the opposite direction, as though on a zigzag path.

        a. Our career at a company is not moving toward the anticipated point B, but is instead headed in the other direction.

        b. The business we started is losing ground rather than advancing toward point B.

        c. The point B of marriage is as far away as it ever was.

        d. We're asked to do things other than the point B ministry we believe we're called to.

    4. Today I want us to see that sometimes, with God, the shortest distance between two points is a zigzag. [*]

    5. I want us to see that sometimes God deliberately leads us on a zigzag path; I want us to see why he does it; and finally I want us to see how he encourages us when we don't seem to be making any progress toward the goal. **[Preview, letting the listener know there will be additional points after the demonstration of the take-home truth in point I.]**

    6. In order to see that God sometimes deliberately takes us on a zigzag path, we're going to look at a time in Israel's history when God deliberately leads them on a zigzag path.

    7. Please turn to Exodus 13:17.

I. God sometimes deliberately takes us on a zigzag path to the good plans he has for us.

II. The reason for this zigzag path is because some obstacle on the straight-line path would keep us from reaching the goal.

III. God keeps us encouraged along this zigzag path by giving us reminders of his good intentions and a tangible sense of his presence.
   A. God encourages us with reminders of his good intentions.
   B. God encourages us with a tangible sense of his presence.

3. If the overall sermon structure/focus is inductive, with the introduction raising a single question, and the main points are a list that cumulatively answers the question, no preview is necessary, since each main point is itself a partial answer to the question.

> Introduction
> 1. Elders are to shepherd God's people.
> 2. In what ways should elders carry out this shepherding responsibility? [**Inductive, raising of a single question; no preview is necessary since the plural word ways signals to the listener that a list is coming, and that each Roman numeral will be clearly connected to the inductive focus as a partial answer to the question.**][5]
>
> I. Elders should shepherd willingly.
>
> II. Elders should shepherd selflessly.
>
> III. Elders should shepherd humbly.

4. If the overall sermon structure/focus is inductive, with the introduction raising a single question, and the main points are a progression (i.e., a sequence of connecting thoughts leading to the take-home truth at the end), you need to preview the coming sequence of thoughts so that the listener will not expect your first Roman numeral to answer the question that was raised.[6]

---

5. Had the speaker, however, phrased the question in the singular—"*How* should elders carry out this shepherding responsibility?"—a brief preview (e.g., "Our passage gives three ways") would be helpful in that it would prevent the listener from assuming that point I would give the total/full answer to the question.
6. For one example, see the message on 2 Chronicles 28–29 that opened this chapter (pp. 221–23).

This message on Matthew 14:13–21 asks a single inductive question (introduction point 3), but the take-home truth answer doesn't appear until points III and IV are developed. The necessary preview tells the listener not to expect the answer in point I.

> Introduction
> 1. Sometimes we feel like God has asked us to do something impossible.
>   a. Example/application
>   b. Example/application
> 2. We may argue that we don't have the ability to do what he wants, but his request remains unchanged.
> 3. How can we accomplish the seemingly impossible tasks God has given us? [**Inductive, raising of a single question; but since the answer doesn't emerge immediately, the following preview prepares the listener for the progression that will lead to the answer.**]
> 4. Today we'll look at a time when Jesus gave the disciples a seemingly impossible task. We'll see them argue that they are unable to do what he wants.[7] But we'll discover in his dealing with them that there is a way by which we can accomplish the seemingly impossible tasks God gives us.
>
> I. Jesus gives the disciples the seemingly impossible task of feeding fifteen thousand people.
>
> II. They object that they are unable to do what he has commanded.
>
> III. When given a seemingly impossible task, we should offer God whatever resources we have.
>   A. Jesus directs the disciples to bring him the five loaves and two fish they do have.
>   B. We should make available to him whatever resources we have.

---

7. Note the wrap pattern (cf. pp. 176–81), in which the relevancy of the first two Roman numerals has been "front-ended" into the introduction, leaving points I and II to be stated historically rather than timelessly.

IV. God will expand and empower those resources until they are more than sufficient for the task he has given us.
  A. Jesus multiplies the loaves and fish until they are more than sufficient to feed the people.
  B. God will multiply our resources until they are more than adequate to do the task he has given us.

5. If the overall sermon structure/focus is inductive, with the introduction raising a single question, but only the first Roman numeral answers the question, no preview is necessary since the listener immediately hears the answer to the question. But since the listener also might think that this answer is the end of the sermon (since it satisfied the question raised), an extremely strong transition is needed in order to clearly take the listener into the unexpected point II.

  Introduction
    1. Some people go "from bad to worse." Rather than responding to pleas for kindness or decent treatment, their level of abuse actually increases.
    2. What accounts for this? [**Inductive, single question raised, which is answered by point I, requiring no preview.**]
    3. The answer is given in Romans 9:14.

  I. God himself has hardened their hearts.

  Transition: But why would God deliberately harden someone's heart? [After several minutes of explanation and illustration on point I, this transition would need to be rephrased and restated several times in order to regear the listener to the fact that there's more message coming.]

  II. The reason God would deliberately harden someone's heart is because . . .

6. If the overall sermon structure/focus is inductive, with the introduction raising multiple questions, and each of the Roman numerals answers

one of the questions, no preview is necessary since the multiple questions themselves serve as the preview.

In this message on Ephesians 5:15–21, the inductive focus raises three questions in introduction point 3. Since the following Roman numerals will sequentially answer each of these questions in order, no separate preview is necessary. (Note the biblical author's thought order[8] of the Roman numerals—v. 18b is handled first, before vv. 15–18a; *what* it means comes before *how* we get it.)

Introduction

1. There's a lot of confusion about what it means to be "filled with the Spirit."
2. Some think it means to be spiritually energetic or aggressive; others think it means to have charismatic experiences.
3. Today we'll see what it really means; then we'll see how it happens; and finally we'll see what we experience when it takes place. [**Multiple inductive questions. Since each of the questions is answered in order below, no separate preview is necessary; the questions themselves serve as a preview.**]
4. Please turn to Ephesians 5:15–21.

I. To be filled with the Spirit means to be filled with the fullness of Christ (5:18b; cf. 1:23; 3:19).

II. We become filled by living obediently in a sinful culture (5:15–18a).

III. (When we are filled, we experience joy, gratitude, and harmonious relationships [5:19–21]).[9]
    A. The evidence of the Spirit's filling is joy (5:19).
    B. The evidence of the Spirit's filling is gratitude (5:20).

---

8. See pages 56–64.

9. The parenthesis indicates that the listener will not hear this statement orally at this spot in the message but inductively will put it together as the subunits accumulate. See appendix A, guideline 5, for proper outlining.

C. The evidence of the Spirit's filling is harmonious relationships
    (5:21).

7. If the overall sermon structure/focus is inductive, with the introduction raising multiple questions, but only some of the Roman numerals answer the questions, then you need a preview to show how the other Roman numeral(s) fit into the flow.

Returning to our sermon on Mark 4:35–41, note that introduction point 2 raises two questions, which are answered in the body of the message by points II and III. A preview is necessary to prepare the listener for point I, before the message starts answering the two questions.

Introduction
1. Sometimes we obey God, and the bottom falls out of everything.
    a. Example/application
    b. Example/application
2. We despair, and wonder, "God, why is this happening, and what do you want me to do?" [**Inductive, raising of two questions, which will be answered in points II and III below.**]
3. Today we'll see the disciples in a similar situation and learn why such things happen and what our response should be. [**This preview tells the listener there will be a point I concept before the message starts answering the two questions.**]
4. Please turn to Mark 4:35–41.

I. The disciples obey Jesus and find themselves in a life-threatening storm that fills them with despair (4:35–38).

II. The reason such things happen may be that Satan is attempting to prevent God's purposes.
    A. The storm is Satan's attempt to prevent the growth of the kingdom.
    B. Our difficulties may be Satan's attempt to prevent what God wants to do through us.

      1. Example/application
      2. Example/application

III. We should resist Satan's efforts and trust God's power.
    A. Jesus rebukes the demonic activity behind the storm and encourages the disciples to trust God's power (4:39–41).
    B. We should resist Satan's efforts and trust God's power.
      1. Example/application
      2. Example/application

The preview gives the listeners whatever help they need to clearly follow the message as it moves from the introduction into the body of the material. If you simply ask yourself, "When I give my first Roman numeral, will the listener clearly be able to connect it to what I've said in the introduction?" then you'll sense whether you need a preview or not. If in doubt, consult the chart on page 225 and make the necessary adjustments.

Once you've determined that you need a preview, you're ready to look at the second question: "How do I phrase it?"

If I Do Need a Preview, How Do I Phrase Its Separate Elements?

All previews contain multiple parts, or elements, each of which prepares the listener for one of the Roman numerals to come. These separate preview elements can be phrased either deductively or inductively.

Since we've encountered the concepts of deduction and induction before, let's take a moment to note that these concepts operate at four different places in a message:

- In chapter 8 we saw the first place—at the overall macrostructural level. Deduction/induction at this level is determined by whether the introduction states the take-home truth or raises a question.
- Now we're going to look at the second place where deduction/induction operates in a message—in the phrasing of the preview elements.
- Later we'll see a third place—in unfolding individual Roman numerals.
- Finally, we'll consider a fourth spot—in reading Scripture verses within the body of the message.

In each of these four spots, the essential meaning of the concepts remains the same:

- Speakers are *deductive* when they make an *assertion* (e.g., a take-home truth) that will be developed.
- Speakers are *inductive* when they raise a *question* that will be answered.

Here, at this second place in the sermon where these concepts show up, a deductively phrased preview element will sound like an assertion, like a complete sentence. It will usually contain or imply the word *that* and will lead to a complete thought: "I want you to see *that* . . ."

This deductive phrasing usually will occur in the first preview element, when the engaging section of the introduction already has suggested the content of the first Roman numeral, as happens in the wrap pattern. When the essential concept of point I has already been revealed in the introduction, the purpose of the first preview element is simply to say to the listener, "I'm going to show you in Scripture *that* what I've been saying is true."

An inductively phrased preview element usually will contain or imply one of the interrogatives—*who, what, when, where, why,* or *how.* Most preview elements will be phrased inductively, so as to anticipate a coming Roman numeral without giving away the actual content or assertion of the point. In other words, you preview what you're going to talk about, but you don't reveal what you're going to say about it.

In the following examples, note that when the first preview element is stated deductively (with the force of *that*), it's because the introduction already has revealed the first Roman numeral concept. Otherwise, all the other preview elements are phrased inductively.

Here's an example from the sermon on Exodus 13:17–22.[10]

> [**Engage**] Early in geometry we learned that "the shortest distance between two points is a straight line." That means, if I'm at point A and I want to get to point B, the shortest distance between these two points is a straight line.

---

10. See appendix C for the full outline and manuscript of this message.

Now that may be true in geometry, but as you and I think about what God is doing in our lives, we wonder if God doesn't think that "the shortest distance between two points is a zigzag." And by that I mean, we're at point A . . .

For example, you may have just started an entry-level job at a particular company . . .

Maybe you've started a business, and your business is at point A. But as you think about the growth of your business, the Spirit of God gives you a mental picture of point B—a certain volume, a certain size of your company . . .

For you, point A may be "single" and point B is "married" . . . But if God is taking you there, he's on a very erratic path, because romantic possibilities are coming and going, and coming and going, mostly going.

[**Focus: take-home truth**] Today I want us to see _that_ sometimes, with God, the shortest distance between two points is a zigzag.

[**Preview of coming hunks**] I want us to see that God sometimes deliberately takes us on a zigzag path. Knowingly, intentionally, purposefully he takes our lives on an alternate route. I want us to see _why_ he does this—what's his reason, what's his purpose, what's he trying to accomplish? And then, finally, _how_ does he keep us encouraged? How does he sustain us on the way? In the midst of the zigs and zags, when we don't seem to be making any progress, how does God keep us moving expectantly and joyfully toward the goal?

The first preview element above—"I want us to see _that_ God sometimes deliberately leads us on a zigzag path"—is stated deductively, since the earlier paragraphs of the introduction already have made that point. Phrasing it inductively—"Today let's see how God sometimes leads us"—would seem foolish to the listeners, who would think, "You've already told us how he leads—on a zigzag path."

The second and third preview elements, however, are stated inductively with interrogatives—"_why_ does he do it?" and "_how_ does he keep us encouraged?"—to reveal what the Roman numerals will talk about but without giving away the content of what will be said about it.

In the Mark 4:35–41 message that follows, the introduction makes the point _that_ we sometimes obey God only to see disaster occur. It then raises

I. What
II. Why
III. How

[handwritten: I. What? / II. Why? / III. How?]

two inductive questions—*why* does this happen, and *what* should we do. Before these questions will be answered in points II and III, however, the speaker needs to show that the disciples are having a similar experience to what has been asserted about our contemporary world. So, in introduction point 3, the first preview element has the force of a deductive statement— "We're going to see *that* the disciples faced a similar situation." The second and third preview elements are inductive—revealing what the coming points will be about but not revealing any content or truth assertions about them.

Introduction

1. Sometimes we obey God, and the bottom falls out of everything.
   a. Example/application
   b. Example/application
2. We despair, and wonder, "God, why is this happening, and what do you want me to do?" [Focus: Inductive, raising of two questions, which will be answered in points II and III below.]
3. Today (1) we'll see the disciples in a similar situation and (2) learn why such things happen and (3) what our response should be. [**The first preview element is deductive, since the "situation" already has been described earlier. The second and third are inductive—they raise questions that the later points will answer.**]
4. Please turn to Mark 4:35–41.

I. The disciples obey Jesus and find themselves in a life-threatening storm that fills them with despair (4:35–38).

II. The reason such things happen may be that Satan is attempting to prevent God's purposes.
   A. The storm is Satan's attempt to prevent the growth of the kingdom.
   B. Our difficulties may be Satan's attempt to prevent what God wants to do through us.

[handwritten: II.]

    1. Example/application
    2. Example/application

How III. We should resist Satan's efforts and trust God's power.
    A. Jesus rebukes the demonic activity behind the storm and encourages the disciples to trust God's power (4:39–41).
    B. We should resist Satan's efforts and trust God's power.
       1. Example/application
       2. Example/application

The abbreviated outline below on James 1:2–4 shows only inductive previews, since neither of the concepts has been developed earlier in the introduction:

Introduction
    1. Often, through no fault of our own, we find ourselves facing various trials in life.
      a. Example/application
      b. Example/application
Inductive   2. How should we react to such situations, and why should we react that way? [**Two interrogative previews, to set up points I and II, which will provide the answers.**]

How? I. We should face trials with joy. *why?*

    II. We should face trials with joy because God is in the process of making us more like Christ.

ANNOUNCE THE PASSAGE, GIVING CHAPTER AND VERSE

Once the preview elements have established the hunks to come, the listener is ready to turn to the specific passage that will reveal God's truth on the issue(s) raised. This is the time to announce the passage, giving chapter and verse.

Let me offer a few suggestions regarding this final part of the introduction:

1. Repeat the reference more than once.

    Many listeners will not get it the first time. They may get the biblical book and perhaps the chapter, but they will miss the verse. So repeat it several times.

2. Give them time to find their place before you continue talking.

    Don't talk while they're attempting to find the reference, because they won't hear what you're saying. They can't listen to you and hunt for a passage at the same time. Their brains will focus on one or the other. If they focus on finding the passage, this means they won't hear any of the essential comments you make as you lay out point I and probably subpoint I.A. When they finally tune into you again, they've missed plugging into the whole first movement of the message.

    After announcing the passage, wait in silence until you see their heads bobbing up with an open Bible before them. If you can't stand the twenty to thirty seconds of "silence," periodically repeat the reference. Or better yet, help them find it:

    "First Timothy, chapter 2, beginning at verse 1. First Timothy 2, verse 1 . . . toward the back part of your Bible . . . after Ephesians, Philippians, Colossians, Thessalonians. If you come to Hebrews or James, you've gone too far. First Timothy, chapter 2, verse 1."

    If there are pew Bibles available, positively direct the listeners toward the page number.[11]

3. Use this part of the introduction to subtly and gently communicate, "I expect you to bring your Bibles to church."

    Some people, of course, will not have brought their Bibles and may be slow to move toward a pew Bible. By waiting in silence and by glancing with a quiet smile at those faces that are looking at you rather than searching in a Bible for the passage, you reinforce the implied message: "I really want you to bring a Bible to church. It's so important to me that you have your Bible in front of you that I'm stopping my whole message and not saying another word, until I know you've had time to look it up. Nothing that I'm going to say

---

11. Not negatively—"If you forgot your Bible this morning . . ."—but rather, "If you're using the Bible in the pew rack in front of you, you'll find it on page 1,738." Then repeat the page number as often as you repeat the chapter and verse.

is as important as your eyes seeing what God himself has said in his Word." After a period of weeks of averting your gaze, they will finally get the point and start bringing a Bible.

Some churches attempt to solve the problem by putting the Scripture on a screen for all to read. But there are a couple of drawbacks to this:

- You're reinforcing the message, "We don't expect you to bring a Bible."
- You're perhaps unintentionally communicating that the Bible is like the newspaper—snippets from columns that have nothing to do with the article above them or the feature below them. You may be losing the essential concepts of: ① there is a continuous flow of thought through this Book; ② this Book in its entirety is a "canon," the revealed Word of God; and ③ you should be used to the feeling of having it in your hands and reading from it at home.

I liked how one church handled it. Since they had flexible seating in their auditorium, without pew racks, they developed a marvelous way of getting Bibles to the people who needed them. Just before introducing the guest speaker, the pastor would say something like:

"In a moment, Dr. Sunukjian's going to come and give us the message for the morning. But before he comes, we want to make sure all of you have a Bible to look at while he's talking. If you don't have a Bible with you, our ushers are coming down the aisles with copies that they'll be glad to slip down the row to you. If you don't own a Bible, please accept this one as our gift to you. Put your name on it, take it home, read it, bring it back next Sunday. If you do have a Bible but just not with you today, take one from the ushers, and, when the service is over, leave it on the table at the rear, and someone else will use it next week."

Through this natural flow—engaging the listeners' attention and interest, providing the point of focus for what God will say that day, setting the stage biblically, previewing the coming hunks, and announcing the chapter and flow—the speaker gathers the listeners from the wide concerns of life and leads them to the living Word of God.

And as the Scriptures are opened, the listeners are prepared and eager to hear how God's truth will speak to the realities of contemporary life.

13

Prepare the
Conclusion and Title

IN THIS CHAPTER WE'LL TALK about preparing the last thing the listeners will hear, and the first thing the listeners will see—the conclusion and the title.

Though both of these, in some form, may have entered our mind earlier in the process of preparation, this is the logical spot in the preparation process to pin them down.

PREPARE THE CONCLUSION

The Purposes of the Conclusion

The conclusion has two purposes: to summarize and to exhort—that is, to give a sense of unity and wholeness to the message, and to urge our listeners to make its truths a part of their lives.

The conclusion tells the listeners where we have been and where we want them to go. As Calvin Pearson, a friend and colleague, once aptly put it: "The conclusion is what we want them to do with what we want them to know."

In summarizing, the conclusion gives the listeners the sense, "We've finished what we set out to do; we've come full circle; the message is complete." Without re-preaching the whole sermon, we briefly review the broad strokes or hunks that have brought us to this point, sometimes gathering them together and expressing them in some fresh way.[1]

---

1. See the example on James 2:1–13 (pp. 244–45) for a summary that brings the concepts together in a fresh way by repeating the same sentence structure for several sentences.

But we don't want to end the message with just a look back. We also want to urge the listeners to carry its truths forward. We want them to "go for it!" We may or may not "apply" in the conclusion; in many cases the relevancy or application has already occurred earlier in the message. But in the conclusion we want to encourage, or exhort, or motivate them to base their lives on the truth they have heard. There may or may not be some action for them to do. There may, instead, be a promise for them to embrace, a gift for them to enjoy, a divine work for which they can increasingly be thankful, or a forgiveness in which they must always be secure. But one way or another, we are pressing God's good Word into the way they will live in the future.

Effective Ways of Concluding

Effective conclusions are as varied as the messages themselves. Good speakers often combine several of the following elements into a single conclusion, while seeking to avoid a predictability or sameness every week.

Tell a Story That Shows the Truth Occurring in Real Life

In a sermon on Ephesians 6:18–20 titled "What's the Word I'm Looking For," I developed two major points: pray for the weapons to stand your ground against Satan (6:18), and pray for the words to take Satan's ground away from him (6:19–20). Then in the conclusion I told the following story:

> Several years ago I was watching a program on television in which an interviewer was with Billy Graham and Woody Allen, the screenwriter and actor. The conversation was flowing, and many subjects were being discussed. Then, at one point, the interviewer said to Woody Allen, "Woody, would you have made a good evangelist?" My instinctive reaction was to snort! But Billy Graham immediately spoke up. "I can answer that," he said. "Yes, he would have made a wonderful evangelist—he's creative, he's insightful into human situations, and he works with words so effectively. He would make a wonderful evangelist."
>
> And I thought, "What grace. What a wonderful way to put it. Instead of letting Woody answer the question and maybe dismiss spiritual things, Billy steps in and praises him. He praises Woody's

honest skills. He doesn't praise his lifestyle. But he praises what Woody could do for the Lord. And he almost hints that, 'Wouldn't it be good, Woody, if your wonderful abilities were used for eternity rather than for things that don't really matter?'"

And I thought, "Billy, how did you know to say that? How did you come up with that on the spot? I know you didn't know what questions were going to be asked. Where did you come up with such a perfect way of putting it? How did you know exactly what to say?"

I think if I had had a chance to ask Billy about it, I think he would have said, "You know, I didn't know what was going to come up in that interview. But I knew it was a big opportunity; I knew that millions of people would be watching—people who would never come to a crusade or watch one on television. I didn't know what would come up during the discussion. So I just prayed beforehand, 'Lord, put your words in my mouth, so that I can do good for your kingdom.' I didn't really plan what to say. That answer just sort of came out of my mouth. It was honest and natural, and I said it freely, easily. And Satan lost ground that day, didn't he?"

Visualize How They Might Obey the Truth in the Future

At the end of a message on "Impartial Love," based on James 2:1–13, I visualized how my listeners might put the truth into practice on the following Sunday.[2]

Maybe next Sunday you'll find yourself near someone who looks out of place, alone, uncertain. Maybe it's a young couple in the parking lot, struggling to get all their gear and small children together. Maybe it's an elderly person walking slowly with a cane, hoping not to get bumped, trying to open a door. Maybe it's a teenager with skin problems and shirttail flapping. It may be someone who weighs too much, or talks too loud, or smells too strong.

But here, among God's people, they are loved—loved for who they are and not for what they can do.

---

2. The visualization returns to a situation similar to the one mentioned in the introduction (see pp. 213–16). See appendix C for the full outline and manuscript of this message.

Repeat the Same Sentence Structure for Several Sentences

After the visualization, the James 2 conclusion continued with a summary of the concepts of the message, bringing them together in a fresh way through a repeated sentence structure.[3]

> But here, among God's people, they are loved—loved for who they are and not for what they can do.
>
> Loved, without thought of gain, because God controls all that.
> Loved, because, unknown to us, God may be doing wonderful things in their lives.
> Loved, because our greatest desire is to do all that our God has said.
> Loved, because we too are all so aware that, though we are unworthy, God's mercy and love never come to an end in our life.
>
> Here, among God's people, there's no favoring one over another. There's only impartial love.

End with an Apt Quotation

A sermon, "Life in the 'Fast' Lane," first described the practice of fasting (i.e., voluntary; of various lengths; and sometimes partial, refraining from certain foods and drinks but not others) and then developed, through biblical example and contemporary application, two reasons for a prayerful fast:

- To seek God's wisdom or guidance for a particular situation
- To seek God's powerful intervention in a particular situation

---

3. See appendix C for the full outline and manuscript of this message. The four major concepts are:
   I. When we love impartially, we show our deep trust in God—that he is in control of our lives (2:4).
   II. When we love impartially, we show our wisdom about people—that it's usually the poor who have the closest walk with God (2:5–7).
   III. When we love impartially, we show our submission to God's Word—that we will obey everything God has said (2:8–11).
   IV. When we love impartially, we show our desire for God's grace—that we want his mercy instead of his judgment (2:12–13).

The message ended with a summary, a personal account, and an apt quotation:

> We humble ourselves in fasting before him, admitting that we are dependent on him. We have no wisdom. We have no power. We appeal to him.
>
> It's fair that I tell you how this works in my life.
>
> Nell and I have five grown children. Some of them have spouses. There are two grandchildren and more on the way. With all of these children, every so often there come some deep aches—lost jobs, career frustrations, struggles with temptation, eating difficulties, health scares, yearnings to be with child if they have a spouse, yearnings to be married if they don't—the periodic aches of life.
>
> Sometimes Nell and I can do something. Sometimes we can say something. But most of the time we have no wisdom or power for the situation. And so for us, every Wednesday is a day to fast and pray. We eat nothing for breakfast or lunch. Around noon Nell calls me at my office, and for thirty to forty minutes we pray through everyone in the family, thanking God for his gifts and grace and asking for help that only he can give. And as we have done this over the past few years, little by little we have seen God's power bring the things we have prayed for.
>
> It may be that God will lead you to fast and pray—to come with a recognition that you are dependent on him and to ask for his wisdom and his power. Someone has put it well:
>
> > The pleasures of eating are fleeting.
> > The pleasures of fasting are lasting.

Quote a Short Poem or Hymn

Malachi 3:13–4:3 speaks of God "eavesdropping" from heaven. He listens to some people complaining that it is futile and profitless to serve him, but he also overhears others remaining true and encouraging one another. God then promises a day when the faithless wicked will burn like stubble, but the steadfast righteous will experience healing and joy, and will become God's treasured possession. After encouraging the listeners to remain steadfast, I closed the sermon with the first verse and chorus of "When We See Christ," following a quote from C. S. Lewis's *Screwtape Letters.*

C. S. Lewis, in his *Screwtape Letters,* has a senior demon explain to his trainee, "Our cause is never more in danger than when a human, no longer desiring, but still intending, to do our Enemy's will, looks round upon a universe from which every trace of Him seems to have vanished, and asks why he has been forsaken, and still obeys."[4]

Complete a Visual Aid That Has Been Unfolding Through the Message

Genesis 29:31–30:24—the birth of Jacob's children—tells how God began fulfilling his promise that Jacob's descendants would be as the dust of the earth (Gen. 28:13–14). In the extended chiastic structure, everything has been moving toward the birth of these children, and everything will flow out from it.

> Promise given, family scheming (25:19–34)
> Deception and strife with foreigners (26:1–35)
> Blessing stolen, flight from the land (27:1–28:9)
> Encounter with God: dream (28:10–22)
> Arrival at Laban's house (29:1–14)
> Deception about wages (29:15–30)
> Birth of the children (29:31–30:24)
> Wealth through wages (30:25–43)
> Departure from Laban (31:1–55)
> Encounter with God: wrestling (32:1–32)
> Blessing replaced, return to the land (33:1–20)
> Deception and strife with foreigners (34:1–31)
> Promise renewed, family scheming (35:1–29)

The truth of this central section (29:31–30:24) is that God faithfully works his good purposes in our lives through times of sorrow and heaviness (29:31–35) and through times of strife and conflict (as revealed through the Hebrew meaning of the children's names in 30:1–13), as we feebly attempt to cooperate with his plans (30:14–24). Along the way, we,

---

4. C. S. Lewis, *The Screwtape Letters* (New York: MacMillan, 1959), 39.

like Jacob, may think that life is a noisy, chaotic mess, but God is putting the pieces of his plan together.

As the message progresses, pieces of a puzzle are thrown randomly and haphazardly on the screen—from one of those plastic puzzles where six or seven differently shaped pieces must be put together into a square or star. Then, as the speaker says the concluding words—"Perhaps, unknown to you, bit by bit God has been adding the pieces of his plan for you. Despite your times of sorrow, strife, and small obedience, it will come together into his good promise for your life"—the differently shaped pieces are formed into the perfect image.

Focus Crisply on the Take-Home Truth

Malachi 2:10–16 teaches that God's child is to marry the right kind of person (a believer) and then live with that person the right kind of way (continuing the lifelong commitment promised at marriage). The final sentence of the message might put this into a crisp take-home truth: "Marry one of God's own, and love that one all of your life."

Offer a Benediction or Doxology

A first-person dramatic sermon on the book of Esther[5] presents the idea that "God, unseen, sovereignly controls the events of our lives for good." The benediction that ends the message also serves to apply it:

> Now to the God who never slumbers, never sleeps; to the God who knows your coming in and your going out; to the God who hovers around you to preserve you from harm and to give you the future he's planned for you; to our great and good God be glory and praise forever. Amen.

Ineffective Ways of Concluding

As I mentioned at the start of the chapter, a conclusion that only summarizes or recaps the points is generally unsatisfying to the listener. In adding an exhortation, however, you should avoid two other generally ineffective ways of ending a message.

---

5. Donald Sunukjian, "A Night in Persia," in *Biblical Sermons,* ed. Haddon W. Robinson (Grand Rapids: Baker, 1989), 71–80.

Introspective Questions

Avoid asking an introspective question in the last line of the message—a question that supposedly asks the listeners to examine themselves and come up with an answer. Examples of such introspective questions might include:

- "So ask yourself, 'Am I the kind of parent that is producing a godly child?'"
- "Have you been living a holy life, one that is pleasing to the Lord?"
- "Are you watching and waiting for his return?"

The listeners probably will not seriously engage such questions, since the likelihood is too great that the answer will be no. It's far better to turn the question into an exhortation:

- "From this day forward, let's determine that we will be the kind of parent who seeks to raise a godly child."
- "He is our Lord, the one who has given us life and will give us eternity. Let us live pleasing to him!"
- "He's coming! Let's watch alertly and wait eagerly!"

A decision question is marginally better, but even it might be more effective as an encouragement or an exhortation rather than as a question. "Will you today commit to giving a tithe to the Lord?" does have the advantage of forcing the issue and pressing for a decision. But it also has the disadvantage of reinforcing rebellion if the listener's answer is no. Instead, how about, "Let today be the day you take this step that will forever change your life."

An affirmation question is entirely appropriate, since it has more the force of an assertion than the force of a question. A final question that affirms or reinforces a truth could be quite effective:

- "If God be for us, who can be against us?"
- "Who can fear to fall into the hands of such incredible love?"
- "Will we ever be able to thank him enough for all he's done for us?"

Long Poems or Quotes

Long poems, quotes, or readings are seldom effective in a conclusion. They were originally written to be read, not to be heard; they were composed for the eye, not for the ear. Their sentence structure is literary rather than conversational and requires a thoughtful pacing and an occasional rereading to get the sense.[6] For this reason, it's extremely difficult for a speaker to convey them clearly or for a listener to track them orally.

Some General Principles

In addition to the specific kinds of materials to use or avoid in a conclusion, here are some general principles to keep in mind.

Plan the Conclusion

Don't leave the conclusion for the spur of the moment; don't depend on "the Spirit's leading." The Spirit can lead just as easily on Thursday in the study as on Sunday in the pulpit.

Failure to plan will often leave the speaker feeling like the pilot of a small plane, circling for a landing. The first attempt at a conclusion seems bumpy and unsmooth, so he goes aloft again for another try. Subsequent attempts also lack the desired grace or finesse of an appropriate ending, so he keeps circling and searching. Finally, in desperation and weariness, anxious to end it all, he simply crashes and burns.

Know exactly what you're going to say and how you're going to say it in the conclusion. If there are any lines in the sermon that ought to be memorized, they are the first lines of the introduction and the last lines of the conclusion.

Don't Announce That You Are Concluding

Announcing that you are concluding has two undesirable effects on the listeners: it calls their attention to the mechanical skills of constructing a message, and it makes them refer to their watches to see how long you've spoken.

The content of your thought (from summary to exhortation) and the manner of your speaking (whether more deliberate or more passionate) should make it clear that the message is drawing to a close.

---

6. We'll look at the differences between literary and oral sentence structures in the next chapter when we talk about writing for the ear.

Maintain Eye Contact with the Listeners

The conclusion is not a time for "housekeeping"—putting your watch back on, collecting your notes into your Bible, or picking up a hymnal in anticipation of a final song. It's a time to look directly and continuously at the listeners, your heart to their heart, without distraction.

End Positively on a Note of Encouragement and Hope

Some passages will inevitably lead to negative messages—exposing failure, denouncing sin, or warning of judgment. On rare occasions the preacher may want to end on such a prophetic note. But assuming that most of the time we will be speaking to struggling believers who deep in their hearts want to please the Lord, it might be better to end with the same loving spirit of our Lord: "A bruised reed he will not break, and a smoldering wick he will not snuff out" (Matt. 12:20, quoting Isa. 42:3).

Sometimes you can turn a negative message into an encouraging one by stating the major points positively. Even though the movements in the text are expressed in negative terms, they can be rephrased into positive ones. The negative content of the text will still be exposed in the subpoints of the message, but the dominant truth statements become ones that point the listener in a positive direction. In other words, from bad examples we can learn positive actions.

For instance, a message on 2 Kings 5:19–27 could be outlined in a negative fashion.

    I. A godly man does not lie.
        A. Gehazi lied.
        B. We should not lie.

    II. A godly man is not greedy.
        A. Gehazi was greedy.
        B. We should not be greedy.

But it can end on a more positive and encouraging note if the major points are phrased positively, yet allowing the text's negative example to come through in the subpoints.

    I. A godly man tells the truth.

A. Gehazi lied.
B. We should tell the truth.

II. A godly man is content.
A. Gehazi was greedy.
B. We should be content.

Or, suppose you're speaking on the third commandment—"You shall not misuse the name of the LORD your God" (Exod. 20:7)—and you want to conclude with some applications. A negative set of points might leave the listeners feeling beaten down:

Conclusion: There are several ways in which we disobey this command.
1. We disobey when we swear falsely by God's name.
2. We disobey when we speak carelessly of God's name.
3. We disobey when we live dishonorably by God's name.

How much better to apply on a positive note:

Conclusion: There are several ways in which we can obey this command.
1. We obey when we swear truly by his name.
2. We obey when we speak reverently of his name.
3. We obey when we live honorably for his name.

Sometimes you will want the main points to retain their negative force. But even then the conclusion can bring in themes of mercy and grace, and an invitation to turn and begin anew. End the message, not on a scolding for the past, but on a wooing to the future.

For example, in the message on Malachi 1:6–14,[7] the main points were phrased in the same negative language of the text, and the applications exposed how the audience was guilty of the same sins as Israel. But the conclusion appealed for and suggested a better response:

---

7. See pages 187–91.

> God has loved you with an everlasting love. He has chosen you, and he will never let you go. Such love ought to lead us to awe and adoration, to honoring him above all else in life.
>
> > When I survey the wondrous cross,
> > On which the Prince of glory died,
> > My richest gain I count but loss,
> > And pour contempt on all my pride.
> >
> > Were the whole realm of nature mine,
> > That were a present far too small;
> > Love so amazing, so divine,
> > Demands my soul, my life, my all.[8]
>
> He is the great King. Among the nations of the earth, he is honored and praised with an overwhelming awe.
>
> Here in our church, we too reveal our honor when we offer him our best, and when our heart says, "I wish I could do even better."

Provide a Natural Connection to Whatever Follows the Message

The conclusion should flow naturally into any invitation, hymn, or observance of the Lord's Supper that will come after the message. In some way the theme of the message should be carried through with whatever follows.

For example, any given sermon might easily find its major thrust carried through into one of these rich themes in the Lord's Supper:

- His body was broken for us to pay the penalty for past sin.
- His blood was shed for us to provide the power over future sin through the internal Spirit of the new covenant.
- We need to examine ourselves as we approach this observance to be sure we are eating and drinking in a worthy manner.
- Through this ceremony, we "proclaim the Lord's death until he comes."

---

8. Isaac Watts, "When I Survey the Wondrous Cross," 1707.

- Some day we will "drink it anew" with him in the Father's kingdom.

In the Malachi 3:13–4:3 message,[9] after quoting the hymn, the message transitions into the Lord's Supper by recalling the experience of Christ, developing the following thoughts: He too might have wondered if serving God was worth it—he ministered to thousands at the beginning, but none stood with him at the end. Even God seemed to have forsaken him. But he remained faithful and did God's will. As a result, God highly exalted him to the highest place, giving him a name above every other name. And someday every knee will bow and every tongue will confess that he is Lord, to the glory of God the Father. And in observing this Supper, we declare our faithful commitment to him, until he comes.

CREATE AN INTRIGUING TITLE

When listeners enter the church, settle in their seats, and open their bulletins to see what the sermon is about, the title should cause them to say, "Ah, this sounds interesting." And they may add, "I wonder what this will be about." The main goal of a title is to create curiosity and interest.[10]

Sometimes the title can raise this curiosity or interest by highlighting an intriguing phrase in the passage. A message on Proverbs 3:5–10 is titled "Health to Your Navel," from the literal meaning of the Hebrew in verse 8, reflected in the King James translation. "A Lion in a Pit on a Snowy Day" would probably make listeners interested in hearing a message on 2 Samuel 23:20–23.

Some titles grab attention through a play on words or by slightly twisting a common expression. Here are several from Genesis and Malachi:

- "It is Wells with My Soul" (Gen. 26:12–33)
- "Marry Christians, Merry Christians" (Gen. 26:34–35; 27:46–28:9)
- "The Bind that Tithes" (Gen. 28:10–22)

---

9. See pages 246–47.
10. If titles are published the week before the sermon, a secondary goal might be to encourage attendance at the service. A third goal, obviously, is to have a reference name for reproducing copies of the message.

- "The Spots and Stripes Forever" (Gen. 30:25–43)
- "How Do I Love Thee? Let Me Count the Way" (Mal. 1:1–5)
- "Tithe if You Love Jesus—Anyone Can Honk" (Mal. 3:7–12)

Watch out for a title that may give away more than you want at the start. A message inductively structured in the introduction to ask, "What is God looking for more than anything else?" might lose some of its steam if the listener sees the advance title—"A Pure Heart."

Times when it might be appropriate for the title to deductively give away the take-home truth would be when the same take-home truth as the title appears in the introduction (i.e., a deductive structure) and both raise some developmental question in the listener.[11] For example, "The Shortest Distance Between Two Points Is a Zigzag" is an appropriate title for the message on Exodus 13:17–22. That same statement will be repeated relatively early in the introduction, and both pique the curiosity of the listener, raising a form of the first developmental question—"I wonder what that means; he's going to have to explain that."

A good title gets them ready to hear, and a good conclusion gets them ready to act.

---

11. See pages 156–59.

14

Write for the Ear

AT THIS POINT IN THE preparation process, you've put together a complete and substantive outline. You have the following:

- An introduction that engages the listener, focuses the message, sets the stage biblically, previews the coming hunks, and announces the chapter and verse
- A sermon outline that unfolds the biblical author's flow of thought and applies it relevantly to the listener, using some combination of structural (inductive or deductive) and relevancy (at the end, interspersed, or wrapped) patterns
- A conclusion that summarizes and exhorts

You conceivably could preach your message without any further preparation, if the pressure of time or circumstances required you to do so. But if you did, your wording would likely be inexact, awkward, and overly verbose. And your oral clarity would be spotty and elusive.

That's why we want to talk about writing for the ear in this chapter and planning for oral clarity in the next one.

The rewards of writing out a message are inestimably worth the additional time it takes. Writing brings a wonderful precision and appropriateness to your language—you not only know what you want to say; you also know exactly how you want to say it. You also can judge from the page length how long it will take you to say it, and you have a complete record in case you want to say it again.

Writing out the message also frees you for a more spontaneous and

A first draft.

dramatic delivery. Far from producing a stilted or wooden presentation, an exact and internalized manuscript enables the speaker to concentrate on the audience and to totally engage in all the natural nuances of delivery that bind them to him. It's because the stage actor so thoroughly knows his lines that he's able to give an eighty-fifth performance that seems totally spontaneous and made-up on the spot!

A written-out message has an amazing effect on both you and the listeners. It gives you the quiet confidence that you will communicate God's truth exactly as you planned and hoped. And it makes your listeners intensely attentive, as they realize how lovingly and thoroughly you've prepared on their behalf. Your careful wording makes their ears open to hear.

As you write out the message, keep the following two guidelines in mind: write like you talk, and be sensitive to the emotional overtones of your language.

WRITE LIKE YOU TALK

Write the way you talk, not the way you write. Make the sentences as easy to speak as they are to read.

Usually when we write something, we're writing for someone's eye to read it. We turn in papers for teachers to grade, we leave notes for spouses to find, we submit estimates for customers to see, we lay out bulletins for church members to read. Inevitably, and subconsciously, we write for the eye.

And in writing for the eye, we've been taught to obey all kinds of rules:

> No sentence fragments. None. Run-on sentences are an abomination and you should never use them because you'll get marked down when the teacher grades your paper. Don't use contractions. It's not a good idea to ever split infinitives. A preposition is something you should never end a sentence with. And don't begin sentences with "and." Never, never, never repeat yourself.[1]

---

1. G. Robert Jacks, *Just Say the Word! Writing for the Ear* (Grand Rapids: Eerdmans, 1996), 2. Note how every sentence breaks the very rule it advocates.

The problem is, we don't follow these rules when we talk. None of them. We talk in short sentences. Fragments. Easy-to-follow phrases.

We don't use big words. We don't sound literary; we sound normal. We talk so that eleven-year-olds can understand us.

So when it's time to write a sermon, we have to make a conscious effort to write like we talk. We have to write for the ear. This means we should follow several rules.

Use the Active Voice Rather Than the Passive and Verbs Rather Than Nouns

The following sentence is hard to grasp because of the improper passives and nouns:

> An improvement in speaking that has too heavy a dependency on nouns can be achieved by making a note of each noun and posing a question to yourself as to whether a replacement of it with a verb could be made.

Note the improvement when the passives are changed to actives, and when many of the nouns are made into verbs:

> To improve speaking that depends too heavily on nouns, note each noun and ask yourself if you can replace it with a verb.

In a sermon on James 4:13–16,[2] it would be difficult for the listeners to transition into the concept of verse 14b if the speaker's language sounded like this:

> The second reason why you would be considered arrogant in your planning is because not only do you lack knowledge of what will occur in the future, but you also lack knowledge of whether you will have a life in the future. Not only are you deprived of an ability to exercise control over the future, but you also have been kept in ignorance as to whether you will even have an existence in the future. Your planning will be deemed arrogant because you don't really have any knowledge as to the length of your life.

---

2. See pages 152–54 for the full sermon outline.

But when the passives are changed to actives and some nouns are changed to verbs, the whole paragraph becomes easier to say and to hear:

> The second reason it's arrogant to plan with certainty is because, not only do you not know what the future will be like, you don't even know for certain that you'll be here for the future. Not only are you unable to control tomorrow, you don't even know for sure you'll be around tomorrow. Your planning is arrogant because you don't really know how long you have to live.

The active voice and verb in "God knows everything you do" is certainly better than the passive voice and noun in "The attribute of omniscience is possessed by God regarding your daily activities."

Put the Important Information or Words Early in the Sentence, and Use Short Sentences Rather Than Long Ones with Dependent Clauses

In the following sentences, the listener would be confused all the way through each sentence as to what the speaker was talking about, since the key information comes at the end of each sentence.

> Sometimes, when I come home after a hard day at work, when the garage door is closed, and bicycles and other toys are in the driveway, I yell at the kids. Storming into the house, I take it out on the kids because I'm frustrated that I can't park the car.

Rather than allowing dependent clauses to delay the important information, put the key concepts at the start, and use several short sentences:

> Sometimes I yell at the kids. I come home after a hard day at work. The garage door is closed. Bicycles and other toys are in the driveway. I'm frustrated that I can't park the car. So I storm into the house and take it out on the kids.

The following might be appropriate as an announcement to be *read* in the bulletin:

There will be a meeting this Saturday at 9:00 AM in the Fireside Room for those of you who are interested in starting an Awana program at the church.

But as an announcement to be *heard* from the pulpit, putting the key information at the start of the sentence would make it orally clearer:

Those of you interested in starting an Awana program at the church—you're invited to a meeting this Saturday at 9:00 AM in the Fireside Room.

Create Conversations, Have Characters Dialogue, Use Quotation Marks

As Israel exits Egypt for Canaan, they find themselves on an uncharted journey in the opposite direction of Canaan, their promised destination (Exod. 13:17–22).[3] To keep them from becoming discouraged as they head away from their promised destination, God provides the people with a continual reminder of his good intentions—a coffin containing the bones of Joseph. Four hundred years earlier Joseph had made the sons of Israel swear that they would take his bones with them when God took them out of Egypt into the Promised Land (Gen. 50:24–26). His coffin reminds the nation of God's commitment to place them in their own land.

Notice how conversations and sentences in quotations help explain the text and convey the applications.[4]

As they leave Egypt and head toward the Red Sea, the coffin that contains the bones of Joseph leads the way. And I can hear some little kid turn to his mother and say, "Why are those men carrying that box?" "That's not a box, honey. That's a coffin." "What's a coffin?" "Well, it has the bones of a dead man in it." "Oh—gross! But why are we taking it with us?" "Well, honey, we're taking it to Canaan." "But we're not headed to Canaan." "Yes we are—Yes we are. That coffin's going to Canaan."

---

3. See appendix C for the full sermon manuscript of this message.
4. Speakers can simulate a conversation by simply turning their head from side to side to represent each person as they speak.

Every day as they started the march, no matter where the zigs and zags led them, the coffin was a continual reminder that God was taking them to point B. That coffin was going to Canaan.

My friend, in the midst of your zigs and zags, if the dream is of God, God will give you continual reminders of his good intention. If the destiny is of God, if point B is of God, then God will find ways of coming to you and letting you know that he's still taking you to his promised destination. Perhaps someone out of the blue—someone who doesn't know what God has put in your heart—perhaps that someone will say something to you. Not knowing your dream, the person won't realize the significance of what he or she is saying, but in that person's words you'll hear God's voice reminding you of his good intentions. The person will use the exact words that God has previously impressed upon you. And your heart will leap as the Spirit affirms to you, "The dream is alive."

It may be, as you're seemingly buried in some side cubicle, and nobody knows you work for the company—it may be that somebody you've helped in the past phones the company and gets transferred to you. Someone you've dealt with previously. And as you come on the line, the person suddenly blurts out, "Are you still at that same desk? Are you still doing this job? My goodness, with all of your ability, I'd have thought by now you'd be—." And out of the blue, of all the positions in the company, the caller will pick point B. Even though you've never breathed a word about it to anyone, the person will pick the very position you feel God is taking you to. And in your heart you'll hear God saying, "I'm reminding you of my good intentions."

It could be in the business you've started. You'll come home one day and hit the "play" button on the answering machine. And the recorded voice will say, "Is this phone still taking your messages? With the quality work you do, I would have thought by now you'd be—." And out of the caller's mouth will come a description of the magnitude or volume of business you believe God intends for you.

It could be you're single. And some dear lady will come up to you after church and say, "You know who I think would make a good couple? You and—." And you'll silently say, "Lord, I think so too. Are you telling me something?"

Putting material into quotations also can add interest and intensity to a sermon from a didactic or epistolary section of Scripture. Notice how a message on James 2:1–13 uses dialogue or conversation as it moves into verses 8–11, the third major point:[5]

> There's a third reason, James says, why you should love equally. A third reason why you should love impartially—because it shows your submission to God's Word, that you will obey everything God has said. When you obey this command—the command to love, which is the supreme command—when you obey this greatest of all commands, you show your willingness to obey all of God's commands.
>
> But if we disobey this command, the most important of all commands, we're essentially saying to God, "I don't care what you command; I'm going to do what I want. I don't care what your Word says; I'll break any of your laws if I feel like it or if I think it will serve my purposes." When we break this greatest command—the command to love—we reveal deep down that our heart is not submissive to God and that we will break or transgress any of his laws whenever it suits us.

Use Simple, Familiar Words; Avoid Showing Off Either Through Vocabulary or Alliteration

Keep asking yourself, "How would I say this if I were talking one-on-one to an eleven-year-old?" Whatever words you would use, and however you would put the sentence together, is probably what you want to do in your message.

Listen to the newscasters on television, or the President of the United States when he gives his State of the Union address. The vocabulary is simple; the sentence structures are uncomplicated. They speak in everyday language so that all may easily understand.

Think how much effort it takes for you to figure out the following:

- Compounds of hydrogen and oxygen in the proportion of two to one that are without visible movement invariably tend to flow with profundity.

---

5. See appendix C for the full sermon manuscript of this message.

- Each mass of vapory collection suspended in the firmament has an interior decoration of metallic hue.
- A body of persons abiding in a domicile of silica combined with metallic oxide should not carelessly project small geologic specimens.
- Do not utter loud or passionate vocal expressions because of the accidental overturning of a receptacle containing a whitish, opaque, and nutritive fluid.
- It is pointless to attempt to edify an elderly canine with novel maneuvers.

Halfway through the list you probably figured out that these were common proverbs, which have come down to us in the simple everyday language of:

- Still waters run deep.
- Every cloud has a silver lining.
- People who live in glass houses shouldn't throw stones.
- Don't cry over spilt milk.
- You can't teach an old dog new tricks.

Franklin Roosevelt once got a draft from one of his speechwriters that contained the line, "We are endeavoring to construct a more inclusive society." Roosevelt crossed it out and wrote instead, "We're going to make a country in which no one is left out."

What would you say instead of the following:

- An inextricable predicament
- It behooves us
- We are cognizant of the fact that[6]

How would you say: "The fact is that the love of Christ has been demonstrated toward this individual and this is well documented in the

---

6. Hopefully you'd come up with something like:
   - a no-win situation
   - we ought to
   - we know that

premises set forth in the Holy Scriptures"? The children's song says it this way: "Jesus loves me, this I know, for the Bible tells me so."[7]

One stylistic feature that has enticed preachers through the decades is that of alliteration—using the same letter of the alphabet to convey parallel points in an outline. Speakers imagine this will help the listeners to remember the points.

Apart from the fact that speakers don't remember their own points a week later, there are several dangers in an alliterated outline:

- It may use a word nobody knows and thus be unclear.
- It may change the biblical author's meaning and thus be biblically inaccurate.
- It may highlight the outline more than the central truth and its relevance.
- It may draw more attention to the cleverness of the speaker than to the truth of God's Word.[8]

BE SENSITIVE TO THE EMOTIONAL OVERTONES
OF YOUR LANGUAGE

Some words or phrases, while accurately communicating your concept, may convey negative overtones to your listeners. If you are alert to these, you can give thought to other less offensive, yet equally accurate, ways of stating your thoughts.

For example, as a young pastor of a few months, I found myself in a church board meeting listening to a discussion of whether a Christian academy started by the church five years earlier should be kept under the church's umbrella and oversight, or whether it should separate from the church for the sake of broader financing and enrollment growth. After considerable discussion, the general consensus was to release the academy so that it could serve God more effectively. In order to bring the matter to a proper vote and decision, one of the younger board members made the motion, "I move that the Christian academy split off from the church." Before the chairman could ask for a second to the motion, one of the older board members quickly spoke up: "No, no, Tom, no, that's not what you

---

7. Jacks, *Just Say the Word!* 28.
8. See appendix B for a full discussion of these dangers.

want to move. What you want to move is 'that the church establish the Christian academy as an independent Arizona corporation.'" Tom agreeably rephrased his motion, and it was seconded and passed.

The older board member was wisely sensitive to how the phrase *split off* might sound if read in the board minutes some years later. He recognized that in church circles the word *split* almost always has negative connotations—it's inevitably the result of bitter disagreements and of prideful actions. He wanted language to communicate to future readers that the board's action was harmonious, unanimous, and for the benefit of God's work. "Establishing an independent corporation" was the right language to do this.

A few months later I found myself preparing a message from 1 Samuel 2 on Eli's failure to discipline his sons for their sins at the altar. Because Eli as a parent honored his sons more than he honored God (v. 29), all his descendants would die in the prime of life, and his family's priestly ministry before the Lord would end. I wanted to encourage parents to care more about obeying God than protecting or sheltering their children. As I prepared the message, I wrote, "We must let our children suffer the consequences of their actions." A day later as I was reading over and rehearsing the message, I winced when I came to that sentence. I thought, "No parent wants to see his or her child 'suffer.' People will have an unconscious emotional reaction to that word. How can I say it so they'll be more likely to nod their heads rather than recoil in their hearts?" And I rewrote the sentence, "We must allow our children to experience the consequences of their behavior." "Yes," I thought, "that's better; we're all for 'experiences.'" That way of saying it was just as accurate but did not have negative overtones.

When we tell women they are to *submit* to their husbands, the word seems harsh and demeaning. It has overtones of, "Keep your mouth shut and do what you're told," which is far from the picture presented of godly women in Scripture. How much better to use the English word *yield*,[9] which has positive overtones of, "You may be going the right way, but in order to avoid a 'collision' in the marriage, be prepared to yield. Argue

---

9. The Greek verb *hupotassō* is repeatedly used in the New Testament for a "voluntary yielding in love"—of Jesus to his parents (Luke 2:51), of Christ to God (1 Cor. 15:28), of wives to their husbands (Col. 3:18; Titus 2:5; 1 Peter 3:1, 5), and of us all to godly leaders (1 Cor. 16:16) and to each other (Eph. 5:21).

your case as best as you can with your husband, but ultimately, in order to keep your marriage united and to incline your husband toward God, be ready to yield, trusting God to protect you and your family, even as he deals with your husband's obstinacy."[10]

Even in fairly neutral matters, we can emotionally color our listeners' perceptions by the words we choose. Notice, for example, the emotional overtones that different translations convey by their rendering of a key word in Matthew 14:13:

- "When Jesus heard of it, he departed thence by ship into *a desert place* apart" (KJV). *A desert place* connotes heat, sand, cacti, scorpions—an inhospitable, torturous place.
- "Now when Jesus heard it, He withdrew from there in a boat, to *a lonely place* by Himself" (NASB). *A lonely place* suggests a sad place, a place that affects you adversely, a place you wouldn't want to be.
- "When Jesus heard what had happened, he withdrew by boat privately to *a solitary place*" (NIV). *A solitary place* speaks more to Jesus' purpose—to have time alone with his disciples—than to the physical nature of the location.

Though the NIV translation avoids the negative and inaccurate connotations of the first two renderings, it probably would be even more accurate to describe the site as an "uninhabited place, away from human settlements, a remote out-of-the-way spot where they can have some time to themselves without the press of people."

Over the course of a ministry, the careful choice of words each week will either diminish or increase the joy of a congregation. A speaker who urges his listeners to "*endure* through hardships" may be creating a spirit of defeat. His wording suggests that they are victims, that there's nothing they can do about what's happening to them, and that they should just hope it ends some day.

On the other hand, a speaker who urges his listeners to "*persevere* through hardships" is probably building up their resolve. His wording

---

10. "Yield and trust God" is exactly Peter's point as he urges wives to "put their hope in God" and "not give way to fear," citing the example of Sarah, who "obeyed" Abraham, considering him her "master," even when he was leading unwisely (1 Peter 3:1–6; cf. Gen. 12:10–20; 18:1–15; 20:1–18).

suggests that there's a reason for the ordeal that will be revealed in the end, and that in the meantime they have control over how they approach the situation and a strength that will enable them to triumph.

Writing your message will make you a good speaker. Examining what you have written for how it will strike the ear and the emotions will make you an even better one.

15

Plan for Oral Clarity

AN OLD JOKE HAS A MAN stopping to shake his pastor's hand on the way out of a church service. "Pastor, you're smarter than Einstein!" the man says. The pastor, taken off guard but flattered, thanks Bill for the compliment. Later in the week, however, the pastor begins to think to himself, "I'm not smarter than Einstein. Bill knows I'm not smarter than Einstein. I wonder what he meant?" So, next Sunday, the pastor gets hold of Bill and asks, "Bill, what did you mean last week when you said I was smarter than Einstein?" "Pastor, I heard Einstein was so smart there were only ten people in the world who could understand him!"

Or as a church member once said to another pastor, "Pastor, your preaching is like the peace of God—it passes understanding."

Where does such humor come from? What gives rise to it? Apparently there's an underlying reality that produces such caricatures—the reality that people sometimes have no idea what their pastor is trying to get across. They may understand all the individual words, but the way the sentences or paragraphs connect to each other and how the flow of thought is being developed remains a mystery to them. They simply cannot track clearly with their pastor over an extended period of time.

This inability to follow the pastor is not because people today have shortened attention spans; they can easily track a two-hour movie. Nor is it because pastors are disorganized in their thinking. Pastors who work diligently in preparation usually have some sense in their own mind of what they're trying to accomplish and how the parts fit together.

Then why the problem? The answer lies in the difference between written clarity and oral clarity. All our lives we've been taught to write clearly—that is, to write so that *readers* can clearly follow what we're saying. Our educational system, and especially our English composition courses, has taught us to write for the eye, not for the ear. And because of this training, when pastors write their messages, they unconsciously write so that the material is clear on the printed page.

But when we take what was originally written for the eye and attempt to speak it for the ear, our *listeners* often have difficulty following us. The reason for this is because as soon as we begin to speak orally we lose a lot of "built-in aids to clarity" that were available through the written form.

For example, we lose paragraph indentations, the most powerful built-in aid to clarity in written material. From childhood you've been trained so that, whenever you see white space at the beginning of a line (i.e., a paragraph indentation), your brain automatically signals to you, "You are about to start a new thought." From your years and years of reading, you know that the first sentence after the white space will most likely be a topic sentence—a sentence that will give you the main thought of the whole paragraph. You also know that the lines that follow this first sentence will in some way explain or enlarge upon this main thought. And finally, when you come across another white space at the end of the paragraph, you unconsciously think to yourself, "End of that thought. Get ready for another one."

Even though you haven't yet read a single word of the paragraph, your brain has powerfully and clearly organized a large body of material for you. But what is the equivalent of white space in oral communication? Not a pause—the listeners will think you simply forgot what you wanted to say.

In addition to paragraphs, we lose other built-in aids to clarity that are present in written material. We lose the ability to reread it again if we didn't get it the first time. Many times you've gone over a page several times in order to make sure you clearly understood what the author was saying. But your listeners cannot "rewind you" and play you back again if they had difficulty understanding you the first time.

We lose punctuation—symbols that signal grouping of words (commas), completion of thoughts (periods), explanatory thoughts (colons), and equivalent thoughts (semicolons).

We lose the ability to leave the printed page to look up a word we're unfamiliar with and to find the page in the same place when we return. If your listeners wander from you mentally for a brief period of time, you're not in the same place when they return—you've talked several "paragraphs" ahead, and they're lost.

We lose the ability to distinguish homonyms—words that sound alike but are spelled differently (e.g., rain, reign).

Because oral communication lacks these built-in aids that written communication has, speakers must give special attention to oral clarity. We must consciously *plan* for it by incorporating specific features into our message that will translate into oral clarity when we preach.

We're going to talk about six principles of oral clarity. Not all of the six principles need to be used in every message. But if you summarize them on a three-by-five card and use the card as a checklist for your sermon manuscript, you'll easily discover which ones will help in any given message. The whole process of checking and adjusting your material will not take more than a few minutes of time, but it will make all the difference in your oral clarity.

Your three-by-five card might look something like this:

- Restate critical sentences
- Key language or phrasing
- Rhetorical questions as transitions
- Roman numerals deductive
- Mini-synopsis of verses before reading
- Physical movement

Let's look at each of these more fully.

RESTATE CRITICAL SENTENCES

Two types of sentences in your message are more important, more critical than other sentences—those that communicate the essential *concepts* of the message, and those that reveal the unfolding *structure* of the message. The first type of sentence conveys the major thoughts and ideas of the message—for example, the Roman numerals, significant subpoints, and the take-home truth. The second type helps the listener to organize the material, and arrange the sequence of thought—for example, previews, reviews, and transitions. There are probably fifteen to twenty such crucial sentences within a message.

Concepts
Structure

The first principle of oral clarity is this: whenever you come to one of these key sentences in your message, restate it—immediately say the same thing in different words. Right away, before you go any farther in the message, find other words to get across the same idea. Whenever you speak one of these crucial sentences that either convey a significant concept or reveal the organizational framework, before you say anything else, use different terms to communicate the same thought. (Notice how I just restated this point three times.)

Restatement is not the same thing as repetition. Repetition is saying the exact same thing in the exact same words. Repetition is saying the exact same thing in the exact same words. Restatement is saying the exact same thing in different words. Repetition may be valuable on occasion; restatement is necessary in every message.

Restatement is not the same thing as returning to a particular thought later in the message. Again, returning to a thought may be helpful on occasion. But restatement is immediately saying the same thing, only using different words.

Restatement is finding synonyms for the words and phrases in the original sentence and immediately rephrasing the thought using those synonyms. It's as though the speaker is temporarily "running in place"—giving the listener the same thought three or four times in a row. It's as though the listener is smoothly progressing through the message but then comes to a critical juncture where a yellow light in the road blinks the same sentence several times before letting the listener proceed.

Restating gives the listener's ear more than one chance to grasp those sentences that are critical to the content or structure of the message. Just as the *reader's eye* can go over a page several times in order to be clear, so restatement allows the *listener's ear* to hear something more than once in order to lock onto it. *Readers* highlight crucial sentences with a yellow marker; *speakers* highlight crucial sentences with restatement.

Let's look at some examples.

Exodus 20:12

Introduction[1]

1. Today I want to talk about the fifth commandment—"Honor your father and your mother."

---

1. See pages 148–49 for the full sermon outline.

2. Some of you are thinking, "Oh good, I hope the kids are listening."
3. This commandment, however, was not primarily addressed to children but to a nation of adults gathered at the base of Mount Sinai.
4. We tend to think of the commandment in terms of children because of Paul's words in Ephesians 6:1–3.
    a. Paul tells children to "obey your parents" and cites this commandment.
    b. But Paul's words do not limit "honor" to "obedience." Rather, what Paul is saying is, "When you are a child, this is how 'honor' shows up—through 'obedience.'"
5. *Honor* is a broad, encompassing word, meaning "attach weight to," "hold in high regard," "publicly esteem."
6. This overall meaning, however, shows itself in different specific ways, depending on how old we are.
    a. When we are children, living under our parents' roof, we honor them by obeying them.
    b. But a man "leaves father and mother," a woman transfers her allegiance from her father to her husband, and honor no longer shows itself through obedience.
7. What does honor look like at the other end of life—when our parents are aged—which is what God most of all had in mind when he gave the command to adults at Sinai?
8. The answer is: When our parents are aged, to honor them is to support them financially [*].
9. Let's look at a couple of Scriptures that will show that this is primarily what God had in mind, and then let's consider some specific steps we might take to follow through on it.

While several sentences in the above introduction might be profitably restated, it would be absolutely critical to restate points 8 and 9. Point 8 is the take-home truth; point 9 is the preview that organizes the rest of the message.

Restating point 8 might sound something like this:

> When our parents are aged, to honor them is to support them financially, to assist them economically. When they're in the sunset years of life, when they're on a fixed income, when they can no longer go out and add to their income, to honor them means to make sure they lack for nothing in the way of food, housing, clothing, or anything necessary for a comfortable existence. To honor our parents in their latter years is to be ready to supplement their income in any way that is needed.

Such restatement gives the listener more than one chance to clearly grasp the central truth that is the point of the whole message.

Stating and restating the preview in point 9 might sound something like this:

> This morning I want to do two things. The first thing I want to do is to look at a couple of Scriptures where we will see the word *honor*. We'll see that the word is used in a financial context. And we'll find that when God said, "Honor your father and your mother," more than anything else he meant, "Be ready to support them financially."
>
> And then, after we've looked at a couple of Scriptures, the second thing I want to do is to suggest some specific steps we can take to put it into practice. If we have a heart to do what the Scriptures say, if our thought is, "I may not have known that the Bible was so explicit about it, but I've always felt that's what should be done," then I want to suggest some specific ways we can put it into practice, some concrete actions we can follow through on. I want us to think about three tangible steps we can take to make it happen.[2]

Matthew 7:7–11

Introduction

1. Our Lord encourages us to pray, to ask God for things, and to expect him to give them to us. (Quote Matt. 7:7–8.)

---

2. Notice how the wording of the preview carefully distinguishes the statements, "I want to do *two things*" and "I want to look at a *couple of Scriptures*." If I had carelessly said, "I want to do two things; I want to look at two Scriptures," the listeners might have mistakenly concluded that the "two Scriptures" were the "two things." Using the word "couple" in the second statement avoids this potential confusion.

2. Someone says, "I've tried that; it doesn't work. I asked; God didn't give it to me. I don't buy it."

3. For the sake of that person, and for the sake of all of us who would like to be encouraged in our praying, let's turn to Matthew 7:7–11 and see what Jesus is saying. (Read Matt. 7:7–11.)

Talk-home truth 4. In these verses Jesus is telling us, "Ask, and if it's a good thing, God will give it to you" [*].

Preview 5. In order to be encouraged in our praying, let's see who this is a promise to, and what it's a promise of.

Who is this a promise to?

Transitional I. (This is a promise for genuine children who are trying to please the Father.)[3]

Subpoint idea A. First of all, this is a promise for those who are genuine children of God.

1. Jesus refers to "your Father in heaven."

2. If you have been "born again" through faith in Christ, this promise is for you.

B. But more specifically, this is a promise for those children who are trying to please their Father.

1. This promise occurs toward the end of a lengthy sermon in which Jesus has been describing the behaviors that please the Father.

2. If your desire is to obey God and please him in whatever way you can, this promise is for you.

What is this a promise of?

II. This is a promise that God knows how to give you good gifts even more than you know how to give your children good gifts.

A. You know how to give good gifts to your children—bread, fish.

B. You know how to do this, despite being "evil"—i.e., despite having human imperfections and limitations.

---

3. The parentheses indicate that this particular sentence will not be spoken orally at this point but instead will form itself in the listener's mind after all the subpoints have been presented. See appendix A, guideline 5, for proper outlining.

    C. God, having no imperfections or limitations, knows even more what good gifts to give you.

III. Come, therefore, with all the spontaneity of a child, asking for what you want and expecting that, if it is good for you to have it, your Father will say yes.

In the outline above, point 2 in the introduction already has its brief restatements. But from point 4 in the introduction through I.A in the body of the message, the flow of thought progresses rapidly through four key sentences of *concept* and *structure*:

- Take-home truth (concept)
- Preview (structure)
- Transitional question (structure)
- First subpoint idea (concept)

If the speaker said each of these four key sentences only once, the listener would probably not be able to aurally follow the rapid progression of thought. In print you might be able to follow it, but if you were listening, it would be difficult to catch everything if it came to you in the following form.

> In these verses Jesus is telling us, "Ask, and if it's a good thing, God will give it to you." In order to be encouraged in our praying, let's see who this is a promise to, and what it's a promise of. Who is this a promise to? First of all, this is a promise for those who are genuine children of God. Notice how in verse 11 Jesus refers to "your Father in heaven."

But if instead the speaker restates each of the key sentences several times, the listeners clearly grasp these crucial sentences and absorb both the meaning and movement of the whole message:

In these verses Jesus is saying, "Ask, and if it is good, God will say yes. Ask, and if it is good for you to have it, God will give it to you. Come like children, who spontaneously, effervescently ask for what

> they want, trusting their father's wisdom. You too have a 'Father in heaven' who loves you and is wise. Ask, and if it is good, God will say yes."
>
> Today, in order to be encouraged in our praying, let's see who this is a promise to, and what it's a promise of. Who is Jesus talking to, and what is he saying to them? Who can claim this promise, and what promise can they claim?
>
> First, who is this a promise to? "Ask and it will be given to you"—who's the "you"? "Seek and you will find"—who's the "you"? Who is Jesus talking to?
>
> There's a twofold answer to that question. First of all, he's talking to those who are genuine children of God. He's talking to those who have been "born again" and have become sons and daughters of God. He's talking to those who by faith in Christ have become part of God's family; God is their Father. Notice how in verse 11 he refers to "your Father in heaven."

At this point the message stops progressing swiftly through different concepts; the speaker slows down to explain the text, and restatement is no longer necessary.

In a message on James 2:1–13, notice how the *concept* of point I and the *transition* to point II are restated several times.[4]

> If you are really committed to following Christ, James says, if your belief in Christ is central to your life, and you find yourself in this situation—the influential and insignificant, the attractive and unattractive, the rich and poor are both in your church—if you are really committed to following Christ, you must treat them absolutely the same. [**Restating the concept of point I.**] You must treat them equally, without thought of gain, without regard for benefit you might receive. You must love them impartially, not for what you can get from them. If you are really committed to following Christ, you must not show favoritism.

---

4. See appendix C for the full outline and manuscript of this message.

That's what James stresses in verse 1: "My brothers, as believers in our glorious Lord Jesus Christ, don't show favoritism." Do not pay attention to people based on what they can do for you. Do not treat them differently based on what you might get from them. Be absolutely impartial. Love them equally.

Now why does James stress that? [**Restating the transition to point II.**] Why is it so important that we love impartially, without thought of gain? Why does James want us to be as ready to love the poor man as the rich man, as quick to pay attention to the insignificant as to the influential? Why is it so important that we love impartially?

The value of such restatement is that you not only highlight the importance of what you've just said, but you also add to the listener's understanding of what you just said.

First of all, you highlight the importance of a thought. Saying something more than once calls the listener's attention to the concept and says, "You need to get this!"

But if, while saying something more than once, you simply use the same words each time, your listeners might realize the concept is important but still not understand its meaning. For example, if I point to a clock on the wall and excitedly say to a friend, "That's a lumigal clock. A lumigal clock! It's lumigal!" My friend would probably think to himself, "He sure is hot on that being 'lumigal,' whatever that means." My using the same word doesn't add to my friend's understanding.

But if I use different words—if I restate—I not only indicate the importance of a thought, but I also make it more understandable. So I say, "That's a lumigal clock! It's not plastic; it's lumigal! It's not wood; it's lumigal!" The phrases help my friend grasp my meaning, and he thinks: "Whatever lumigal means, it has to do with material. We're not talking size, we're not talking shape, we're not talking brand name, and we're not talking accuracy. We're talking material—what it's made of."

Restatement—immediately saying the same thing in different words—is God's gift to oral communicators. Of all the six principles we're going to look at, it's the one you'll use in every message.

CONSISTENTLY USE THE SAME KEY LANGUAGE OR PHRASING

In order for a listener to aurally connect the unfolding parts of a message, you need to consistently use the same key language or words or phrasings of any larger unit as you progress through its subunits. This principle—consistently use similar wording—shows up at three different levels in your message: introduction and main points, sequential items in a list, and single paragraphs. Let's look at each of these.

Introduction and Main Points

The key words or phrases that are used early in the introduction (i.e., the engage section) should filter through the rest of the introduction (i.e., the set-the-stage-biblically and preview sections) and into the roman numerals.

In the following sermon outline on Exodus 13:17–22,[5] notice (1) how the key language of "shortest distance between two points is a zigzag" filters through the rest of the introduction and into the Roman numerals, and (2) how the key words in the point 5 preview section—"deliberately," "[reason] why," and "encourage"—reappear in the Roman numerals:

> Introduction
> 1. Early in geometry we learned, "The shortest distance between two points is a straight line."
> 2. But sometimes, as we look at what God is doing in our lives, we wonder if he doesn't think that the shortest distance between two points is a zigzag.
> 3. We find ourselves at some point A, and though we believe God intends to take us to a point B, we seem instead to be headed in the opposite direction, as though on a zigzag path.
>   a. Our career at a company is not moving toward the anticipated point B, but is instead headed in the other direction.
>   b. The business we started is losing ground rather than advancing toward point B.
>   c. The point B of marriage is as far away as it ever was.

---

5. See appendix C for the full outline and manuscript of this message.

        d. We're asked to do things other than the point B ministry we believe we're called to.

    4. Today I want us to see that sometimes, with God, the shortest distance between two points is a zigzag.

    5. I want us to see that sometimes God deliberately leads us on a zigzag path; I want us to see why he does it; and finally I want us to see how he encourages us when we don't seem to be making any progress toward the goal.

    6. In order to see that God sometimes deliberately takes us on a zigzag path, we're going to look at a time in Israel's history when God deliberately leads them on a zigzag path.

    7. Please turn to Exodus 13:17.

I.   God sometimes deliberately takes us on a zigzag path to the good plans he has for us.

II. The reason for this zigzag path is because some obstacle on the straight-line path would keep us from reaching the goal.

III. God keeps us encouraged along this zigzag path by giving us reminders of his good intentions and a tangible sense of his presence.

    A. He encourages us with continual reminders of his good intentions.

    B. He encourages us with a tangible sense of his presence.

Watch what happens in the following abbreviated introduction to a sermon on Psalm 27 when the speaker stops using consistent key language to connect the unfolding sequence of thought.

> In the comic strip *Peanuts*, the character Linus always has to have his security blanket. Linus lives in an insecure world, and he needs security.
>
> We live in an insecure world, and we desire to have security (develop examples).
>
> The psalmists also lived in an insecure world, and they too desired security. In many of the psalms, the psalmist would cry

> out in fear, and God would answer him. Psalm 27 is written after
> one of those experiences.
>
> As we examine Psalm 27:1–3, let's first look at how the psalmist
> views God, and then let's see how this view changed his life.

You easily followed the speaker through the early paragraphs above.
But by the time you reached the end of the last paragraph, you were uncertain what the message would be about. That's because the speaker stopped using the key word *security* to help you connect the unfolding thought.
Note how the following is so much clearer:

> In the comic strip *Peanuts*, the character Linus always has to have
> his security blanket. Linus lives in an insecure world, and he needs
> security.
>
> We live in an insecure world, and we desire to have security (develop examples).
>
> The psalmists also lived in an insecure world, and they too desired security. In many of the psalms, the psalmist would cry out in
> his insecurity, and God would bring him security. Psalm 27 is written after one of those experiences.
>
> As we examine Psalm 27:1–3, let's first look at how the psalmist
> found God as his security, and then see how this security changed
> his approach to life.

The speaker plans for oral clarity by continuing the same key wording
from the engage section through the set-the-stage-biblically and preview
sections.[6]

Here's another example. Notice your jolt of confusion when the first
biblical concept (the last sentence) seems to have no connection to the
introduction:

> Hudson Taylor, the great missionary to China, gave up all his
> rights for the sake of the gospel. He gave up his right to wear Western
> dress; instead he wore the fashions of the people he ministered to. He

---

6. See pages 209–19 for additional examples of using the same key language from the engage section in the set-the-stage-biblically section.

> gave up his right to a Western haircut; instead he shaved the front part of his head and grew the braid that was common among the men of that culture. Hudson Taylor gave up his personal identity, all of his rights, for the sake of the gospel.
>
> What would make someone do that? What would make someone give up his rights for the sake of the gospel? What would make you give up your rights for the sake of your ministry?
>
> The answer to that question is found in 1 Corinthians 9, verses 1–23. Would you turn there please?
>
> The first thing we see in verses 1–6 is Paul's role as an apostle . . .

As a listener you wonder what Paul's role as an apostle has to do with giving up our rights.

The speaker, however, was clear in his own thinking. In his study of the passage, he had noticed Paul's claim to be an apostle and the rights that came with such a position (1 Cor. 9:1–6):

> Am I not free? Am I not an apostle? Have I not seen Jesus our Lord? Are you not the result of my work in the Lord? Even though I may not be an apostle to others, surely I am to you! For you are the seal of my apostleship in the Lord.
>
> This is my defense to those who sit in judgment on me. Don't we have the right to food and drink? Don't we have the right to take a believing wife along with us, as do the other apostles and the Lord's brothers and Cephas? Or is it only I and Barnabas who must work for a living?

Given this correct understanding of the text, instead of transitioning into the first biblical concept with "Paul's *role* as an apostle," it would have been better to use the same consistent language of the introduction—"The first thing we see in verses 1–6 are Paul's *rights* as an apostle." Even better yet, let the Roman numeral convey *truth* rather than *history*. Establish the timeless concept, then go to the text to show where you got it from.

> What would make someone do that? What would make someone give up his rights for the sake of the gospel? What would make you give up your rights for the sake of your ministry?

The answer to that question is found in 1 Corinthians 9, verses 1–23. Would you turn there please?

The first thing we see in verses 1–6 is that we do have rights. As ministers, we have certain rights.

In verses 1–6 Paul says that he as an apostle had certain rights. Let's read what those were . . .

You too have rights. You have the right to . . .

Here's an outline for a message on Judges 7. Again, as it progresses from introduction to Roman numerals, the listener becomes unclear because of an inconsistent use of language.

> Introduction
> 1. There may be times when God will ask you to do something that seems impossible. You feel like you're the last person on earth God should be asking to do that. (Develop examples.)
> 2. Gideon felt God was asking him to do something impossible—to save Israel out of Midian's hand.
> 3. When God asks us to do something impossible, how should we respond?
>
> I. God often puts us in seemingly impossible situations in order to show us his power (Judg. 7:1–8).
>
> II. These impossible situations may cause us to fear, but God will reassure us (Judg. 7:9–14).
>
> III. When God asks us to do something seemingly impossible, we should respond with obedience and anticipate victory (Judg. 7:15–25).

The difficulty is that points I and II don't sound like responses. The use of language is not consistent.

There are two ways to correct this. One way would be to change the Roman numerals so that they sound like responses:

Introduction

1. There may be times when God will ask you to do something that seems impossible.
2. Gideon felt God was asking him to do something impossible.
3. When God asks us to do something impossible, how should we respond?

I. We should look to God rather than ourselves.

II. We should listen for God's reassuring voice.

III. We should obey God and anticipate victory.

While these changes bring consistency and oral clarity, they unfortunately also manipulate the text, changing divine indicatives (*God* desires to show his power; *God* will reassure) into human imperatives (*We* should . . .). This becomes "interrogative-keyword-list" preaching, which does not reflect the exact meaning of the text.[7]

Since the original Roman numerals accurately reflect the text, the second way to correct the outline would be better: change the point 3 preview in the introduction so that it is consistent with the main points:

Introduction

1. There may be times when God will ask you to do something that seems impossible.
2. Gideon felt God was asking him to do something impossible.
3. Today we're going to see why God puts us in these seemingly impossible situations, what he'll do for us in the midst of them, and how we should respond so as to accomplish his purposes.

I. God often put us in seemingly impossible situations in order to show us his power.

---

7. See pages 81–83.

II. These impossible situations may cause us to fear, but God will reassure us.

III. When God asks us to do something impossible, we should respond with obedience and anticipate victory.

When the key words or phrases that are used early in the introduction (i.e., the engage section) filter through the rest of the introduction (i.e., the set-the-stage-biblically and preview sections) and into the Roman numerals, the message becomes orally clear.

Sequential Items in a List

The key words or phrasings that are used to start a list must be used again each time a new item in the list is brought up.

Often one of the hunks or Roman numerals of a message will start a list of some sort. For example, the third hunk of a sermon on Ephesians 5:15–21 seeks to answer the question:[8]

> What does it look like to be filled with the Spirit, with the presence of Christ? How does this filling show up? What do we experience when we are filled with the presence of Christ?[9]

Coming to this third movement or hunk, the speaker then sets up a list of "three things that show up when we are filled with the presence of Christ." This key language—"three things that show up"—becomes the umbrella concept intended to cover all the items in the ensuing list (i.e., the subsequent subpoints). The beginning of point III in the message would correctly sound something like this:

> That brings us to the third question. What does that life look like? How does it show up? When we are filled with the Spirit, with the life of Christ, what do we experience?
>
> The verses that follow tell us three things that show up when we are filled with the presence of Christ. In verses 19, 20, and 21, through

---

8. See pages 232–33 for the full sermon outline.
9. Note the restatement of the preview questions.

> a series of participles, Paul says that when we're filled with the life of Christ, we experience three things—this . . . and this . . . and this.
>
> First, he says, when you're filled with Christ, you experience joy—a joy that bubbles up in some musical way as you find yourself thinking about some spiritual truth. When you're filled with Christ, you have a pervasive happiness. And at different moments you find yourself kind of spontaneously singing or humming some truth of God's Word.[10]

The speaker would then talk for four to six minutes on this first point—explaining, illustrating, and applying how we speak to ourselves in psalms, hymns, and spiritual songs, singing and making melody in our hearts to the Lord (Eph. 5:19).

If the speaker then continued,

"Second, we have contentment . . ."

the listener might think: "'Second' *what*? What are we talking about? What's this list about? I forgot the overall category." Though the speaker is clear in his own mind on what the list is about, the intervening minutes of explanation on the first item have blurred the listener's memory as to the umbrella language that covers *all* the items.

So the speaker must use the same key words or phrases to bring up the next item on the list: *Each time...*

> There's a second thing that shows up when we're filled with the Spirit. There's a second thing you experience when you're filled with the presence of Christ. You experience contentment. You find yourself content, grateful, thankful for all the good things God has given you. Verse 20—you find yourself "always giving thanks to God the Father for everything." Look at it again: it's a pervasive, wide-ranging contentment—"always giving thanks . . . for everything."
>
> When you're filled with Christ, you have this wonderful contentment in life. You don't feel this terrible itch or frustration to

---

10. Notice the restatements of the transitional question in the first paragraph, of the preview in the second paragraph, and of the new concept itself in the third paragraph.

> have something you don't have. You're not bitter, you're not re-
> sentful, you're not envious. You look at what you have, and you're
> grateful and content.

In this way, by repeating the key words—"things we experience when
we are filled"—the speaker keeps the listener clear on what the whole list
is about.

Single Paragraphs   *Old & New Contract*

The key words or phrasings that occur toward the end of one paragraph
should reappear fairly quickly in the next paragraph.

In order for listeners to follow a speaker's train of thought through several paragraphs, they must *aurally* hear some connection in the wording
or language as one paragraph flows into the next. In the example below,
the italicized words highlight the thought-connections of the paragraphs
as language from the end of one paragraph appears fairly early in the suc-
ceeding one:

> Five years ago a man named Timothy McVeigh pressed the but-
> ton on a bomb, a bomb that crushed a nine-story federal building in
> Oklahoma City. He killed nineteen children who were in a day care
> in the building. He killed another 147 people who were working or
> visiting in the building. That was *five years ago.*
>
> *Three months from now,* on May 16, he will be put to *death* by
> chemical injection.
>
> One woman who is glad that Timothy McVeigh is going to *die*
> is Janie Cloverdale, a sixty-three-year-old grandmother. Her two
> grandsons, Elijah and Aaron, ages two and five, were killed in the
> day care that day. She says, "I've got *questions about the death penalty,*
> but not in this case."
>
> But other people do have *questions about the death penalty,* even in
> Oklahoma City, where it happened . . .

The listeners are following your message with their ears. As their ears hear
the same sounds—the same words, the same key phrasings—they are able to
clearly track with you through your introduction into the body of the message, through separate items on a list, and from one paragraph to another.

24v

5 USE RHETORICAL QUESTIONS TO TRANSITION FROM ONE MAJOR MOVEMENT TO THE NEXT

Asking a rhetorical question (i.e., a question you don't expect the listeners to answer out loud) is an effective means of transitioning from one major thought to the next. The listener hears the restated[11] question, and thinks, "I may have become a bit foggy over the last several minutes, but I bet for the next four or five minutes you're going to answer that question, aren't you?" Rhetorical questions help the listener to focus in again, to pick up your train of thought again.

For example, in a sermon on Exodus 13:17–22,[12] after summarizing Roman numeral I, you might ask rhetorical questions as a means of preparing the listener for Roman numeral II:

> So we see that God deliberately takes Israel on a zigzag path. Not the direct, shorter road toward Canaan, but in a southerly direction, toward the Red Sea. Knowingly, purposefully, intentionally, God takes Israel on a zigzag path.
>
> Sometimes God takes our life on an alternate path to his promised destination.
>
> But why does he do that? What's his reason? What's his purpose? What's accomplished by taking us on a roundabout route?

You could likewise use rhetorical questions to transition from point II to point III later in the same message:

> But sometimes this alternate path can be hard on us. We start to lose heart. In the midst of the zigs and zags, as we don't seem to be making any progress toward the goal, we get discouraged. In fact, if our progress is too slow, or if sometimes we seem to be going in the opposite direction, we not only become discouraged, but we even begin to doubt. We begin to doubt there ever was a point B. We begin to think, "Maybe that's not God's goal. Maybe I just imagined it.

24s

---

11. Transitions, as well as summary reviews, are among those crucial structural sentences that need to be restated (see pp. 270–71).
12. See appendix C for the full outline and manuscript of this message.

Maybe I just wanted it so bad I psyched myself into it. Maybe it was just my pipe dream, and not God's destiny."

In the midst of doubt and discouragement, how does God encourage us? How does he sustain us on the way? In the midst of the zigs and zags, when we don't seem to be making any progress, how does God keep us heading expectantly and joyfully toward the goal? How does he keep us moving ahead with faith and stamina?

In the sermon "Honoring Your Father and Mother," restated rhetorical questions would keep the listeners clearly tracking with you as you transitioned from the first major point to the second:[13]

So from the Scriptures we see that when God said, "Honor your father and your mother," more than anything else he meant, "Be ready to support them financially in their latter years."

Now if you and I have a heart to do that, how would we put it into practice? What specific steps could we take? What tangible actions could we follow through on? Let me suggest three—three practical steps we might take.

Asking a question that your next point is going to answer is a great aid to oral clarity.

PRESENT EACH NEW MAIN POINT IN A DEDUCTIVE MANNER, UNLESS ITS SUBUNITS ARE A LIST

As you progress through your message and come to a new major point, present the new hunk deductively[14]—that is, *give full sentences asserting the complete thought* before you go into any discussion of its subpoints. State and restate its full concept before you read any relevant verses or explain any passage details.

---

13. See pages 148–49 for the full sermon outline.
14. This is the third place in a message where the concepts of deduction and induction operate.
    ✓ The first place is at the overall macrostructural level—your introduction either deductively states the take-home truth or inductively raises the topic/question (chap. 8).
    ✓ The second place is in the preview elements—you give the listener an overview of the major hunks that will come in the body of the message (pp. 234–38).

(244)

Speakers sometimes make the mistake of presenting a new Roman numeral inductively—they use a rhetorical question to transition to the new point, but instead of immediately answering the question before they go into the discussion (a deductive approach), they allow the discussion itself to progressively lead up to the answer at the end (an inductive approach). *inductive approach* In other words, the listener goes into the discussion or explanation with a question in mind rather than an assertion.

As a hypothetical example, suppose you hear something like the following:

> What's the first reason you and I should be joyful in trials? What's the first reason we should have a sense of excitement, of anticipation, as we encounter some difficulty? What's the first reason Paul gives?
>
> The answer is found in verses 1–5. Let's look at it.
>
> In verse 1, Paul says he came to Corinth to preach the gospel. He came to this port city—this maritime, commercial center—to bring the message of salvation. He came to this crossroads of the Mediterranean world, through which passed merchants and sailors from every corner of the earth, in order to tell them about a Savior who loved them and gave his life for them.
>
> But verse 2 says that no one welcomed him. No one seemed interested in what he was saying. No one came to hear him . . .

Now stop. What did the speaker say his point was about? Did you have to look at the top of the paragraph to recall it? In the space of nine lines (thirty seconds), did you lose what the main thought was about—the first reason to be joyful in trials?

In an oral presentation of the above, almost everyone in the audience would lose what the new hunk was about during those thirty seconds

---

✓ This is the third place—you choose whether to present a Roman numeral by deductively stating its concept at the start of the discussion or by inductively building to its concept at the end of the discussion.

✓ At the end of this chapter, we'll look at the fourth place—the reading of Scripture verses within the body of the message.

As mentioned previously (p. 235), the essential meaning of the concepts remains the same in all four places: You are *deductive* when you make an *assertion* that will be developed; you are *inductive* when you raise a *question* that will be answered.

because they wouldn't be hearing anything that sounded like an answer to the question. In outline form, what they'd be hearing is:

III. The first reason we should be joyful in trials is given in verses 1–5. [Note: In essence this is not an "assertion," but rather an inductive "question"—What is the first reason given in verses 1–5?]
   A. Paul came to Corinth to preach the gospel.
   B. No one welcomed him.
   C.
   D.

In his own mind, the speaker is clear—he knows he's leading up to the answer. Mentally, he visualizes his flow of thought:

III. The first reason we should be joyful in trials is given in verses 1–5.

~~Sub unit~~ - A. Paul came to Corinth to preach the gospel.
~~Sub unit~~ - B. The trial[15] he faced is that no one welcomed him.
~~Sub unit~~ - C. This trial forced Paul to turn to the Lord.
~~Sub unit~~ - D. Paul rejoiced to learn the Lord's sufficiency.

At the end of the discussion the speaker intends to give the answer— "The reason you should rejoice in trials is because you're going to learn something of the adequacy of your God."

But though the speaker clearly knows where he is heading, the listener does not. At subpoint B, the speaker knows what's coming up through the "pipeline," but the listener cannot penetrate a mental pipeline. All the listener can work with are the words already spoken into the air. And at subpoint B, since none of those words sounds like an answer to the question raised at the start, the listener loses the train of thought.

Instead, the speaker should state and restate the new point deductively, as in the following: *immediately answer to rhetorical question asked...*

---

15. Did you originally understand that subpoint B was the trial, or did the absence of this key word further contribute to the confusion? See pages 278–84.

1.e

> What's the first reason you and I should be joyful in trials? What's the first reason we should have a sense of excitement, of anticipation, as we encounter some difficulty?
>
> The answer is that we should be joyful in trials because that trial is going to reveal something to us about our God. **[Restate]** We should rejoice in trials because we're going to learn something of the adequacy of our God—that he is sufficient for all things. **[Restate]** We should be joyful in trials because we're going to discover that God himself is all we need.
>
> That's what Paul discovered as he faced a trial in Corinth—that God was all he needed. Let's look at verses 1–5 to see that we should rejoice in trials because we are going to learn the adequacy of our God.
>
> In verse 1, Paul says he came to Corinth to preach the gospel. He came to this port city—this maritime, commercial center—to bring the message of salvation. He came to this crossroads of the Mediterranean world, through which passed merchants and sailors from every corner of the earth, in order to tell them about a Savior who loved them and gave his life for them.
>
> But verse 2 says that no one welcomed him. No one seemed interested in what he was saying. No one came to hear him . . .

In this way the new concept is deductively stated and restated at the start of the point, before going into the details of explanation. The listener is then able to clearly understand and integrate the details in light of the larger concept.[16]

This clarity principle of presenting each new main point in a deductive manner should be followed whenever the subunits of the larger point are a progression—that is, whenever the subunits unfold in some unalterable sequence, such as a narrative story or a reasoning chain of thought. The

---

16. The outline would correctly be written as follows:
    I. The first reason we should be joyful in trials is because they reveal the adequacy of our God.
        A. Paul learned the adequacy of God through his trial at Corinth.
            1. He came to Corinth to preach the gospel.
            2. He faced a trial of hostility and indifference.
            3. This trial forced him to turn to the Lord.
            4. He rejoiced to learn the Lord's sufficiency.
        B. We too can rejoice in our trials, knowing they will reveal the adequacy of our God.

tip-off that such a progression or sequence is occurring is that only the last subunit will contain the same key phrasing as the larger concept, the main point.

In the example above, the subunits are a narrative chain, and only the last subunit (D) contains the same language as the main point—"joyful/ rejoice."

Occasionally the subunits of a main point will be a list—all the subunits will have the same language as the larger concept, their sequence could be changed without logical or narrative damage, and there is an obvious "counting" through the subunits.

For example, a Roman numeral might instead have content such as:

III. Why should we be joyful in trials?
   A. We should be joyful in trials because they develop perseverance.
   B. We should be joyful in trials because they prompt the kindness and compassion of other believers toward us.
   C. We should be joyful in trials because they reveal the adequacy of our God.

In the above, the subunits are a list—an enumeration of parallel (not progressive) concepts, all containing the same language as the larger concept ("joyful in trials"), the order of which can be reversed or interchanged without disrupting the flow of thought.

When the subunits are a list such as this, it would be more natural to present the new main point in an inductive manner—that is, let the discussion cumulatively build toward the complete thought at the end: "We should be joyful in trials because they develop perseverance, prompt kindness and compassion from others, and reveal the adequacy of our God." This inductive approach—asking a question at the start of the movement, and then allowing the subsequent subunits to progressively unfold the complete answer—will sustain greater interest than if you deductively give away all the subunit answers at the start of the point.[17]

---

17. The outline would be correctly written as follows (see appendix A, guideline 5, for proper outlining):

   Transition: Why should we be joyful in trials?
   I. (We should be joyful in trials because they develop perseverance, prompt kindness and compassion from other believers, and reveal the adequacy of our God.)

There's one exception to the above discussion. It is possible to present a progression in an inductive manner *if you immediately preview* the progression that will take you to the answer. In other words, you would ask a question and then immediately give an overview of the coming subunits that will eventually lead to the full answer.

Using the example above, it might sound something like this:

What's the first reason you and I should be joyful in trials? What's the first reason we should have a sense of excitement, of anticipation, as we encounter some difficulty?

The next few verses will give us the answer. We'll see that Paul came to Corinth to preach the gospel. We'll see a trial he encounters, and what that forces him to do. And then we'll see why he finds joy in that trial. And from his experience we'll learn the first reason why we can rejoice in trials.

Let's look at verses 1–5 to see this. Notice in verse 1 that Paul came to Corinth to preach the gospel . . .[18]

The following chart is a helpful checklist for whenever you find yourself asking a question during any part of your message.

WHEN YOU ASK A QUESTION

Whenever you ask a question (whether in the introduction or as an internal transition from one major point to the next), the next few sentences immediately following the question must do one or another of the following:

    A. We should be joyful in trials because they develop perseverance.
    B. We should be joyful in trials because they prompt the kindness and compassion of other believers toward us.
    C. We should be joyful in trials because they will reveal the adequacy of our God.

18. Previewing a progression is essentially what makes a macro-inductive structure work. See the similar discussion on pages 229–30, point 4: When your sermon's macrostructural pattern is inductive, and you have a single question setting up a progression of main points, you must have a preview in the introduction in order to be clear. While this inductive progression works easily at the macrostructural level, it seems cumbersome at the Roman numeral level. In the example above, the deductive progression seems preferable.

- The next few sentences must give *a partial answer* to the question.

  If the subunits that answer the question are a list, you can leave it as an inductive question, since the language of the first subunit will sound like a clear partial answer to the question.

- The next few sentences must give *the full answer* to the question.

  If the subunits that follow are a progression, you need to immediately provide the full answer to the question, creating a deductive statement at the start of the discussion. This statement will invariably contain the language of the last subunit in the progression.

- The next few sentences must give *a preview of the progression* that will take you to the answer.

  If the subunits that follow are a progression, you may leave it as an inductive question if you preview the path that will eventually lead to the answer.

GIVE A MINI-SYNOPSIS OF THE POINT OF ANY VERSES BEFORE YOU READ THEM

During your message, when you come to some verses that you intend to read, first give a mini-synopsis, or summary, of what the listener will learn in the reading. State and restate the point of the verses *before* you read them.[19]

This is the fourth place[20] at which either induction or deduction operates in a message. In this case, before reading any verses, you should first

---

19. I'm not referring to the Scripture reading, which may occur earlier in the worship service or before the start of the message, but rather to those internal spots during the unfolding message when you wish to read the next verse(s) that will advance the message.
20. See footnote 14 of this chapter, pages 288–89, for a summary of the four places.

make several deductive statements about what the listener can expect to find in the reading.

Speakers frequently make the mistake of inductively asking a question and then expecting the listener to pick out the answer while the speaker reads some verses. It often sounds like this:

> What else does Paul have to say about temptation? What else can we learn about temptation? Let's read verses 11–16 to find out.

Some conscientious listeners will make a valiant attempt to discover the answer from the reading, but most will go mentally blank within a verse or two, saying to themselves, "He's going to tell me what it says anyway when he finishes, so why should I try to figure it out from the reading?"

Further, the fact that many speakers read poorly, not having practiced the reading out loud beforehand, soon leads listeners to adopt the mental attitude in church, "I can't ever get anything out of the Bible from reading it, which is why I don't try to have devotions at home."

A final drawback to this "figure-it-out-while-I-read-it" approach is that when the speaker finally gives the answer or concept after the reading is finished, the listeners' understanding of the answer is divorced from the text. They didn't see the answer during the reading; they only heard it after the reading. And their faith is now in the words of the speaker rather than in the words of Scripture.

But if the speaker states and restates the point of the verses before he reads them, the listeners are encouraged to look for that clearly asserted concept in the reading. They experience satisfaction in perceiving the point in the reading, and they are able to visually connect the concept with the actual words in the verses.

Stating and restating the point before you read will sound something like the following:

> When are we most vulnerable to temptation? When is it most likely to strike us?
>
> In verses 11–16 Paul goes on to say that we are most vulnerable to temptation right after a spiritual victory. Right after we have done something significant for God, we are most likely to be lifted up with pride, and Satan has an entry. That's what happened to him, he says.

> Right after he preached, and hundreds responded, he found himself vulnerable to Satan's attack.
>   Let's read verses 11–16 to see how we are most vulnerable to temptation right after a spiritual victory . . .

When you read, only read as many verses as your immediate next point is going to address. Save reading the subsequent verses for when you come to their spot in the message.[21]

USE PHYSICAL MOVEMENTS TO MARK OFF MAJOR UNITS OR CONCEPTS IN THE MESSAGE

Your physical gestures and bodily movements can greatly aid your oral clarity. By the direction you turn your face, or the steps you take, you can visualize the hunks of a message.

For example, imagine how the physical movements in the parenthetical descriptions below, along with the restatements, would combine to clearly preview the coming three hunks in a message on Exodus 13:17–22.[22]

> Today I want us to see that sometimes God does indeed take us on an alternate path to reach his intended destination. Sometimes, with God, the shortest distance between two points is a zigzag.
>   (*The speaker looks to his right or takes a few steps in that direction.*) I want us to see that God sometimes deliberately takes us on a zigzag path. Knowingly, intentionally, purposefully he takes our lives on an alternate route.
>   (*Looking to the middle or stepping back to the center of the speaking area.*) I want us to see why he does this—what's his reason, what's his purpose, what's he trying to accomplish?
>   (*The speaker faces his left or takes a few steps in that direction.*) And then, finally, how does he keep us encouraged? How does he sustain us on the way? In the midst of the zigs and zags, when we don't seem to be making any progress, how does God keep us moving expectantly and joyfully toward the goal?

---

21. The sample sermons in appendix C illustrate how the verse hunks are progressively read as the message unfolds.
22. See appendix C for the full outline and manuscript of this message.

> (*Returning to the speaker's right so that the discussion of point I physically coincides with the above placing of the first preview element.*) In order to see that God deliberately takes us on a zigzag route, we're going to turn to a time in Israel's history when he deliberately takes them on a zigzag path. Israel is at point A . . .

In the example above, the speaker could actually step a few feet in each direction, restating the appropriate preview element several times at each spot.

In a message on Matthew 7:7–11, the speaker would probably stand in the center of the speaking area and simply turn his face back and forth as he alternated his hand motions to emphasize the preview restatements:

> In these verses Jesus is saying, "Ask, and if it is good, God will say yes. Ask, and if it is good for you to have it, God will give it to you. Come like children, who spontaneously, effervescently ask for what they want, trusting their father's wisdom. You too have a Father in heaven who loves you and is wise. Ask. If it is good, God will say yes."
>
> Today, in order to be encouraged in our praying, (*the speaker faces his right*) let's see who this is a promise to, and (*the speaker faces his left*) what it's a promise of. (*Facing right*) Who is Jesus talking to, and (*facing left*) what is he saying to them? (*Facing right*) Who can claim this promise, and (*facing left*) what promise can they claim?
>
> First (*facing right, motioning to the physical spot where the first preview element was placed each time, and restating*), who is this a promise to? "Ask and it will be given to you." Who's the "you"? "Seek and you will find." Who's the "you"? Who is Jesus talking to?

It's important that all physical movements or gestures be done from the standpoint of how the listener would view them—which means in most cases they should move or advance from the listener's left to the listener's right, the natural way a listener would count, read, or move forward in time.

You as a speaker must remember just the opposite: all progressions, sequences, time lines, numbers, or lists should move from your right to your left.

For example, here are the opening paragraphs to a message on Exodus 13:17–22, with the movements from the speaker's right to left in parentheses.[23]

Early in geometry we learned that "the shortest distance between two points is a straight line." That means, if I'm at point A *(take a few steps to the speaker's right, establish the spot as point A)* and I want to get to point B *(then turn and motion toward a point B on the opposite side of the stage; this establishes point A on the listener's left, with point B on the listener's right)*, the shortest distance between these two points will be a straight line *(stride across the stage from point A to point B, listener's left to listener's right)*.

Well *(walk back to point A)*, that may be true in geometry, but when you and I think about what God is doing with our lives, we wonder if God doesn't think that "the shortest distance between two points is a zigzag." By that I mean, we're at point A, and we sense that God is taking us to point B *(from the point A spot, face and repeatedly gesture toward point B)*—that's his will for our lives, that's what the Spirit of God has affirmed to our hearts, that's the dream, that's the vision. And as far as we're concerned, the shortest distance between where we are and where we believe God is taking us is a straight line. But if God's taking us there, he must think the shortest distance is a zigzag.

For example, *(standing at the point A spot)* maybe you've just started working for a certain company in an entry-level position. But as you think and pray about your future with the company, *(face the point B spot)* you get some sense of what God's plans may be. Somehow in your mind you sense that God may take you to that corner office on the second floor *(point to an office on the second floor of point B)*, with the windows and a gold nameplate on the door. Something inside you says, "That's where I'm going to end up someday."

Now, in your mind, the shortest distance between your entry-level position and the second floor office is a straight line. It goes something like this *(take a couple of steps in the direction of point B, stop)*: You get assigned to some project that is central to what the company

---

23. See appendix C for the full outline and manuscript of this message.

does. You do well. As a result, *(take another couple of steps in the direction of point B, stop)* you're put in charge of a certain task force that's working on another project. And again you do well—bringing it in under budget and on time. *(Take another couple of steps.)* This good track record brings you to the attention of the decision-makers in the company, and you get labeled as a comer, someone to watch, on the fast track. And the higher-ups begin moving you around to different positions so that you gain experience with the whole operation. And then, when the corner office becomes vacant, *(take the last few steps, arriving at point B, on the listener's far right)* you're the natural choice for it. A nice straight line.

But if God is taking you there, he's on a strange path. Because *(go back to point A)* instead of getting assigned to something central to what the company does, you got assigned to something peripheral *(face or step to the speaker's right to simulate losing ground rather than advancing)*. Instead of coming to the attention of the decision-makers, *(move further to the speaker's right to suggest regression away from point B)* you're in some side cubicle, and nobody knows you even work for the company.[24]

If you fail to make your movements or gestures from the standpoint of the listeners—from their left to their right—you'll end up, in their eyes, with the past and future reversed (you'll have put historical events on your left and "eternity" on your right), with maps drawn backward (you'll have started Abraham's travels from Ur with your right hand moving toward your left), and with ascending graphs rising in the wrong direction (you'll have "invested in a stock when it was low and watched it climb" from your left to your right).

These six principles of oral clarity will enable you to take your message from the printed page, which is read by the eye, and send it into a live auditorium, where ears are ready to hear and hearts are ready to respond.

---

24. Additional contemporary situations could be probed, each one similarly paced off to contrast the "zigzag" from the expected straight line—starting a business, wanting to be married, desiring a particular ministry.

– 16 –
Deliver with Freedom

PERIODICALLY, IN CLASS OR AT A seminar, I involve students or pastors in a fun exercise. I place a three-by-five card upside down in front of about fifteen different people. Each card has a number on it, the name of a biblical character, and a passage of Scripture that describes that character in some action or situation. Examples of such cards are:

1. Zacchaeus meeting Jesus (Luke 19:1–6)
2. Peter walking on water (Matt. 14:28–31)
3. David slaying Goliath (1 Sam. 17:38–51)
4. One of the disciples participating in the feeding of the multitude (Mark 6:35–43)
5. Woman with a hemorrhage approaching Jesus (Mark 5:25–34)

I tell those who have received the cards that when we return after a brief break, they are to pantomime or charade the person on the card, doing the action described. Simply by their movements and expressions, without using any words, they are to act out the scene in such a way that we can guess who their character is.

The following fifteen to twenty minutes are a riot, as each person creatively and humorously mimes the character and the event. The others in the room uproariously shout out the biblical names as each presenter finishes.

When it's all over and I return to the front of the class or seminar, I suggest three things that they learned from the exercise.

First, they see how much information can be communicated without any words—emotions, character, actions, physical objects, and so on.

Second, they see how interesting it is when the speaker is alive, moving, animated.

Third, they see that *they* can do it! They can move, bend, raise their arms, hug their stomachs, or simulate climbing, rowing, slinging, or marching. They can be animated and alive and move with natural freedom.

My goal in the exercise is to break past the objection, "It's not my personality to be expressive and move around." Most of us have grown up with a mental image of a speaker standing relatively immobile behind a podium, continually referring to notes while he speaks. We therefore expect that when our time comes to speak, that's what we'll do as well. And if someone tries to get us to do something different—walk away from the podium, or act out some part of our message—our objection is, "That's not my personality." But it *is* our personality—God made every one of us to act naturally and joyfully and freely.

If someone in the room still doubts—even after the exercise with the three-by-five cards—that "animated moving" is their personality, I might point to him and say, "If I asked your wife, 'When does your husband talk loud, move fast, or get excited?' what would she say? She'd say, 'Oh, you ought to see him when—' Finish the sentence for us. What would she say?" And inevitably the one I point to will sheepishly offer some situation in which he erupts or explodes or moves with abandonment: "She'd say 'when he's watching a ball game,' or 'when someone cuts him off on the freeway,' or 'when he's wrestling with the kids' or—" We're all naturally spontaneous and expressive.

The question is not, "Is it our personality?" The question is, "What's preventing our real personality from coming out while we preach? What's stopping or hindering the real us from showing up while we speak?"

And the answer is: We're copying generations of bad models. We've spent decades watching other speakers in church, and Satan has gotten it into our heads, "Be natural everywhere else in life, but don't be the real you in church—people might listen."

The simple truth is, there's no communication advantage to standing immobile behind a box. The large podium box actually interferes with your communication. It impedes your arm motions, hides you from the listeners, and somehow mysteriously causes your feet to grow roots into the ground. Talk-show hosts do not come out and do their monologues behind a box; awards presenters on TV do not stand behind a box; the best campaign speeches are not given behind a box. There's no communication advantage to standing behind a box.

"But I need a place for my notes," someone says. And the gentle reply to that is, "Why do you need notes? Why not learn your message well enough so that you can deliver it without notes—speaking directly and continuously to the listeners, without a single break in eye contact, with no lapse of energy and enthusiasm?"

Do we visualize Peter with notes on the Day of Pentecost? Paul with notes on Mars Hill? Would we go to a contemporary drama where the actors on stage used notes to help them remember their lines? Of course not.

I'm not suggesting that you memorize your message. But I am suggesting that if you have a clear outline, have worked on your wording, and have gone over the message several times—out loud, so that you have internalized it and become comfortable with it—then you *will* be able to deliver it freely without notes. And you will find that 80 to 90 percent of the words you wrote easily come to mind as you speak.[1]

Will this take extra work and preparation on your part? Yes. Writing it out and going over it out loud several times will add some hours of preparation. But God has created and called the real you to present his eternal truth, and he and his people are worth your best.

Here are several practical suggestions:

- To develop greater freedom in delivery, rehearse in front of a mirror. This gives you an audience—you, the person in the mirror—to speak directly and urgently to and helps you see your level of energy and animation. As you watch yourself in the mirror, add intensity and expressiveness until you like what the mirror is doing.
- Any opportunity to watch yourself on video also will reveal ways to make your delivery even more effective.

---

1. Becoming more alive and animated in delivery will actually help you to remember your words more easily. Research psychologists are discovering that gesturing while speaking helps us to remember what we intended to say and frees us to speak more easily. People talking on cell phones gesture even though the person they're talking to can't see them. Even blind people gesture with their hands while talking to other blind listeners. There's something about having our whole body naturally involved that makes our communication more effective.

- When the time comes to speak, walk purposefully to the front of the room. Pause. Smile briefly as your eyes take in the whole room, as if to say, "I'm glad I'm here. I'm glad you're here. I have something good to say to you."
- Rather than standing behind a large box, arrange for a small music stand, or stool, to be slightly to one side, as a place for your Bible when you're not holding it or using it. Keep the music stand close enough to you so that you can easily lift the Bible from it, always conveying that the Scriptures are central to your message.
- Thoroughly know your two opening and closing paragraphs. If there are any sentences that you want to come out exactly as you intend, it's these. By speaking confidently and distinctly at the start, you convey to your listeners that you're prepared and know exactly what you want to say. You also subconsciously send a signal to yourself—"I'm off to a good start"—that helps you to relax and enjoy the rest of the message. And finishing well gives both you and the listeners the satisfying sense that you've accomplished what you set out to do.

Preach accurately, clearly, relevantly, and energetically. And when you are finished, each heart will whisper, "Look at what God has said to us!"

– Appendix A –

Outlining Procedures

IN ORDER TO DEVELOP GOOD outlines that result in clear and unified messages, you must follow certain essential guidelines.

1. ESTABLISH ALL OF THE ROMAN NUMERALS BEFORE YOU WORRY ABOUT ANY SUBORDINATE LEVELS IN THE OUTLINE

First get all your big hunks, your broad strokes. Once these are determined, then add the next level throughout the outline—the capital letters. After these first two levels are established, you can then fill in the rest of the subordinate levels in any order you wish.

Speakers sometimes make the mistake of putting down one Roman numeral, then one capital, and then stringing out several more indentations, without knowing what the next big hunk is going to be. Instead of creating the outline "from the top, down," they make the mistake of creating it "from the side, in."

I.
  A.
    1.
      a.
        i.
        ii.

When they run out of things to say in this long streak, they then take a "flying squirrel leap" back to Roman numeral II without any sense of how the material connects.

Anchor yourself first to all of the big hunks before you go into the smaller units. This will ensure the necessary unity of the passage and the connections of the parts to each other.

2. DISTINGUISH SUPERIOR, SUBORDINATE, AND COORDINATE IDEAS FROM EACH OTHER

Main ideas are superior to their subpoints. They summarize the content and include all the verses of their subordinate points. They are umbrellas that cover everything under them.

Incorrect

    I.   Hardships come unexpectedly (v. 5).
        A. Hardships develop godliness (vv. 6–7).
        B. Persecution develops trust (v. 6).
        C. Uncertainty develops patience (v. 7).

Correct

Book Theme	*Common Heading	Text Ref	Main item	Titles / Complete Thoughts

    I.   Hardships come unexpectedly (v. 5). *(titles / complete thoughts)*

    II. Hardships develop godliness (vv. 6–7).
        A. Persecution develops trust (v. 6). *supporting details*
        B. Uncertainty develops patience (v. 7). *from verses that make up complete thought*

If an idea supports another idea, it is a subordinate idea. Each subordinate idea should directly and logically amplify, explain, illustrate, or apply the larger heading beneath which it stands.

Coordinate ideas are ideas of equal weight or importance that support the same larger heading.

(Note: Any sequence of either time or logical progression can occur only at coordinate levels. When you tell what comes next, do not move to a subordinate level. Remain at the same coordinate one, or else go to the next superior level for the new unit of thought.)

Incorrect

   I. Abraham journeyed with Isaac to the top of the mountain (Gen. 22:3–8).
      A. Next, Abraham built an altar and put Isaac on it (v. 9).
      B. Next, Abraham took a knife to slay his son (v. 10).

Correct

   I. Abraham journeyed with Isaac to the top of the mountain (vv. 3–8).
      A. He took two servants and wood (v. 3).
      B. He made the servants stay below (vv. 4–5).
      C. He climbed the mountain with his son (vv. 6–8).

   II. Abraham prepared to sacrifice his son (vv. 9–10).
      A. He built an altar and put Isaac on it (v. 9).
      B. He took a knife to slay his son (v. 10).

3. USE CONSISTENT SYMBOLS

While the choice of outline symbols is arbitrary, custom has established the following general use: Arabic numerals and small letters are used in the introduction and conclusion; Roman numerals and capital letters are reserved for main points in the body of the message:

   Introduction
       1.
          a.
          b.
      2.
      3.

   I.
     A.
       1.
       2.

a.
b.
    i.
    ii.
B.
C.

II.
A.
B.

Conclusion
1.
2.

4. WRITE FULL, COMPLETE SENTENCES FOR ALL POINTS IN THE OUTLINE

An effective outline deals with whole ideas, full truths, complete assertions, not phrases or fragments or questions. Each point in the outline, at whatever level of subordination, and including illustrations, should be a grammatically complete sentence.

A title or phrase outline is not sufficient. The outline should do more than label the verses (e.g., "Promises") or give the topics discussed without stating what is actually said about them (e.g., "The Work of God"). Such outlining lacks the necessary assertions that turn points into ideas.

Watch out for complete sentences that are really no better than a phrase since they express no actual content about the topic. They are content-less.

Incorrect: Paul discusses the work of God.
Correct: The work of God began in eternity past.

Incorrect: Two features of genuine obedience are described.
Correct: Genuine obedience is voluntary and thorough.

If an outline point is an example or illustration, the full-sentence statement should show the purpose and point of the illustration:

Incorrect:	The story of the yellow bird.
Correct:	The story of the yellow bird proves (purpose) we cannot live free without some restrictions (point).

Incorrect:	Going off to college.
Correct:	The mixture of emotions when you go off to college is an example (purpose) of how you can feel fear and excitement at the same time (point).

5. AVOID QUESTIONS AS OUTLINE POINTS

Each outline point should be a declarative or imperative sentence, not a question.

A question is not an idea; it is a *transition* to an idea.

Sometimes in oral communication the speaker will lead into a new major unit with a transitional question, such as, "We've looked at man's power and seen that it is harsh and ignorant. Now let's look at God's power. *How does God's power differ from man's? What is God's power like?*"

This transitional question should not be written as the outline point.

II. What is God's power like?
   A. Loving
   B. Wise

While the speaker would undoubtedly be clear in such a short example, in longer or larger examples, the lack of an "idea" at the main point level makes it too easy for imprecision and vagueness to creep in.

To ensure clarity of thought, you should make a practice of outlining as follows:

- If you intend to immediately provide *the full answer* to the transitional question, then write the outline so that a grammatically complete sentence appears in the Roman numeral:

Transition: What is God's power like?

II. God's power is loving and wise.
   A. God's power is loving.
   B. God's power is wise.

- If you intend to immediately provide *only the first subpoint answer* to the transitional question, with the remaining subpoints building cumulatively to the complete answer, then put the Roman numeral point in parentheses.

Transition: What is God's power like?
II. (God's power is loving and wise.)
   A. God's power is loving.
   B. God's power is wise.

- The parentheses indicate that this particular sentence will not be heard aurally at this point but instead will be formed in the listener's mind after all the subpoints have been presented. The parentheses signal that the speaker will take an inductive approach to the material. (See the several discussions of deduction and induction in the chapters.)

The Dangers of Alliteration

WOODY HAYES, LEGENDARY FOOTBALL coach at Ohio State (1951–1978), ran an offense that the sportswriters dubbed "three yards and a cloud of dust." When asked, "Woody, why don't you ever throw a forward pass?" Hayes replied, "Three things can happen when you throw a forward pass, and two of them are bad."

In that same vein, I would like to suggest: "Four things can happen when you alliterate, and four of them are bad."

Alliteration, in ordinary writing, is the literary device of repeating the same initial sound or letter several times in rather close succession (e.g. "conspicuous consumption," "nattering nabobs of negativism").

In homiletics, alliteration is most frequently used to convey the major outline points of a sermon.

There are times, of course, when alliteration is appropriate and effective in preaching. Succinct and accurate words can crisply communicate the concepts of a *short* outline—for example, "Today we're going to look at the *cause* and the *cure* of our problem." (Note—"crisply communicate the concepts," a serendipity.)

But when a sermon outline extends to multiple main points, the use of alliteration runs the risk of four bad things.

- It may use a word nobody knows and thus be unclear.
- It may change the original author's meaning and thus be biblically inaccurate.
- It may highlight the outline more than the central truth and its relevance.

- It may draw more attention to the cleverness of the speaker than to the truth of God's Word.

First, alliteration may cause the speaker to use a word nobody knows and thus to be unclear. In order to sustain the same alphabet letter, the speaker searches his thesaurus. Unfortunately, the only word that accurately conveys his concept is a word few of his listeners are familiar with:

A PERSPECTIVE ON PRAYER

   I.   The purpose of prayer
  II.   The power of prayer
 III.   The perspicacity of prayer

The speaker may be accurate to the text, but he is unclear to the listener.

Second, alliteration runs the danger of changing the author's meaning. If the speaker resolves to alliterate with only familiar words, he may find himself finessing or manipulating the true meaning of the text in order to remain intelligible to the listener. The speaker may be clear, but now he is biblically inaccurate.

CHARACTERISTICS OF A LEADER
(1 Samuel 17:17–51)

    I.   Cooperative (17:17–24)
   II.   Curious (17:25–27)
  III.   Consistent (17:28–30)
  IV.   Courageous (17:31–37)
   V.   Careful (17:38–40)
  VI.   Confident (17:41–47)
 VII.   Conclusive (17:48–51)

"Cooperative," "consistent," and "careful" do not accurately reflect what is happening in the text. "Obedient," "persistent," and "wise" come closer to describing David's actions in those verses.

Worse than changing the meaning of a small paragraph within the text, alliteration sometimes violates the author's entire flow of thought as the speaker turns the biblical progression of ideas into an artificial list of parallel points.

It is doubtful that the author of 1 Samuel said to himself as he came to chapter 17, "I will now write about the seven characteristics of leadership." Such an approach to preaching is far from the intent of the author—namely, showing that a young man from the tribe of Judah, believing the covenant promises of God, finishes the task God gave his tribe by removing the "uncircumcised" from "Gath," thus qualifying himself for leadership among God's people.

Alliterated list preaching not only violates the author's theological intent but also inevitably presents supposed "truths" that are easily contradicted elsewhere in Scripture. Abundant examples could be found of biblical leaders who are uncooperative (Peter refusing the Sanhedrin), inconsistent (Joshua changing strategy at Ai), fearful (Gideon preparing for the Midianites), and rash (Jonathan charging the Philistine outpost).

Alliteration runs a third danger. Not only may it lead the speaker to be unclear or unbiblical, but it also suggests to the listeners that the most important thing in the message to remember is the outline. It subtly says to the listeners, "Get this outline! Remember it!"

But what the listeners really need to "get" is the central truth and its relevance for their lives. They should walk away from the message, not with an outline, but with an awareness of how a biblical truth bears on their lives. Their minds should be engaged, not with "points," but with how they, in some concrete way, are going to think or act differently as a result of their time with God.

Worse yet, the alliterated outline, which has been unwisely highlighted, all too often is content-less—it communicates no content. If the listeners do manage to remember the points, they still doesn't *know* anything.

PREACHING THE GOSPEL

I. The process for preaching
II. The practice in preaching
III. The product of preaching

Taken from 1 Thessalonians 1:4–8, the speaker's message conveys the following thoughts:

- When preaching the gospel, we must remember that God elects and the power of the Spirit saves.

- We must practice what we preach.
- The gospel cuts through human suffering, causing joy and growth.

But none of these thoughts are accessible by remembering the outline. The alliterated outline terms are unnecessary "middlemen" that the listeners must mentally jump over in order to form the concepts in their minds.

If remembering the outline is important, a nonalliterated, content-full set of points (i.e., in complete declarative sentences) would be more effective:

PREACHING THE GOSPEL

I. We don't need to sell it.
II. But we must live it.
III. It will change lives.

The final bad thing that can happen when we alliterate is that the listeners' attention may be drawn more to our cuteness and cleverness than to the truth of God's Word. They may appreciate our skill more than they absorb God's message.

The words of an ancient divine still ring true: "No man can at one and the same time give the impression that he is clever and that Christ is mighty to save."

Alliteration? We could say:

- It misproffers.
- It misleads.
- It misdirects.
- It mishonors.

But it seems better to say:

- It may be unclear.
- It may be unbiblical.
- It may highlight the outline more than the truth.
- It may draw attention to the cleverness of the speaker.

– Appendix C –
Sample Sermons

HERE ARE TWO SAMPLE SERMONS (with outlines)—one from an Old Testament narrative and one from a New Testament epistle.

These sermon manuscripts reflect how they would be preached orally—with repetitions, sentence fragments, and other conversational features.[1]

Each sermon appears first in an uninterrupted form, so that you can "hear it" as a message from God's Word. Then it appears a second time with bracketed bold-print insertions identifying the use of specific homiletical features, along with any page numbers where these may be discussed in the book.

THE SHORTEST DISTANCE BETWEEN TWO POINTS IS A ZIGZAG

Exodus 13:17–22 *Wrap*

Outline

Introduction

Engage 1. Early in geometry we learned, "The shortest distance between two points is a straight line."

contradiction 2. But sometimes, as we look at what God is doing in our lives, we wonder if he doesn't think that the shortest distance between two points is a zigzag.

---

1. All of these would be deleted if the sermon were to be made available in written form.

(handwritten: Restat) 3. We find ourselves at some point A, and though we believe God intends to take us to a point B, we seem instead to be headed in the opposite direction, as though on a zigzag path.

(handwritten: what does it look like) a. Our career at a company is not moving toward the anticipated point B but instead is headed in the other direction.

(handwritten: ") b. The business we started is losing ground rather than advancing toward point B.

(handwritten: ") c. The point B of marriage is as far away as it ever was.

(handwritten: ") d. We're asked to do things other than the point B ministry we believe we're called to.

(handwritten: THT + Restate) 4. Today I want us to see that sometimes, with God, the shortest distance between two points is a zigzag.

(handwritten: Preview (deductive) restate) 5. I want us to see that sometimes God deliberately leads us on a zigzag path; I want us to see why he does it; and finally I want us to see how he encourages us when we don't seem to be making any progress toward the goal.

(handwritten: Preview (inductive) restate) 6. In order to see that God sometimes deliberately takes us on a zigzag path, we're going to look at a time in Israel's history when God deliberately leads them on a zigzag path.

(handwritten: Set the stage Biblically) a. The ten plagues have devastated Egypt; Pharaoh capitulates; Israel prepares to exit Egypt.

b. Israel could get from Egypt (point A) to Canaan (point B) in eight to ten days, following a straight-line path.

c. But instead God deliberately leads them on a zigzag path in the opposite direction.

(handwritten: Announce Passage) 7. Please turn to Exodus 13:17.

(handwritten: Mini - synopsis + Rhetorical transition)

(handwritten: Topic (passage)) I. God sometimes deliberately takes us on a zigzag path to the good plans he has for us. *(handwritten: (main point progression - restate))*

(handwritten: time (passage) Timeless) A. God purposefully takes Israel from Goshen to Canaan by an indirect route (13:17–18). *(handwritten: (mini - synopsis) (summary of Restate, Told Home truth))*

B. He does the same for us. *(handwritten: (Restate, Told Home truth))*

(handwritten: what does it look like? THT what does it look like? THT what does it look like? what does it look like?)

II. The reason for this zigzag path is because some obstacle on the straight-line path would keep us from reaching the goal.

   A. The reason God takes Israel on a zigzag path is because they would encounter war on the straight-line path and would never reach their destination (13:17).

      1. The war might be from Egyptian defenses along the trade route or from the Philistines as Israel went through their territory.

      2. God knows that his people, facing war without military skills, would return to Egypt instead of continuing to Canaan.

      3. God first must take his people into the desert to convince them of his faithfulness and commitment before taking them into Canaan.

   B. The reason God sometimes takes us on a zigzag path is because some obstacle along the direct route would prevent us from ever reaching the goal.

      1. Our career advancement might be delayed until a difficult person is removed or necessary skills are learned.

      2. Our company might not grow until we're past the danger of becoming a workaholic or materially focused.

      3. Marriage might be put off until past issues no longer threaten a stable and long-lasting relationship.

      4. Ministry opportunities might wait until pride is less of a danger.

III. (God keeps us encouraged along this zigzag path by giving us reminders of his good intentions and a tangible sense of his presence.)[2]

---

2. The parentheses indicate that this sentence will not be spoken orally at this point but instead will form itself in the listener's mind as its two subpoints progressively emerge. See appendix A, guideline 5, for proper outlining. This inductive handling of point III works because III.A and III.B are a list (see pp. 288–94).

    The subunits of point III could have been outlined differently. Instead of grouping both "Israel and us" under each individual concept (III.A and III.B), as above, I could have handled both concepts ("intentions" and "presence") together, first under "Israel" and then under "us." Viz:

III. God encourages us with reminders of his good intentions and a tangible sense of his presence.

A. God encourages us with continual reminders of his good
   intentions.

   1. Someone's off-hand comment may remind us of God's
      good intentions.[3]

      a. Someone at another company might wonder why
         we're not yet in the "point B" office.

      b. A client might be amazed that the business we started
         is not yet doing a "point B" volume of business.

      c. A woman in church might comment that we and
         some "point B" person would make a nice couple.

      d. A spiritual leader might predict that someday we'll be
         serving the Lord doing "point B."

   2. Joseph's coffin reminded Israel of God's good intentions
      (13:19).

      a. Years earlier Joseph made Israel promise they would
         take his bones to Canaan when they left Egypt (Gen.
         50:24–26).

      b. The coffin is a reminder that God will eventually take
         them into the land he's promised them.

B. God encourages us with a tangible sense of his presence.

   1. The column of cloud represents God's tangible presence
      with Israel.

      a. Through this cloud, God leads them on the unchart-
         ed journey (13:20–22).

A. God encourages Israel with reminders of his good intentions and a tangible sense of
   his presence.
   1. Joseph's coffin reminds Israel of God's good intentions.
   2. The column of cloud represents God's tangible presence.
B. God encourages us with reminders of his good intentions and a tangible sense of his
   presence.
   1. Someone's off-hand comment may remind us of God's good intentions.
   2. During our zigs and zags, God will encourage us with a tangible, palpable sense
      of his presence.

The former way of grouping the material—both "Israel and us" under each individual
concept—is almost always preferable since it keeps each concept's application more closely
attached to its explanation. The latter grouping would inevitably require you to remind the
listeners of previous material as you return to apply a concept explained considerably earlier.

3. For variety's sake, I reverse the normal sequence of explanation/application under III.A and
   instead give the contemporary applications before explaining the biblical details.

          i. As they leave Succoth, they enter uncharted desert territory.

          ii. A column of cloud, capable of becoming luminescent at night, gives them around-the-clock direction and visibility for their travels.

          iii. The cloud remains with them until they finally cross the Jordan River into the Promised Land (point B).

      b. Through this cloud God protects them from the Egyptians (Exod. 14:19–20) and from the burning sun (Psalm 105:39).

      c. Through this cloud God speaks to them (Exod. 19:16–19).

(*truth*) 2. During our zigs and zags, God will encourage us with a tangible, palpable sense of his presence.

Conclusion

    1. God sometimes leads us on an alternate path to get to the promised destination.

    2. Sometimes the shortest distance between two points is a zigzag.

    3. Follow him without fear; you can never be harmed by God.

Sermon

Early in geometry we learned that "the shortest distance between two points is a straight line." That means, if I'm at point A and I want to get to point B, the shortest distance between these two points is a straight line.

Now that may be true in geometry, but as you and I think about what God is doing in our lives, we wonder if God doesn't think that "the shortest distance between two points is a zigzag." And by that I mean, we're at point A, and we sense that God intends to take us to point B—that's his will for our life, that's the dream, that's the vision, that's what the Spirit of God has affirmed to our heart. And as far as we're concerned, the shortest distance between where we are and where we believe God is taking us is a straight line. But if God *is* taking us there, he must think the shortest distance is a zigzag.

For example, you may have just started an entry-level job at a particular company. As you think about your future with the company, you sense that someday God may have you in that corner office on the second floor—the one with the windows and the gold nameplate on the door. Something in your heart says, "That's where I'm going to end up some day; that's the position I'm eventually going to have in this company." And in your mind, the shortest distance between your entry-level job and the second-floor office is a straight line. It goes something like this:

- You get assigned to some project that's central to what the company does. You do well.
- As a result, the next time you're put in charge of a different task force working on another major project. You finish the project on time and under budget.
- This good track record brings you to the attention of the decision-makers in the company. They label you as a comer, someone to watch, someone who's on the fast track for promotion.
- The higher-ups start moving you around to different positions so that you can gain experience with the whole operation.
- And then, when that corner office becomes vacant, you're the natural choice for it.

That's the route you visualize—a nice straight line.

But if God is taking you there, he's on a strange path. Because instead of being assigned to something central to what the company does, you got assigned to something peripheral to the company's operations. Instead of coming to the attention of the decision-makers, you're stuck in some side cubicle, and nobody even knows you work for the company.

Maybe you've started a business, and your business is at point A. But as you think about the growth of your business, the Spirit of God gives you a mental picture of point B—a certain volume, a certain size of your company. For you, the shortest distance between your start-up business and point B would be a straight line. It might look something like this:

- You win the bid on some small project, and you make a decent profit.

- Because of that profit, you hire another worker and are able to successfully bid on a larger project.
- The two of you continue to do well, and soon you find yourself hiring more people and bidding on larger jobs. You're also buying more trucks and stocking larger inventory.
- And it's not too long before you find yourself at point B, bidding on county or government projects.

But if God is taking you there, he seems to be on an alternate route, because instead of making a profit on that first project, you lost money. And instead of hiring somebody to work with you, you've had to let your part-time secretary go, and now a machine is answering your phone.

For you, point A may be "single" and point B is "married." That's what God seems to be witnessing to your heart—that you're going to be married. Now the shortest distance from point A "single" to point B "married" goes something like this:

- An attractive eligible person visits your church.
- After the service that person is invited to join the rest of the singles for lunch at a local restaurant. You sit next to the visitor at lunch, and the two of you thoroughly enjoy the conversation and laughter. You hope your new friend will show up again next week.
- Your friend does. But this time, as the singles talk about where to go for lunch, the two of you quietly decide, "Why don't we go to lunch by ourselves somewhere else?" And before you leave after that second lunch, you've made a date for Friday night.
- Many Friday (and weekday) dates have occurred since then. You've made the obligatory visit to meet each other's parents and to pass inspection.
- Finally, you show up in the pastor's office, "Pastor, this coming June 19, Saturday, at two o'clock—we hope you have the date open." Tum-tum-de-dum. Here comes the bride.

There it is—a nice straight line.

But if God is taking you there, he's on a very erratic path, because romantic possibilities are coming and going, and coming and going, mostly going.

For you, point B may be something you want to do for the Lord. As you think about your future and what you can do to serve God, you see yourself in a certain ministry for the Lord. The shortest distance to that point is:

- Your church asks you to do something in that area.
- You enjoy doing it, and you do it well.
- God's people are blessed, and the leaders ask you to do it again.
- Soon you're put in charge of that particular ministry. Maybe you're even full time.
- You get some additional biblical training to help you, and there you are—serving the Lord in this area, point B.

But if God is taking you there, he doesn't seem to be moving in a straight-line path. Because instead of being asked to do something in the area you wanted, you were asked to do something in an area you weren't interested in or good at. You reluctantly agreed because of the need, and you did the best you could. But it didn't come out well, and the leadership never asked you to do anything again.

Today I want us to see that sometimes God does indeed take us on an alternate path to reach his intended destination. Sometimes, with God, the shortest distance between two points is a zigzag.

I want us to see that God sometimes *deliberately* takes us on a zigzag path. Knowingly, intentionally, purposefully he takes our lives on an alternate route. I want us to see *why* he does this—what's his reason, what's his purpose, what's he trying to accomplish? And then, finally, how does he keep us *encouraged*? How does he sustain us on the way? In the midst of the zigs and zags, when we don't seem to be making any progress, how does God keep us moving expectantly and joyfully toward the goal?

In order to see that God deliberately takes us on a zigzag route, we're going to turn to a time in Israel's history when he deliberately takes them on a zigzag path. Israel is at point A. They know what point B is. And they know for sure that God's going to take them there. Yet God purposely, deliberately takes them in the opposite direction.

Point A for them is the land of Goshen in Egypt, where they've been slaves for four hundred years. Pharaoh has just capitulated. The ten plagues have decimated Egypt. Wailing and mourning echo through the land because of the death of the firstborn. Pharaoh gives up. "Get out! Leave! Go!" he says to Moses.

Israel rendezvous in the land of Goshen, point A. Point B is Canaan, Palestine, *the Promised Land.* There's no question that's their destiny. That's where Abraham, Isaac, and Jacob are buried. That's the goal. That's where God is going to take them.

Now the shortest distance between point A, Goshen, and point B, Canaan, is a relatively straight line—an international trade route that goes from Goshen, along the Mediterranean seacoast, through Philistine territory, and into Canaan. Israel can get from point A to point B in eight to ten days following that international highway—a straight line.

But instead, God takes them in the opposite direction. Let's turn to Exodus 13:17, where we'll see God deliberately taking Israel on a zigzag path. Exodus 13:17.

In Exodus 13:17–18 we read that God deliberately takes Israel on a zigzag path, heading them in the opposite direction:

> When Pharaoh let the people go, God did not lead them on the road through the Philistine country, though that was shorter. For God said, "If they face war, they might change their minds and return to Egypt." So God led the people around by the desert road toward the Red Sea. The Israelites went up out of Egypt armed for battle.

God deliberately takes them on a zigzag path. Not the direct, shorter road toward Canaan, but in a southerly direction, toward the Red Sea. Knowingly, purposefully, intentionally, God takes Israel on a zigzag path.

Sometimes God takes our lives on an alternate path to his promised destination.

But why does he do that? What's his reason? What's his purpose? What's accomplished by taking us on a roundabout route?

The answer is, God sometimes takes us on a zigzag path because he knows if he took us on the straight-line route, we'd never make it. There's something in the straight-line path that would stop us from getting to point B. God, in his wisdom, takes us on an alternate route because it's the only sure way to reach our destination.

In Israel's case, there was some fighting, or "war," on the straight-line path that would prevent them from making it to Canaan. Notice verse 17 again: *"When Pharaoh let the people go, God did not lead them on the road through the Philistine country, though that was shorter. For God said, 'If they face war, they might change their minds and return to Egypt.'"*

The Scripture doesn't specify what this "war" is. It could be Egyptian defenses along the direct route, because the international trade route also was the international invasion route. Egypt's enemies to the north—Syria, Nineveh, Babylon—would invade along that same route, and Egypt had built fortifications to repel them. Or the reference could be to the "warlike" Philistines, through whose territory Israel would have to pass. One way or another, God knows there's some obstacle along the straight-line path that would prevent his people from ever reaching their destination.

God says, "My people are not ready for war. They have no military skills; they've been slaves for four hundred years. They have no social cohesion, no political organization. Their organizational chart is: Moses—two million! If I were to take them on that straight-line path, they would encounter something they're not yet prepared for, and they'd never make it to the goal. They'd instead go back to point A."

God says, "I need to take them south, into an isolated, desert area. I need to take them to a spot where I can teach them some things and prepare them for their entry into Canaan.

"They need to know, first of all, that they can count on me, that I will provide everything they need. I'll let them exhaust all their food in the desert. And then when they say, 'Unless the God who brought us out here is with us, we will die,' I'll show them that I am with them. I'll rain down a waferlike flake, something they've never seen before. They'll pick it up, look at it, taste it with the tip of their tongue, and say, 'Manna'—in Hebrew 'man-hu,' which means, 'What is it?' And then they'll realize I can provide for them in ways they'd never expect. And when they see me do it again and again and again, they'll know that they can always count on me.

"They also need to see that they are no longer a nation of slaves but instead the most favored nation that has ever existed. They're going to be my treasured possession. I will speak words to them—words of wisdom and life—words that no other nation has ever heard. They will be the most envied people on earth. They will possess the oracles of truth.

"And, finally, I need to develop their military skills. I need to teach them the art of warfare. But I will do it through skirmishes with the Amalekites, with Bedouin tribes, rather than have them face trained armies. And then, when my people are ready, I'll take them into Canaan."

My friend, sometimes God knows there's something in the straight-line path that would stop us from ever reaching our destination, some obstacle that would prevent us from ever getting there. And in his wisdom he takes us on an alternate path in order to safely get us to the goal.

In the company you've joined, God may keep you under the radar until a disgruntled older worker who would be envious of your rapid promotion and determined to sabotage your advancement is transferred or retired. Or God may keep you in place for a while so that you can hone critical skills or develop key networking connections that will help you succeed in the new responsibility. And thus God wisely and lovingly takes you on a zigzag path to protect you from failure and prepare you for the future.

In the business you've started, it may be God knows if he took you to point B in a fast, straight-line way, it would require so many extra hours from you that, at this stage in your family's life, your kids would suffer or foolish financial decisions would be made. Somehow keeping you on the alternate path enables you to have the hours at home, to be involved in family activities, to cement a lifetime of care for your children, and to gradually learn how to responsibly handle the extra income.

If you're single, it may be that God knows the person he's bringing to you is not quite ready yet. That person needs a little more time to work out a few things, to resolve some issues, so that when the marriage comes together, it's secure and joyful instead of troubled and tentative.

Perhaps God knows that if you were too quickly given a prominent role in ministry, you would be vulnerable to pride and a domineering spirit. And if God's people reacted adversely and harshly to you, you might never consider any ministry again.

God in his wisdom knows there's something in the straight-line path that would prevent us from ever reaching the intended destination. And he lovingly leads us on an alternate route, because that's the only safe, sure way to get there. The shortest distance between two points is a zigzag.

But sometimes this can be hard on us. We start to lose heart. In the midst of the zigs and zags, as we don't seem to be making any progress toward the goal, we get discouraged. In fact, if our progress is too slow or if we sometimes seem to be going in the opposite direction, we not only become discouraged, but we even begin to doubt. We begin to doubt there ever was a point B. We begin to think, "Maybe that's not God's goal. Maybe I just imagined it. Maybe I just wanted it so badly I psyched myself into it. Maybe it was just my pipe dream and not God's destiny."

In the midst of doubt and discouragement, how does God encourage us? How does he sustain us on the way? In the midst of the zigs and zags, when we don't seem to be making any progress, how does God keep us heading expectantly and joyfully toward the goal? How does he keep us moving ahead with faith and stamina?

The Scripture says there are two things he will do for us, two things he will give us, two things that will keep us encouraged and pressing ahead.

The first thing, the Scripture says, is that if the dream is of God, then God will give us continual reminders of his good intention. If the destiny is of God, if point B is of God, then God will find ways of coming to you and letting you know that he's still taking you to his promised destination. Perhaps someone out of the blue—someone who doesn't know what God has put in your heart—perhaps that someone will say something to you. Not knowing your dream, the person won't realize the significance of what he or she is saying, but in that person's words you'll hear God's voice reminding you of his good intentions. The person will use the exact words that God has previously impressed upon you. And your heart will leap as the Spirit affirms to you, "The dream is alive."

It may be, as you're seemingly buried in some side cubicle, and nobody knows you work for the company—it may be that somebody you've helped in the past phones the company and gets transferred to you. Someone you've dealt with previously. And as you come on the line, the person suddenly blurts out, "Are you still at that same desk? Are you still doing this job? My goodness, with all of your ability, I'd have thought by now you'd be—." And out of the blue, of all the positions in the company, the caller will pick point B. Even though you've never breathed a word about it to anyone, the person will pick the very position you feel God is taking you to. And in your heart you'll hear God saying, "I'm reminding you of my good intentions."

It could be in the business you've started. You'll come home one day and hit the "play" button on the answering machine. And the recorded voice will say, "Is this phone still taking your messages? With the quality work you do, I would have thought by now you'd be—." And out of the caller's mouth will come a description of the magnitude or volume of business you believe God intends for you.

It could be you're single. And some dear lady will come up to you after church and say, "You know who I think would make a good couple? You and—." And you'll silently say, "Lord, I think so too. Are you telling me something?"

It may be that as you faithfully serve God in whatever ways are open to you, that some wise and discerning leader might comment to you, "You know, you don't really seem to be suited to this particular ministry. Have you ever considered—?" And that one will identify the very ministry you feel God has called you to.

God's first promise is that he will give you reminders of his good intentions.

In Israel's history, his reminder to them is a coffin, a sarcophagus. We learn this through a very strange note that appears as God begins to take them on the zigzag path. We read in verse 19 that as Israel went up out of Egypt,

> *Moses took the bones of Joseph with him because Joseph had made the sons of Israel swear an oath. He had said, "God will surely come to your aid, and then you must carry my bones up with you from this place."*

Israel takes with them the coffin that contains the bones of Joseph. Before he died four hundred years earlier, Joseph had made the sons of Israel swear an oath that they would not leave his body in Egypt.[4] More than four hundred years earlier Joseph was the first to enter that land, sold into slavery by his brothers. He lived to become the number two ruler in the land and to see his father and brothers come under his protection. Soon seventy people came and joined him in Egypt. By the time Joseph died, those seventy had grown to two or three hundred.

And on his deathbed, with those two to three hundred gathered around him, Joseph says to them: "Some day God's going to come to the aid of our people. This is not our home. God's going to take us out of Egypt. He's going to take us back to the Land of Promise. He's going to put us where our ancestors are buried. And when he does, don't leave me here in Egypt. Swear to me that you'll take my bones with you. Swear to me that when

---

4. Genesis 50:24–25.

the day comes that God takes you out of Egypt, you'll take my bones with you. I want to be buried in Canaan with Abraham, Isaac, and Jacob."

Now, four hundred years later, those two to three hundred have grown to two million. And now, as they are getting ready to leave Egypt, several strong men lift the coffin containing the bones of Joseph. And as they head south toward the Red Sea, the coffin leads the way.

And I can hear some little kid turn to his mother and say, "Why are those men carrying that box?" "That's not a box, honey. That's a coffin." "What's a coffin?" "Well, it has the bones of a dead man in it." "Oh— gross! But why are we taking it with us?" "Well, honey, we're taking it to Canaan." "But we're not headed to Canaan." "Yes we are—Yes we are. That coffin's going to Canaan."

Every day as they started the march, no matter where the zigs and zags led them, the coffin was a continual reminder that God was taking them to point B. That coffin was going to Canaan.

My friend, in the midst of the zigs and zags, if the dream is of God, every so often, out of the blue, by someone's words, or by something you read, or by thoughts that come in the night, God will give you a reminder of his good intentions. That's the first thing he says he'll do.

The second thing he says is that he will also give you a tangible sense of his presence. You will have a palpable sense of God's nearness, God's protection, God's guidance. The closeness of God, his being a part of your family—you'll feel it and sense it like you've never felt it before.

In Israel's journey this palpable presence took the form of a column of cloud. It came into their national existence as soon as they stepped out of Egypt. And it stayed with them in a tangible way until they arrived at Canaan. And then it left them.

They described what came to them as *"a pillar of cloud"*—some opaque, swirling, dense mass of shimmering whiteness—a "cloud column" that stretched into the sky. At night, it looked as if there was a fire inside of it. It glowed, it became luminescent, so that it was as visible at night as it was in the day. It was the presence of their God, and it stayed with them on the zigs and zags until they crossed the Jordan River and entered Canaan. And then it was gone.

We read of this tangible symbol of God's presence beginning in verse 20: *"After leaving Succoth they camped at Etham."* Where's Etham? It's *"on the edge of the desert."* What does that mean? It means Etham wasn't the end of the world, but you could see the end of the world from Etham. When they left Etham, they were leaving civilization. They were going out into the trackless desert. No maps. No Thomas Brothers guides. No Global Positioning System. They were going where people don't go.

And as they stepped into nothingness, the tangible, visible, palpable sense of God's presence came into their lives. Look at it in verses 21–22:

> *By day the LORD went ahead of them in a pillar of cloud to guide them on their way and by night in a pillar of fire to give them light, so that they could travel by day or night. Neither the pillar of cloud by day nor the pillar of fire by night left its place in front of the people.*

During all their zigs and zags, whether by day or by night, their God was visibly and tangibly present with them as at no other time in their nation's history. The cloud never left its place in front of the people.

That cloud was their God leading them, guiding them. When it moved, they moved—"Roll up the sleeping bags; pull up the tents. We're on our way!"

That cloud was also their God protecting them, sheltering them. When Pharaoh decided to chase after them, when Israel looked in one direction to see the charging chariots and in the other direction to see an impassible sea, when they feared for their lives—then they saw the cloud insert itself between them and the chariots.[5] The horses couldn't penetrate the dense opaqueness. Then the sea split open, and they walked through. When they were all on dry land on the other side, the cloud lifted. The horses and chariots charged into the water, but the waters returned to cover them. Israel's God was protecting them.

The Bible also says that the cloud protected them or sheltered them when they got out into the heat of the desert. The cloud would invert itself and become a shade canopy against the heat of the sun.[6]

And, finally, it was through that cloud that their God talked to them. When they got to Sinai, that cloud shrouded Mount Sinai. And from it

---

5. Exodus 14:19–20.
6. Psalm 105:39.

came the voice of their God, speaking directly and specifically to them, telling them exactly what he wanted them to know.[7]

My friend, in the midst of the zigs and zags, there will be a tangible, palpable sense of God's presence, a nearness of God, a sense of "You're guiding me, you're protecting me, and your Spirit is telling me what you want me to know."

God in his goodness sometimes leads us on an alternate path to get to the promised destination. Sometimes the shortest distance between two points is a zigzag, because that's the only way to get there. Along the way God gives us reminders of his good intentions and a tangible sense of his presence.

Follow him without fear. You can never be harmed by God.

Homiletical Features ~ i.e p.88

Early in geometry we learned that "the shortest distance between two points is a straight line." That means, if I'm at point A and I want to get to point B, the shortest distance between these two points is a straight line.

Now that may be true in geometry, but [engage, contradiction, 193–99] as you and I think about what God is doing in our lives, we wonder if God doesn't think that "the shortest distance between two points is a zigzag." And by that I mean, we're at point A, and we sense that God intends to take us to point B—that's his "will" for our life [restate, 270–77], that's the dream, that's the vision, that's what the Spirit of God has affirmed to our heart. And as far as we're concerned, the shortest distance between where we are and where we believe God is taking us is a straight line. But if God *is* taking us there, he must think the shortest distance is a zigzag.

For example [what does it look like, 106–12], you may have just started an entry-level job at a particular company. As you think about your future with the company, you sense that someday God may have you in that corner office on the second floor—the one with the windows and the gold nameplate on the door. Something in your heart says, "That's where I'm going to end up some day; that's the position I'm eventually going to have in this company." And in your mind, the shortest distance between your entry-level job and the second-floor office is a straight line. It goes something like this [physical movement, 296–99]:

---

7. Exodus 19:9, 16–19.

- You get assigned to some project that's central to what the company does. You do well.
- As a result, the next time you're put in charge of a different task force working on another major project. You finish the project on time and under budget.
- This good track record brings you to the attention of the decision-makers in the company. They label you as a comer, someone to watch, someone who's on the fast track for promotion.
- The higher-ups start moving you around to different positions so that you can gain experience with the whole operation.
- And then, when that corner office becomes vacant, you're the natural choice for it.

That's the route you visualize—a nice straight line.

But if God is taking you there, he's on a strange path. Because instead of being assigned to something central to what the company does, you got assigned to something peripheral to the company's operations. Instead of coming to the attention of the decision-makers, you're stuck in some side cubicle, and nobody even knows you work for the company.

Maybe [what does it look like, 106–12] you've started a business, and your business is at point A. But as you think about the growth of your business, the Spirit of God gives you a mental picture of point B—a certain volume, a certain size of your company. For you, the shortest distance between your start-up business and point B would be a straight line. It might look something like this [physical movement, 296–99]:

- You win the bid on some small project, and you make a decent profit.
- Because of that profit, you hire another worker and are able to successfully bid on a larger project.
- The two of you continue to do well, and soon you find yourself hiring more people and bidding on larger jobs. You're also buying more trucks and stocking larger inventory.
- And it's not too long before you find yourself at point B, bidding on county or government projects.

But if God is taking you there, he seems to be on an alternate route, because instead of making a profit on that first project, you lost money. And instead of hiring somebody to work with you, you've had to let your part-time secretary go, and now a machine is answering your phone.

For you [**what does it look like, 106–12**], point A may be "single" and point B is "married." That's what God seems to be witnessing to your heart—that you're going to be married. Now the shortest distance from point A "single" to point B "married" goes something like this [**physical movement, 296–99**]:

- An attractive eligible person visits your church.
- After the service that person is invited to join the rest of the singles for lunch at a local restaurant. You sit next to the visitor at lunch, and the two of you thoroughly enjoy the conversation and laughter. You hope your new friend will show up again next week.
- Your friend does. But this time, as the singles talk about where to go for lunch, the two of you quietly decide, "Why don't we go to lunch by ourselves somewhere else?" And before you leave after that second lunch, you've made a date for Friday night.
- Many Friday (and weekday) dates have occurred since then. You've made the obligatory visit to meet each other's parents and to pass inspection.
- Finally, you show up in the pastor's office, "Pastor, this coming June 19, Saturday, at two o'clock—we hope you have the date open." Tum-tum-de-dum. Here comes the bride.

There it is—a nice straight line.

But if God is taking you there, he's on a very erratic path, because romantic possibilities are coming and going, and coming and going, mostly going.

For you [**what does it look like, 106–12**], point B may be something you want to do for the Lord. As you think about your future and what you can do to serve God, you see yourself in a certain ministry for the Lord. The shortest distance to that point is [**physical movement, 296–99**]:

- Your church asks you to do something in that area.
- You enjoy doing it, and you do it well.
- God's people are blessed, and the leaders ask you to do it again.

- Soon you're put in charge of that particular ministry. Maybe you're even full time.
- You get some additional biblical training to help you, and there you are—serving the Lord in this area, point B.

But if God is taking you there, he doesn't seem to be moving in a straight-line path. Because instead of being asked to do something in the area you wanted, you were asked to do something in an area you weren't interested in or good at. You reluctantly agreed because of the need, and you did the best you could. But it didn't come out well, and the leadership never asked you to do anything again.

Today I want us to see that [**focus: take-home truth, 65–83, 199–205; macro-deductive structure, 143–50**] sometimes God does indeed take us on an alternate path to reach his intended destination. [**restate, 270–77**] Sometimes, with God, the shortest distance between two points is a zigzag.

[**preview, 221–24; preview #2, 225–29**] I want us to see [**deductive preview, 234–38**] that God sometimes *deliberately* takes us on a zigzag path. [**restate, 270–77**] Knowingly, intentionally, purposefully he takes our lives on an alternate route. I want us to see [**inductive preview, 234–38**] *why* he does this—[**restate, 270–77**] what's his reason, what's his purpose, what's he trying to accomplish? And then, finally [**inductive preview, 234–38**], how does he keep us *encouraged*? [**restate, 270–77**] How does he sustain us on the way? In the midst of the zigs and zags, when we don't seem to be making any progress, how does God keep us moving expectantly and joyfully toward the goal?

[**physical movement, 296–99**] In order to see that God [**same phrasing as preview, 278–84**] deliberately takes us on a zigzag route, we're going to turn to a time in Israel's history when he deliberately takes them on a zigzag path. [**set the stage biblically, 205–20**] Israel is at point A. They know what point B is. And they know for sure that God's going to take them there. Yet God purposely, deliberately takes them in the opposite direction.

Point A for them is the land of Goshen in Egypt, where they've been slaves for four hundred years. Pharaoh has just capitulated. The ten plagues have decimated Egypt. Wailing and mourning echo through the land because of the death of the firstborn. Pharaoh gives up. "Get out! Leave! Go!" he says to Moses.

Israel rendezvous in the land of Goshen, point A. Point B is Canaan, Palestine, *the Promised Land*. There's no question that's their destiny. That's where Abraham, Isaac, and Jacob are buried. [restate, 270–77] That's the goal. That's where God is going to take them.

Now the shortest distance between point A, Goshen, and point B, Canaan, is a relatively straight line—an international trade route that goes from Goshen, along the Mediterranean seacoast, through Philistine territory, and into Canaan. Israel can get from point A to point B in eight to ten days following that international highway—a straight line.

But instead, God takes them in the opposite direction. Let's turn to Exodus 13:17 where we'll see God deliberately taking Israel on a zigzag path. Exodus 13:17. [announce passage, repeat, wait, 238–41]

In Exodus 13:17–18 [mini-synopsis, only next verses, 294–96] we read that God deliberately takes Israel on a zigzag path, heading them in the opposite direction:

> *When Pharaoh let the people go, God did not lead them on the road through the Philistine country, though that was shorter. For God said, "If they face war, they might change their minds and return to Egypt." So God led the people around by the desert road toward the Red Sea. The Israelites went up out of Egypt armed for battle.*

God deliberately takes them on a zigzag path. Not the direct, shorter road toward Canaan, but in a southerly direction, toward the Red Sea. Knowingly, purposefully, intentionally, God takes Israel on a zigzag path.

Sometimes God takes our lives on an alternate path to his promised destination.

[rhetorical question transition, 287–88] But why does he do that? [restate, 270–77] What's his reason? [same key phrasing as preview, 278–84] What's his purpose? What's accomplished by taking us on a roundabout route?

The answer is [main point deductive, progression, 288–94], God sometimes takes us on a zigzag path because he knows if he took us on the straight-line route, we'd never make it. [restate, 270–77] There's something in the straight-line path that would stop us from getting to point B.

[take-home truth, 65–83] God, in his wisdom, takes us on an alternate route because it's the only sure way to reach our destination.

In Israel's case [mini-synopsis, 294–96], there was some fighting, or "war," on the straight-line path that would prevent them from making it to Canaan. Notice verse 17 again: *"When Pharaoh let the people go, God did not lead them on the road through the Philistine country, though that was shorter. For God said, 'If they face war, they might change their minds and return to Egypt.'"*

The Scripture doesn't specify what this "war" is. It could be Egyptian defenses along the direct route, because the international trade route also was the international invasion route. Egypt's enemies to the north—Syria, Nineveh, Babylon—would invade along that same route, and Egypt had built fortifications to repel them. Or the reference could be to the "war-like" Philistines, through whose territory Israel would have to pass. One way or another, God knows there's some obstacle along the straight-line path that would prevent his people from ever reaching their destination.

God says, "My people are not ready for war. They have no military skills; they've been slaves for four hundred years. They have no social cohesion, no political organization. Their organizational chart is: Moses—two million! If I were to take them on that straight-line path, they would encounter something they're not yet prepared for, and they'd never make it to the goal. They'd instead go back to point A."

God says, "I need to take them south, into an isolated, desert area. I need to take them to a spot where I can teach them some things and prepare them for their entry into Canaan.

"They need to know, first of all, that they can count on me, that I will provide everything they need. I'll let them exhaust all their food in the desert. And then when they say, 'Unless the God who brought us out here is with us, we will die,' I'll show them that I am with them. I'll rain down a waferlike flake, something they've never seen before. They'll pick it up, look at it, taste it with the tip of their tongue, and say, 'Manna'—in Hebrew 'man-hu,' which means, 'What is it?' And then they'll realize I can provide for them in ways they'd never expect. And when they see me do it again and again and again, they'll know that they can always count on me.

"They also need to see that they are no longer a nation of slaves but instead the most favored nation that has ever existed. They're going to be my treasured possession. I will speak words to them—words of wisdom and life—words that no other nation has ever heard. They will be the most envied people on earth. They will possess the oracles of truth.

"And, finally, I need to develop their military skills. I need to teach them the art of warfare. But I will do it through skirmishes with the Amalekites, with Bedouin tribes, rather than have them face trained armies. And then, when my people are ready, I'll take them into Canaan."

My friend [summary review], sometimes God knows there's something in the straight-line path that would stop us from ever reaching our destination [restate, 270–77], some obstacle that would prevent us from ever getting there. And [take-home truth, 65–83] in his wisdom he takes us on an alternate path in order to safely get us to the goal.

In the company you've joined [what does it look like, 106–12], God may keep you under the radar until a disgruntled older worker who would be envious of your rapid promotion and determined to sabotage your advancement is transferred or retired. Or God may keep you in place for a while so that you can hone critical skills or develop key networking connections that will help you succeed in the new responsibility. And thus [take-home truth, 65–83] God wisely and lovingly takes you on a zigzag path to protect you from failure and prepare you for the future.

In the business you've started [what does it look like, 106–12], it may be God knows if he took you to point B in a fast, straight-line way, it would require so many extra hours from you that, at this stage in your family's life, your kids would suffer or foolish financial decisions would be made. Somehow keeping you on the alternate path enables you to have the hours at home, to be involved in family activities, to cement a lifetime of care for your children, and to gradually learn how to responsibly handle the extra income.

If you're single [what does it look like, 106–12], it may be that God knows the person he's bringing to you is not quite ready yet. That person needs a little more time to work out a few things, to resolve some issues, so that when the marriage comes together, it's secure and joyful instead of troubled and tentative.

Perhaps God knows that if you were too quickly given a prominent role in ministry [what does it look like, 106–12], you would be vulnerable to pride and a domineering spirit. And if God's people reacted adversely and harshly to you, you might never consider any ministry again.

[summary review] God in his wisdom knows there's something in the straight-line path that would prevent us from ever reaching the intended destination. And he lovingly leads us on an alternate route, because that's the only safe, sure way to get there. [**take-home truth,** 65–84] The shortest distance between two points is a zigzag.

[**transition**] But sometimes this can be hard on us. We start to lose heart. In the midst of the zigs and zags, as we don't seem to be making any progress toward the goal, we get discouraged. In fact, if our progress is too slow or if we sometimes seem to be going in the opposite direction, we not only become discouraged, but we even begin to doubt. We begin to doubt there ever was a point B. We begin to think, "Maybe that's not God's goal. Maybe I just imagined it. Maybe I just wanted it so badly I psyched myself into it. Maybe it was just my pipe dream and not God's destiny."

In the midst of doubt and discouragement [**rhetorical question transition,** 287–88], how does God encourage us? [**restate,** 270–77] How does he sustain us on the way? [**same key phrasing as preview,** 278–84] In the midst of the zigs and zags, when we don't seem to be making any progress, how does God keep us heading expectantly and joyfully toward the goal? How does he keep us moving ahead with faith and stamina?

The Scripture says [**main point inductive, list,** 288–94] there are two things he will do for us [**restate,** 270–77], two things he will give us, two things that will keep us encouraged and pressing ahead.

The first thing, the Scripture says, is that [**subpoint deductive, progression,** 288–94] if the dream is of God, then God will give us continual reminders of his good intention. [**restate,** 270–77] If the destiny is of God, if point B is of God, then God will find ways of coming to you and letting you know that he's still taking you to his promised destination. Perhaps someone out of the blue—someone who doesn't know what God has put in your heart—perhaps that someone will say something to you. Not knowing your dream, the person won't realize the significance of what he or she is saying, but in that person's words you'll hear God's voice reminding you of his good intentions. The person will use the exact words that God has previously impressed upon you. And your heart will leap as the Spirit affirms to you, "The dream is alive."

It may be [**what does it look like,** 106–12], as you're seemingly buried in some side cubicle, and nobody knows you work for the company—it may be that somebody you've helped in the past phones the company and gets transferred to you. Someone you've dealt with previously. And as you come on the line, the person suddenly blurts out, "Are you still at that same desk? Are you still doing this job? My goodness, with all of your ability, I'd have thought by now you'd be—." And out of the blue, of all the positions in the company, the caller will pick point B. Even though you've never breathed a word about it to anyone, the person will pick the very position you feel God is taking you to. And in your heart you'll hear God saying, "I'm reminding you of my good intentions."

It could be [what does it look like, 106–12] in the business you've started. You'll come home one day and hit the "play" button on the answering machine. And the recorded voice will say, "Is this phone still taking your messages? With the quality work you do, I would have thought by now you'd be—." And out of the caller's mouth will come a description of the magnitude or volume of business you believe God intends for you.

It could be [what does it look like, 106–12] you're single. And some dear lady will come up to you after church and say, "You know who I think would make a good couple? You and—." And you'll silently say, "Lord, I think so too. Are you telling me something?"

It may be [what does it look like, 106–12] that as you faithfully serve God in whatever ways are open to you, that some wise and discerning leader might comment to you, "You know, you don't really seem to be suited to this particular ministry. Have you ever considered—?" And that one will identify the very ministry you feel God has called you to.

God's first promise is that he will give you reminders of his good intentions.

In Israel's history [mini-synopsis, only next verse, 294–96], his reminder to them is a coffin, a sarcophagus. We learn this through a very strange note that appears as God begins to take them on the zigzag path. We read in verse 19 that as Israel went up out of Egypt,

> Moses took the bones of Joseph with him because Joseph had made the sons of Israel swear an oath. He had said, "God will surely come to your aid, and then you must carry my bones up with you from this place."

Israel takes with them the coffin that contains the bones of Joseph. Before he died four hundred years earlier, Joseph had made the sons of

Israel swear an oath that they would not leave his body in Egypt.[8] More than four hundred years earlier Joseph was the first to enter that land, sold into slavery by his brothers. He lived to become the number two ruler in the land and to see his father and brothers come under his protection. Soon seventy people came and joined him in Egypt. By the time Joseph died, those seventy had grown to two or three hundred.

And on his deathbed, with those two to three hundred gathered around him, Joseph says to them: "Some day God's going to come to the aid of our people. This is not our home. God's going to take us out of Egypt. He's going to take us back to the Land of Promise. He's going to put us where our ancestors are buried. And when he does, don't leave me here in Egypt. Swear to me that you'll take my bones with you. Swear to me that when the day comes that God takes you out of Egypt, you'll take my bones with you. I want to be buried in Canaan with Abraham, Isaac, and Jacob."

Now, four hundred years later, those two to three hundred have grown to two million. And now, as they are getting ready to leave Egypt, several strong men lift the coffin containing the bones of Joseph. And as they head south toward the Red Sea, the coffin leads the way.

And I can hear some little kid turn to his mother and say [**write for the ear, conversation, 260–62**], "Why are those men carrying that box?" "That's not a box, honey. That's a coffin." "What's a coffin?" "Well, it has the bones of a dead man in it." "Oh—gross! But why are we taking it with us?" "Well, honey, we're taking it to Canaan." "But we're not headed to Canaan." "Yes we are—Yes we are. That coffin's going to Canaan."

Every day as they started the march, no matter where the zigs and zags led them, the coffin was a continual reminder that God was taking them to point B. That coffin was going to Canaan.

[**summary review**] My friend, in the midst of the zigs and zags, if the dream is of God, every so often, out of the blue, by someone's words, or by something you read, or by thoughts that come in the night, God will give you a reminder of his good intentions. That's the first thing he says he'll do.

The second thing he says is that [**subpoint deductive, progression, 288–94**] he will also give you a tangible sense of his presence. [**restate, 270–77**] You will have a palpable sense of God's nearness, God's protection, God's

---

8. Genesis 50:24–26.

guidance. The closeness of God, his being a part of your family—you'll feel it and sense it like you've never felt it before.

In Israel's journey this palpable presence [mini-synopsis, only next verses, 294–96] took the form of a column of cloud. It came into their national existence as soon as they stepped out of Egypt. And it stayed with them in a tangible way until they arrived at Canaan. And then it left them.

They described what came to them as *"a pillar of cloud"*—some opaque, swirling, dense mass of shimmering whiteness—a "cloud column" that stretched into the sky. At night, it looked as if there was a fire inside of it. It glowed, it became luminescent, so that it was as visible at night as it was in the day. It was the presence of their God, and it stayed with them on the zigs and zags until they crossed the Jordan River and entered Canaan. And then it was gone.

We read of this tangible symbol of God's presence beginning in verse 20: *"After leaving Succoth they camped at Etham."* Where's Etham? It's *"on the edge of the desert."* What does that mean? It means Etham wasn't the end of the world, but you could see the end of the world from Etham. When they left Etham, they were leaving civilization. They were going out into the trackless desert. No maps. No Thomas Brothers guides. No Global Positioning System. They were going where people don't go.

And as they stepped into nothingness, the tangible, visible, palpable sense of God's presence came into their lives. Look at it in verses 21–22:

> By day the LORD went ahead of them in a pillar of cloud to guide them on their way and by night in a pillar of fire to give them light, so that they could travel by day or night. Neither the pillar of cloud by day nor the pillar of fire by night left its place in front of the people.

During all their zigs and zags, whether by day or by night, their God was visibly and tangibly present with them as at no other time in their nation's history. The cloud never left its place in front of the people.

That cloud was their God leading them, guiding them. When it moved, they moved—"Roll up the sleeping bags; pull up the tents. We're on our way!"

That cloud was also their God protecting them, sheltering them. When Pharaoh decided to chase after them, when Israel looked in one direction to see the charging chariots and in the other direction to see an impassible sea, when they feared for their lives—then they saw the cloud insert itself between them and the chariots.[9] The horses couldn't penetrate the dense opaqueness. Then the sea split open, and they walked through. When they were all on dry land on the other side, the cloud lifted. The horses and chariots charged into the water, but the waters returned to cover them. Israel's God was protecting them.

The Bible also says that the cloud protected them or sheltered them when they got out into the heat of the desert. The cloud would invert itself and become a shade canopy against the heat of the sun.[10]

And, finally, it was through that cloud that their God talked to them. When they got to Sinai, that cloud shrouded Mount Sinai. And from it came the voice of their God, speaking directly and specifically to them, telling them exactly what he wanted them to know.[11]

My friend, in the midst of the zigs and zags, there will be a tangible, palpable sense of God's presence, a nearness of God, a sense of "You're guiding me, you're protecting me, and your Spirit is telling me what you want me to know."

God in his goodness sometimes leads us on an alternate path to get to the promised destination. [**take-home truth**, 65–83] Sometimes the shortest distance between two points is a zigzag, because that's the only way to get there. Along the way God gives us reminders of his good intentions and a tangible sense of his presence.

Follow him without fear. You can never be harmed by God.

---

9. Exodus 14:19–20.
10. Psalm 105:39.
11. Exodus 19:9, 16–19.

IMPARTIAL LOVE

James 2:1–13

Outline

Introduction

(handwritten: Situation)

1. Two families come as first-time visitors to the church.
   a. The members of one family are well dressed and influential within the community.
   b. The members of the other are dowdy and no one you've ever seen before.
2. When it appears that both families need help finding seats, which one do you help?
3. That's the issue James poses as he writes to his former church members.
   a. Fifteen years earlier his friends had fled Jerusalem for safety's sake.
   b. But now, in their new communities, they face insurmountable obstacles.
   c. James describes two men who come into their small church.
      i. One is wealthy and influential and can make life easier for them.
      ii. The other is poor and unknown and can do nothing for them.
   d. And James poses the question, "Which one do you go to?"
4. To see James's description of these two visitors and his answer to his question, let's turn to James 2.

(handwritten: (Shift) Topic)

I. James describes two visitors to his readers' church.
   A. One is a wealthy and influential man who could benefit them in some way.
   B. The other is a poor and insignificant man who can do nothing for them.

arch)

vestion II. In such situations, if we're really committed to following Christ, we'll love them impartially, without thought of gain (2:1–3).

between)

issue III.

Transition: Why is it important to love impartially, without thought of gain?

III. (When we love impartially, without thought of gain, we show our trust in God, our wisdom regarding people, our submission to God's Word, and our desire for God's grace.)

    A. When we love impartially, we show our deep trust in God—that he is in control of our lives (2:4).

    B. When we love impartially, we show our wisdom about people—that it's usually the poor who have the closest walk with God (2:5–7).

    C. When we love impartially, we show our submission to God's Word—that we will obey everything God has said (2:8–11).

    D. When we love impartially, we show our desire for God's grace—that we want his mercy instead of his judgment (2:12–13).

to situation)

Conclusion

    1. Next Sunday you may find yourself encountering various individuals.

    2. Love them impartially, not for what they can do, but simply for who they are.

Sermon

Let's suppose we have in the audience this morning some first-time visitors to the church. Let's imagine two different families who have come.

If you were outside when the first family drove up, you would have looked at their car kind of enviously—expensive, new, shiny. "Somebody's doing OK to be able to afford that."

The car of the second family was right behind them. This car—well, you kind of heard it even before you saw it. You know—that noise that tells you "this engine isn't long for this world." And when you looked at the car, it was old and rusty, paint splotchy and faded, sides dented, back trunk held down with rope, windows rolled down because the air-conditioning is broken. "Mmm, things must be tough for them. Low-paying job. Probably hardly making it."

Both cars park, and the two families walk from the parking lot to the door. You're getting your bulletin at the same time they are, and you notice a difference in how the two families are dressed.[12]

> The first family—hey, the latest styles, well tailored, coordinated outfits, matching accessories. I mean we're talking Nordstrom's all the way. The parents both look like they work out—fit, trim. It's obvious the woman's been to the hairdresser—styled, highlighted. Attractive makeup. Their kids—a daughter in college, a son in high school—are well dressed, poised, confident.
>
> The second family is getting their bulletins behind them. The man is in faded corduroys, ill-fitting shirt. Shoes scuffed, slanting to the sides because the heels are worn away, shoelaces dragging. The woman is wearing a housedress. Purse doesn't match. Hair needs work. Their kids—overweight, self-conscious, uncomfortable.

As they're getting their bulletins, you suddenly realize you recognize someone in that first family.

> Maybe the man is the head of an engineering firm or a software company that you'd like to work for or maybe sell something to. It'd be good to establish a contact with him for business reasons.
>
> Or maybe you recognize the wife as a professor at the university, someone who hires research assistants, and your daughter is applying for one of the jobs in her department.
>
> Or maybe you recognize their son—you've seen his picture in the paper—he's the all-state quarterback for the local team. Hmm, be kind of nice if he were part of the youth group.
>
> Or maybe the daughter is beautiful, and your twenty-five-year-old son in grad school standing next to you is one of the leaders of the college group. You're sure he'd love to tell her about the group's activities and maybe see that she gets to the college class and has a good time.

---

12. Sometimes I write my sermon manuscript in a semi-outline block form, to make it easier visually to spot and remember a group of subordinate paragraphs.

The second family? They're nobody you've ever seen before. You're not even sure they live in your bedroom community; maybe they're from one of the apartments in a nearby city.

Both families finally have their bulletins and walk into the back of the auditorium. One steps to the right, the other to the left. Both families kind of stop and hesitate, because they're not sure where they should sit. This is their first time, and they're trying to get the lay of the land and figure out where they should go.

By now you also have come into the back of the auditorium, and you see both families, one on each side. Both of them hesitating, trying to make up their minds and decide what they should do. And it occurs to you that you could offer some help . . . to one of them.

Which family do you go to? Which one do you walk toward? Which family do you give attention to?

> You'd be tempted to go to the first family. "Hi, my name is Don Sunukjian. Can I help you? We don't save seats here, so you can sit anywhere you want. My wife and I normally sit in this section—you can get a good view of the screen, and you can get to the donuts and coffee more quickly afterward. Why don't you join us?"
>
> You'd be tempted to go to that first family, because—you never know—it might lead to a job or a sale, or maybe a job for your daughter, or a date for your son. You'd be drawn to the first family—they're attractive, and they might do something for you. You might benefit in some way.

Two families come into church. Which one would you go to?

That's the same question James poses in a letter he writes to some Christian friends of his—friends he hasn't seen for fifteen years. He used to be their pastor when they attended his church in Jerusalem, before they had left the city. Actually they had fled the city. For a period of time it had become too dangerous to be a Christian in Jerusalem.

> One of the church members, Stephen, had been falsely charged and executed. The authorities were planning similar trumped-up charges against other Christians too. And so, many families had

fled for safety's sake, to other cities and countries, in order to start life over.

But in their new cities, they were viewed with suspicion. They were immigrants, refugees, strangers. Life was tough. The obstacles they faced seemed insurmountable.

- They couldn't find jobs.
- They had trouble getting permits to set up businesses. Even if they managed to open their doors, they found themselves boycotted by the community or trashed by local hooligans.
- At the local markets, their wives were being cheated and hassled.
- At school, their children were being tormented.
- The citizens of the towns hated them because they were Jews, and the Jews of the towns hated them because they were Christians.
- They found themselves isolated and harassed by a hostile society.

On Sundays they gathered in their small church, a fragile minority, looking for comfort from each other in a menacing environment.

And their former pastor writes to them. He knows how vulnerable they are and the temptations that come because of that. And so, as he writes, he imagines a Sunday when two first-time visitors might come to their church. Two different men from the community, checking them out, each one maybe interested in attending the church a bit. One of the first-time visitors is obviously wealthy. They recognize him as an influential man in the community. The other visitor is the opposite; he is poor, and nobody knows him. And James raises the question for his friends, "Which one would you go to? Which one would you pay attention to?"

Let's look at how James describes these two visitors, and at the answer he gives to his question. Please turn to James 2 . . . James 2.

Let's see how James describes these visitors and his answer to the question he raises.

One of the visitors, James says, is obviously wealthy and influential in the community. Notice how James puts it in verse 2: "*Suppose a man comes into your meeting wearing a gold ring and fine clothes.*"

"*A gold ring and fine clothes*"—that's the way the ruling-class Romans were described. "*A gold ring and fine clothes.*" A three-piece suit. *Gold ring, fine clothes*—that was the description of a government official, someone high up, someone who determined the laws and controlled the patronage jobs.

The first visitor, James says, is a man of wealth and influence in the city—the kind of man who could get you a job or a permit. The kind of man who could get the hooligans to lay off. The kind of man who could see to it that you wife and kids were no longer hassled. The kind of man who could do something for you—benefit you in some way.

The second visitor is poor and unknown.

James describes him in verse 2 as "*a poor man in shabby clothes.*" A poor man—his clothes are shabby, nondescript. And maybe even a little bit dirty, for soap was expensive in that day. He's poor and can't afford soap, so his clothes are grimy. They smell of sweat and earth.

Two first-time visitors—one wealthy and influential; the other poor and insignificant. Which one do you go to? Which one do you give attention to? Do you give special attention to the rich one?

That's what James visualizes in verse 3: Do "*you show special attention to the man wearing fine clothes and say, 'Here's a good seat for you'*"? "I've got a spot on the aisle for you, lots of legroom, you can see well, get to the coffee fast." Do you pay special attention to the rich one, because he's the one who can do something for you?

And do you kind of brush off the poor one?

Verse 3: "*but say to the poor man, 'You stand there' or 'Sit on the floor by my feet.'*" "There are some folding chairs over by the wall that you can set up." Or, "Here's a spot, over on the side, right under the loud-speaker." Do you ignore and brush off the poor man?

If you are really committed to following Christ, James says, if your belief in Christ is central to your life, and you find yourself in this situation—the influential and insignificant, the attractive and unattractive,
the rich and poor are both in your church—if you are really committed
to following Christ:

- You must treat them absolutely the same.
- You must treat them equally, without thought of gain, without regard for benefit you might receive.
- You must love them impartially, not for what you can get from
  them.
- If you are really committed to following Christ, you must not show
  favoritism.

That's what James stresses in verse 1: *"My brothers, as believers in our
glorious Lord Jesus Christ, don't show favoritism."* Do not pay attention to
people based on what they can do for you. Do not treat them differently
based on what you might get from them. Be absolutely impartial. Love
them equally.

Now why does James stress that? Why is it so important that we love
impartially, without thought of gain? Why does James want us to be as
ready to love the poor man as the rich man, as quick to pay attention to
the insignificant as to the influential? Why is it so important that we love
impartially?

You might say, "Well, that's the right, Christian thing to do. That's the
way a Christian ought to act." And that would be true.

But the reasons are much more profound than that. The reasons why
we must love impartially, without thought of gain, go far deeper than, "It's
the right thing to do."

In the verses that follow, James probes and searches our hearts and reveals why it is so essential that we love impartially, without regard for any
benefit to us. He gives four answers, four penetrating reasons why it's so
important that we love impartially, without thought of gain.

First, he says, when you love impartially, without thought of gain, you
show your deep trust in God—that he is in control, that he's the one who
determines your future, not the rich and influential of this world. You
show your conviction that your future is in God's hands, not people's—

that he's the one who determines the good things that come to you, not people. When you love impartially, you show your trust in God—that he is in control of your life.

But if you show favoritism in your love, if you're partial to those you think can do something for you, then that shows you're not confident about God's role in your life. You're uncertain whether he's real and in control. You're wavering, vacillating, unsure about what God is able to handle and what people have in their control. And because of your doubts about God, you're now deciding what you will do based on evil, self-centered motives. You're making judgments based on "who can do what for me."

That's what James means in verse 4: When you show favoritism and pay special attention to the rich, *"have you not discriminated among yourselves and become judges with evil thoughts?"*

When he says, *"Have you not discriminated among yourselves?"* the word he uses for "discriminated" is the word for "doubted." Have you not revealed your doubts about whether God is in control? It's the same word he used earlier when he talked about "asking God for wisdom but doubting" while you were doing it. Doubting, vacillating, wavering—asking God for wisdom, but not sure whether he was really in control or not. *Discriminating, doubting*—same Greek word. Look back at chapter 1, verses 5–8, to see the same word:

"If any of you lacks wisdom, he should ask God, who gives generously to all without finding fault, and it will be given to him. But when he asks, he must believe and not doubt"; he must not discriminate in his mind about whether God controls this or that situation, *"because he who doubts"*—the one who wavers, vacillates, discriminates—*"is like a wave of the sea, blown and tossed by the wind. That man should not think he will receive anything from the Lord; he is a double-minded man, unstable in all he does."*

James says when we discriminate in our love, we are revealing our doubts about whether God is in control.

God may not be in control of my job, my career, so I'd better play favorites with this executive and ignore the other family.

God may not be in control of my children's future, so I need to be partial to these people who can hire them or date them and not worry about whether anyone is helping these other people.

And because of our doubts about God, we judge the situation *"with evil thoughts."* We decide what we will do based on unworthy motives—on "who can do what for me," rather than on "what are the needs."

The first reason it's so important to love impartially, without thought of gain, is because it shows our deep confidence in God. It shows we have no doubts about him. To love impartially shows our complete trust in God—that he is in control.

There's a second reason, James goes on to say, why we should love impartially. Not only because it shows our trust in God, that he is in control, but also because it shows our wisdom about people, that it's usually the poor who have the deepest walk with God. When you love without partiality, it's because you know that the poor are usually the ones who are most fully centered on God, whereas the rich have no use for him in their lives. The poor are often the most spiritually rich, whereas the rich are often the most abusive and cruel.

That's what James is saying in verses 5–7: To love impartially shows your wisdom about people—that it's usually the poor who have the deepest walk with God, while it's usually the rich who are cruel and have no use for him. Let's read it—verses 5–7:

> *Listen, my dear brothers: Has not God chosen those who are poor in the eyes of the world to be rich in faith and to inherit the kingdom he promised those who love him? But you have insulted the poor. Is it not the rich who are exploiting you? Are they not the ones who are dragging you into court? Are they not the ones who are slandering the noble name of him to whom you belong?*

If you insult or snub the poor person, if you shun him in your love, you may be snubbing someone that God has chosen, someone God is very close to, someone who has a rich and deep walk with him.

- You may be snubbing a man who daily walks with God in faith, a man who asks God every morning to keep his car running because there's no money for repairs. And every night he returns to thank him for making it last another day.

- If you snub the poor person, you may be snubbing a housewife who doesn't have money to put her elderly mother in a care facility. So she's taking care of her in her own home, and every day she asks God to keep her loving and gentle and patient.

- If you snub the poor person, you may be brushing off the single mother whom God is filling with grace every day—helping her keep up with trips to day care; with her job; with the grocery shopping, the hurried meals, the baths and homework. And then, at night, when she's overcome with weariness and tears and loneliness, he's loving her and consoling her and assuring her of his presence and protection.

- When you snub the poor person, you may be dishonoring the shy teenager who doesn't say much and isn't an athlete or a student leader but who works at McDonald's after school and quietly gives half of his income to feed orphans in India.

Listen, my dear brothers: Has not God chosen those who are poor in the eyes of the world to be rich in faith and to inherit the kingdom he promised those who love him?

Often it's the poor who have the richest and deepest walk with God, and to love them quickly and fully is to discover someone God has chosen, someone who has a deep walk with him.

On the other hand, to show favoritism to the rich is often a fool's errand, for they are usually the most abusive and cruel. Verses 6–7:

Is it not the rich who are exploiting you? Are they not the ones who are dragging you into court? Are they not the ones who are slandering the noble name of him to whom you belong?

- Is the Fortune 500 executive going to do you good? Or is he going to use you for anything he can and then spit you out? Ask his ex-wives. Ask his serial girlfriends. Ask his business lackeys.

- Is it the rich or the poor who cause the business scandals, drag

firms into bankruptcy, and destroy investors while building personal mansions?

- Is it the rich or the poor who take advantage of you in court because they have the deep pockets to hire the lawyers and beat you
back?
- Is it the rich or the poor who use their good-old-boy networks to
get insider tips, government contracts, preferential treatment, and
company perks?
- Is it the rich or the poor who smile to your face and do a hatchet job
to your back, who show up at church for image purposes but never
let it affect their lives in any way?

Not all rich, of course, are this way. But James's point is that more often
they are the ones who have no use for God in their lives. And so, when you
love impartially, you show your wisdom about people—that it's usually
the poor who have the deepest walk with God.

There's a third reason, James says, why you should love equally. A third
reason why you should love impartially—because it shows your submission to God's Word, that you will obey everything God has said. When
you obey *this* command—the command to love, which is the supreme
command—when you obey this *greatest* of all commands, you show your
willingness to obey *all* of God's commands.

But if we disobey this command, the most important of all commands,
we're essentially saying to God, "I don't care what you command; I'm going to do what I want. I don't care what your Word says; I'll break any
of your laws if I feel like it or if I think it will serve my purposes." When
we break this greatest command—the command to love—we reveal deep
down that our heart is not submissive to God and that we will break or
transgress any of his laws whenever it suits us.

To obey this supreme command not only shows your trust in God and
your wisdom about people; it also shows your willingness to obey everything God has said.

That's what James is saying in verses 8–11—that when you obey this
greatest command to love impartially, you show that your entire life is
submitted to God's Word and that your desire is to obey him in every
way:

"If you really keep the royal law found in Scripture," the royal law, the supreme law, the law that means the most to our King, the greatest law he gave—*"if you really keep the royal law found in Scripture,"* the law that says, *"Love your neighbor as yourself"*—if you really keep this law, *"you are doing right."* You are revealing your desire to obey all of God's commands. But if you break this law, *"if you show favoritism, you sin and are convicted by the law as lawbreakers. For whoever keeps the whole law and yet stumbles at just one point is guilty of breaking all of it. For he who said, 'Do not commit adultery,' also said, 'Do not murder.' If you do not commit adultery but do commit murder, you have become a lawbreaker."* You now stand before the law as someone who is not submissive to it.

"For whoever keeps the whole law"—whoever says, "Yeah, I'll do what God says"—*"and yet stumbles at just one point"*—"Oh, except for that, I'm not going to do that"—whoever reveals a rebellious spirit against one of God's commands shows that deep down he's prepared to break or transgress any command whenever it suits him. Whoever *"stumbles at just one point, is guilty of breaking all of it,"* because to deliberately break *one* of them shows you're willing to break any or all of them. Essentially it's saying, "I'll disobey any command whenever I want to."

And this attitude makes you guilty before God, because God considers his law as an unbreakable whole. God views his Word, his commands, like a pane of glass—you can't break one part of it without shattering the whole. All of Scripture, undivided, not piecemeal, is God's perfect will for our lives. *"For he who said, 'Do not commit adultery,' also said, 'Do not murder.' If you do not commit adultery but do commit murder,"* if you pick and choose to break God's commands, you reveal a rebellious heart against God, and *"you have become a lawbreaker."*

To pick and choose whom you will love based on what you can get out of them is to disobey the greatest of all the commands God has given. And deep down it reveals that you are unsubmissive to God, that you will disobey any command whenever it serves your purposes.

But to love impartially, without thought of gain, is to show that your whole life is submitted to God's Word and that you want to obey him in every way you can. Love impartially, James says, because when you obey this greatest command, you show that you are willing to obey all the commands that God has given.

Finally, James says, there's one last reason why you should love impartially.

- It shows your trust in God—that he is in control of your life.
- It shows your wisdom about people—that it's usually the poor that have the deepest walk with him.
- It shows your submission to God's Word—that you will obey everything God has said.

And, finally, to love impartially shows your desire for God's grace— that you want his mercy instead of his judgment. To show mercy toward others, to love them without making judgments about how deserving they are, shows an awareness that you too need God's mercy and not his judgment. And God treats us as we treat others, either acting in judgment against us, or loving us with infinite mercy. We should love others impartially, James says, because mercy is what we need.

That's James's final reason in verses 12–13: To love impartially, he says, shows your desire for God's grace, that you want his mercy toward you to be greater than, stronger than, triumphing over his judgment of you.

> Speak and act as those who are going to be judged by the law that gives freedom, because judgment without mercy will be shown to anyone who has not been merciful. Mercy triumphs over judgment!

This command to love impartially is the command that liberates you. It's the law that gives you freedom—freedom to trust God's control in your life, freedom to focus on those whom he has chosen, freedom to obey all that he has written in his Word, and freedom to live within his mercy.

So speak and act according to this law of impartial love, for your obedience to this law—to show mercy to others without regard of gain—will determine whether you'll be judged as you deserve or whether mercy will continually stream into your life.

If we fail to love impartially, if we fail to show mercy to others, it means that God will act the same way toward us—we will get what we deserve: justice, judgment, with little sense of his love and mercy in our lives.

But when you love impartially, when you show mercy without judging whether people deserve it, then God's love and mercy toward you will be greater than, and will triumph over, any judgment of you. When you love impartially, you show your desire for God's grace—that you want his mercy instead of his judgment.

Maybe next Sunday you'll find yourself near someone who looks out of place, alone, uncertain. Maybe it's a young couple in the parking lot, struggling to get all their gear and small children together. Maybe it's an elderly person walking slowly with a cane, hoping not to get bumped, trying to open a door. Maybe it's a teenager with skin problems and shirttail flapping. It may be someone who weighs too much, or talks too loud, or smells too strong.

But here, among God's people, they are loved—loved for who they are and not for what they can do.

- Loved, without thought of gain, because God controls all that.
- Loved, because unknown to us, God may be doing wonderful things in their lives.
- Loved, because our greatest desire is to do all that our God has said.
- Loved, because we too are all so aware that, though we are unworthy, God's mercy and love never come to an end in our lives.

Here, among God's people, there's no favoring one over another. There's only impartial love.

Homiletical Features

Let's suppose we have in the audience this morning some first-time visitors to the church. [**engage, 193**] Let's imagine two different families who have come.

[**what does it look like, 106–12**] If you were outside when the first family drove up, you would have looked at their car kind of enviously—expensive, new, shiny. "Somebody's doing OK to be able to afford that."

The car of the second family was right behind them. This car—well, you kind of heard it even before you saw it. You know—that noise that tells you "this engine isn't long for this world." And when you looked at the car, it was old and rusty, paint splotchy and faded, sides dented, back trunk held down with rope, windows rolled down because the air-conditioning is broken. "Mmm, things must be tough for them. Low-paying job. Probably hardly making it."

Both cars park, and the two families walk from the parking lot to the door. You're getting your bulletin at the same time they are, and you notice a difference in how the two families are dressed.

> The first family—hey, the latest styles, well tailored, coordinated outfits, matching accessories. I mean we're talking Nordstrom's all the way. The parents both look like they work out—fit, trim. It's obvious the woman's been to the hairdresser—styled, highlighted. Attractive makeup. Their kids—a daughter in college, a son in high school—are well dressed, poised, confident.
>
> The second family is getting their bulletins behind them. The man is in faded corduroys, ill-fitting shirt. Shoes scuffed, slanting to the sides because the heels are worn away, shoelaces dragging. The woman is wearing a housedress. Purse doesn't match. Hair needs work. Their kids—overweight, self-conscious, uncomfortable.

As they're getting their bulletins, you suddenly realize you recognize someone in that first family.

> Maybe the man is the head of an engineering firm or a software company that you'd like to work for or maybe sell something to. It'd be good to establish a contact with him for business reasons.
>
> Or maybe you recognize the wife as a professor at the university, someone who hires research assistants, and your daughter is applying for one of the jobs in her department.
>
> Or maybe you recognize their son—you've seen his picture in the paper—he's the all-state quarterback for the local team. Hmm, be kind of nice if he were part of the youth group.
>
> Or maybe the daughter is beautiful, and your twenty-five-year-old son in grad school standing next to you is one of the leaders

of the college group. You're sure he'd love to tell her about the group's activities and maybe see that she gets to the college class and has a good time.

The second family? They're nobody you've ever seen before. You're not even sure they live in your bedroom community; maybe they're from one of the apartments in a nearby city.

Both families finally have their bulletins and walk into the back of the auditorium. One steps to the right, the other to the left. Both families kind of stop and hesitate, because they're not sure where they should sit. This is their first time, and they're trying to get the lay of the land and figure out where they should go.

By now you also have come into the back of the auditorium, and you see both families, one on each side. Both of them hesitating, trying to make up their minds and decide what they should do. And it occurs to you that you could offer some help . . . to one of them.

[focus: question, 199–205; macro-inductive structure, 150–55] Which family do you go to? [restate, 270–77] Which one do you walk toward? Which family do you give attention to?

You'd be tempted to go to the first family. "Hi, my name is Don Sunukjian. Can I help you? We don't save seats here, so you can sit anywhere you want. My wife and I normally sit in this section—you can get a good view of the screen, and you can get to the donuts and coffee more quickly afterward. Why don't you join us?"

You'd be tempted to go to that first family, because—you never know—it might lead to a job or a sale, or maybe a job for your daughter, or a date for your son. You'd be drawn to the first family—they're attractive, and they might do something for you. You might benefit in some way.

Two families come into church. [focus: question, 199–205] Which one would you go to?

[set the stage biblically, 205–20] That's the same question James poses in a letter he writes to some Christian friends of his—friends he hasn't seen for fifteen years. He used to be their pastor when they attended his church in Jerusalem, before they had left the city. Actually they had fled the city. For a period of time it had become too dangerous to be a Christian in Jerusalem.

One of the church members, Stephen, had been falsely charged and executed. The authorities were planning similar trumped-up charges against other Christians too. And so, many families had fled for safety's sake, to other cities and countries, in order to start life over.

But in their new cities, they were viewed with suspicion. They were immigrants, refugees, strangers. Life was tough. The obstacles they faced seemed insurmountable.

- They couldn't find jobs.
- They had trouble getting permits to set up businesses. Even if they managed to open their doors, they found themselves boycotted by the community or trashed by local hooligans.
- At the local markets, their wives were being cheated and hassled.
- At school, their children were being tormented.
- The citizens of the towns hated them because they were Jews, and the Jews of the towns hated them because they were Christians.
- They found themselves isolated and harassed by a hostile society.

On Sundays they gathered in their small church, a fragile minority, looking for comfort from each other in a menacing environment.

And their former pastor writes to them. He knows how vulnerable they are and the temptations that come because of that. And so, as he writes, he imagines a Sunday when two first-time visitors might come to their church. Two different men from the community, checking them out, each one maybe interested in attending the church a bit. One of the first-time visitors is obviously wealthy. They recognize him as an influential man in the community. The other visitor is the opposite; he is poor, and nobody knows him. And James raises the question for his friends [focus: question, 199–205; same key phrasing as engage section, 278–84], "Which one would you go to? Which one would you pay attention to?"

[preview, 221–24; preview #5, 231] Let's look at how James describes these two visitors, and at the answer he gives to his question. Please turn to James 2 . . . James 2. [**announce the passage, repeat, wait, 238–41**]

[**mini-synopsis, only next verses, 294–96**] Let's see how James describes these visitors and his answer to the question he raises.

One of the visitors, James says, is obviously wealthy and influential in the community. Notice how James puts it in verse 2: "*Suppose a man comes into your meeting wearing a gold ring and fine clothes.*"

> "*A gold ring and fine clothes*"—that's the way the ruling-class Romans were described. "*A gold ring and fine clothes.*" A three-piece suit. *Gold ring, fine clothes*—that was the description of a government official, someone high up, someone who determined the laws and controlled the patronage jobs.
>
> The first visitor, James says, is a man of wealth and influence in the city—the kind of man who could get you a job or a permit. The kind of man who could get the hooligans to lay off. The kind of man who could see to it that you wife and kids were no longer hassled. The kind of man who could do something for you—benefit you in some way.

The second visitor is poor and unknown. [**mini-synopsis, only next phrase, 294–96**]

> James describes him in verse 2 as "*a poor man in shabby clothes.*" A *poor man*—his clothes are shabby, nondescript. And maybe even a little bit dirty, for soap was expensive in that day. He's poor and can't afford soap, so his clothes are grimy. They smell of sweat and earth.

Two first-time visitors—one wealthy and influential; the other poor and insignificant.

[**focus: question, 199–205**] Which one do you go to? [**restate, 270–77**] Which one do you give attention to? Do you give special attention to the rich one? [**mini-synopsis, 294–96**]

> That's what James visualizes in verse 3: Do "*you show special attention to the man wearing fine clothes and say, 'Here's a good seat*

for you'"? [**write for the ear, conversation, 260–62**] "I've got a spot on the aisle for you, lots of legroom, you can see well, get to the coffee fast." Do you pay special attention to the rich one, because he's the one who can do something for you?

And do you kind of brush off the poor one?

Verse 3: "*but say to the poor man, 'You stand there' or 'Sit on the floor by my feet.'*" "There are some folding chairs over by the wall that you can set up." Or, "Here's a spot, over on the side, right under the loud-speaker." Do you ignore and brush off the poor man?

If you are really committed to following Christ, James says [**restate, 270–77**], if your belief in Christ is central to your life, and you find yourself in this situation—the influential and insignificant, the attractive and unattractive, the rich and poor are both in your church—if you are really committed to following Christ [**take-home truth, 65–83; mini-synopsis, only next verse, 294–96**]:

- You must treat them absolutely the same.
- [**restate, 270–77**] You must treat them equally, without thought of gain, without regard for benefit you might receive.
- You must love them impartially, not for what you can get from them.
- If you are really committed to following Christ, you must not show favoritism.

That's what James stresses in verse 1: "*My brothers, as believers in our glorious Lord Jesus Christ, don't show favoritism.*" Do not pay attention to people based on what they can do for you. [**restate, 270–77**] Do not treat them differently based on what you might get from them. Be absolutely impartial. Love them equally.

[**rhetorical question as transition, 287–88; preview #5, 231**] Now why does James stress that? [**restate, 270–77**] Why is it so important that we love impartially, without thought of gain? Why does James want us to be as ready to love the poor man as the rich man, as quick to pay attention to the insignificant as to the influential? Why is it so important that we love impartially?

You might say, "Well, that's the right, Christian thing to do. That's the way a Christian ought to act." And that would be true.

But the reasons are much more profound than that. [restate, 270–77] The reasons why we must love impartially, without thought of gain, go far deeper than, "It's the right thing to do."

In the verses that follow, James probes and searches our hearts and reveals [main point inductive, list, 288–94] why it is so essential that we love impartially, without regard for any benefit to us. [restate, 270–77] He gives four answers, four penetrating reasons why it's so important that we love impartially, without thought of gain.

First, he says [subpoint deductive, progression, 288–94; mini-synopsis, only next verse, 294–96], when you love impartially, without thought of gain, you show your deep trust in God—that he is in control, that he's the one who determines your future, not the rich and influential of this world. [restate, 270–77] You show your conviction that your future is in God's hands, not people's—that he's the one who determines the good things that come to you, not people. When you love impartially, you show your trust in God—that he is in control of your life.

But if you show favoritism in your love, if you're partial to those you think can do something for you, then that shows you're not confident about God's role in your life. [restate, 270–77] You're uncertain whether he's real and in control. You're wavering, vacillating, unsure about what God is able to handle and what people have in their control. And because of your doubts about God, you're now deciding what you will do based on evil, self-centered motives. You're making judgments based on "who can do what for me."

That's what James means in verse 4: When you show favoritism and pay special attention to the rich, *"have you not discriminated among yourselves, and become judges with evil thoughts?"*

When he says, *"Have you not discriminated among yourselves?"* the word he uses for "discriminated" is the word for "doubted." "Have you not revealed your doubts about whether God is in control?" It's the same word he used earlier when he talked about "asking God for wisdom but doubting" while you were doing it. Doubting, vacillating, wavering—asking God for wisdom, but not sure whether he was really in control or not. *Discriminating, doubting*—same word. Look back at chapter 1, verses 5–8 to see the same word:

> *"If any of you lacks wisdom, he should ask God, who gives generously to all without finding fault, and it will be given to him. But when he asks, he must believe and not doubt,"* he must not discriminate in his mind about whether God controls this or that situation, *"because he who doubts"*—the one who wavers, vacillates, discriminates—*"is like a wave of the sea, blown and tossed by the wind. That man should not think he will receive anything from the Lord; he is a double-minded man, unstable in all he does."*

James says when we discriminate in our love, we are revealing our doubts about whether God is in control.

[what does it look like, 106–12] God may not be in control of my job, my career, so I'd better play favorites with this executive and ignore the other family.
     [what does it look like, 106–12] God may not be in control of my children's future, so I need to be partial to these people who can hire them or date them and not worry about whether anyone is helping these other people.

And because of our doubts about God, we judge the situation *"with evil thoughts."* We decide what we will do based on unworthy motives—on "who can do what for me," rather than on "what are the needs."

[review] The first reason it's so important to love impartially, without thought of gain, is because it shows our deep confidence in God. **[restate, 270–77]** It shows we have no doubts about him. To love impartially shows our complete trust in God—that he is in control.

There's a second reason, James goes on to say **[repeating same key words of larger list, 284–86]**, why we should love impartially. Not only because it shows our trust in God, that he is in control, but also **[subpoint deductive, progression, 288–94]** because it shows our wisdom about people, that it's usually the poor who have the deepest walk with God. **[restate, 270–77]** When you love without partiality, it's because you know that the poor are usually the ones who are most fully centered on God, whereas the rich have no use for him in their lives. The poor are often the most spiritually rich, whereas the rich are often the most abusive and cruel.

That's what James is saying in verses 5–7 [**mini-synopsis, only next verse, 294–96**]: To love impartially shows your wisdom about people—that it's usually the poor who have the deepest walk with God, while it's usually the rich who are cruel and have no use for him. Let's read it—verses 5–7:

> *Listen, my dear brothers: Has not God chosen those who are poor in the eyes of the world to be rich in faith and to inherit the kingdom he promised those who love him? But you have insulted the poor. Is it not the rich who are exploiting you? Are they not the ones who are dragging you into court? Are they not the ones who are slandering the noble name of him to whom you belong?*

If you insult or snub the poor person, if you shun him in your love, you may be snubbing someone that God has chosen, someone God is very close to, someone who has a rich and deep walk with him.

- [**what does it look like, 106–12**] You may be snubbing a man who daily walks with God in faith, a man who asks God every morning to keep his car running because there's no money for repairs. And every night he returns to thank him for making it last another day.
- If you snub the poor person, you may be snubbing a housewife who doesn't have money to put her elderly mother in a care facility. So she's taking care of her in her own home, and every day she asks God to keep her loving and gentle and patient.
- If you snub the poor person, you may be brushing off the single mother whom God is filling with grace every day—helping her keep up with trips to day care; with her job; with the grocery shopping, the hurried meals, the baths and homework. And then, at night, when she's overcome with weariness and tears and loneliness, he's loving her and consoling her and assuring her of his presence and protection.
- When you snub the poor person, you may be dishonoring the shy teenager who doesn't say much and isn't an athlete or a student

leader but who works at McDonald's after school and quietly gives half of his income to feed orphans in India.

> *Listen, my dear brothers: Has not God chosen those who are poor in the eyes of the world to be rich in faith and to inherit the kingdom he promised those who love him?*

Often it's the poor who have the richest and deepest walk with God, and to love them quickly and fully is to discover someone God has chosen, someone who has a deep walk with him.

On the other hand [**mini-synopsis, only the next verses, 294–96**], to show favoritism to the rich is often a fool's errand, for they are usually the most abusive and cruel. Verses 6–7:

> *Is it not the rich who are exploiting you? Are they not the ones who are dragging you into court? Are they not the ones who are slandering the noble name of him to whom you belong?*

- [**what does it look like, 106–12**] Is the Fortune 500 executive going to do you good? Or is he going to use you for anything he can and then spit you out? Ask his ex-wives. Ask his serial girlfriends. Ask his business lackeys.
- Is it the rich or the poor who cause the business scandals, drag firms into bankruptcy, and destroy investors while building personal mansions?
- Is it the rich or the poor who take advantage of you in court because they have the deep pockets to hire the lawyers and beat you back?
- Is it the rich or the poor who use their good-old-boy networks to get insider tips, government contracts, preferential treatment, and company perks?
- Is it the rich or the poor who smile to your face and do a hatchet job to your back, who show up at church for image purposes but never let it affect their lives in any way?

Not all rich, of course, are this way. But James's point is that more often they are the ones who have no use for God in their lives. And so, when you love impartially, you show your wisdom about people—that it's usually the poor who have the deepest walk with God.

[**transition; restate, 270–77; use same umbrella language of larger list, 284–86**] There's a third reason, James says, why you should love equally. A third reason why you should love impartially—because it shows your submission to God's Word, that you will obey everything God has said. [**subpoint deductive, progression, 288–94; restate, 270–77**] When you obey *this* command—the command to love, which is the supreme command—when you obey this *greatest* of all commands, you show your willingness to obey *all* of God's commands.

But if we disobey this command, the most important of all commands, we're essentially saying to God [**write for the ear, conversation, 260–62**], "I don't care what you command; I'm going to do what I want. I don't care what your Word says; I'll break any of your laws if I feel like it or if I think it will serve my purposes." When we break this greatest command—the command to love—we reveal deep down that our heart is not submissive to God and that we will break or transgress any of his laws whenever it suits us.

To obey this supreme command not only shows your trust in God and your wisdom about people; it also shows your willingness to obey everything God has said.

That's what James is saying in verses 8–11—[**mini-synopsis, only next verses, 294–96**] that when you obey this greatest command to love impartially, you show that your entire life is submitted to God's Word and that your desire is to obey him in every way:

"If you really keep the royal law found in Scripture," the royal law, the supreme law, the law that means the most to our King, the greatest law he gave—*"if you really keep the royal law found in Scripture,"* the law that says, *"Love your neighbor as yourself"*—If you really keep this law, *"you are doing right."* You are revealing your desire to obey all of God's commands. But if you break this law, *"if you show favoritism, you sin and are convicted by the law as lawbreakers. For whoever keeps the whole law and yet stumbles at just one point is guilty of breaking all of it. For he who said, 'Do not commit adultery,' also said, 'Do not murder.' If you do not commit adultery but do commit murder, you have become a lawbreaker."*

You now stand before the law as someone who is not submissive to it.

"For whoever keeps the whole law"—whoever says [**write for the ear, conversation, 260–62**], "Yeah, I'll do what God says"—*"and yet stumbles at just one point"*—"Oh, except for that, I'm not going to do that"—whoever reveals a rebellious spirit against one of God's commands shows that deep down he's prepared to break or transgress any command whenever it suits him. Whoever *"stumbles at just one point, is guilty of breaking all of it,"* because to deliberately break one of them shows you're willing to break any or all of them. Essentially it's saying, "I'll disobey any command whenever I want to."

And this attitude makes you guilty before God, because God considers his law as an unbreakable whole. God views his Word, his commands, like a pane of glass—you can't break one part of it without shattering the whole. All of Scripture, undivided, not piecemeal, is God's perfect will for our lives. *"For he who said, 'Do not commit adultery,' also said, 'Do not murder.' If you do not commit adultery but do commit murder,"* if you pick and choose to break God's commands, you reveal a rebellious heart against God, and *"you have become a lawbreaker."*

To pick and choose whom you will love based on what you can get out of them is to disobey the greatest of all the commands God has given. And deep down it reveals that you are unsubmissive to God, that you will disobey any command whenever it serves your purposes.

But to love impartially, without thought of gain, is to show that your whole life is submitted to God's Word and that you want to obey him in every way you can. Love impartially, James says, because when you obey this greatest command, you show that you are willing to obey all the commands that God has given.

[**transition, summary review; use same umbrella language as the larger list, 284–86**] Finally, James says, there's one last reason why you should love impartially.

- It shows your trust in God—that he is in control of your life.
- It shows your wisdom about people—that it's usually the poor that have the deepest walk with him.

- It shows your submission to God's Word—that you will obey everything God has said.

And, finally [**subpoint deductive, progression, 288–94**], to love impartially shows your desire for God's grace—that you want his mercy instead of his judgment. [**restate, 270–77**] To show mercy toward others, to love them without making judgments about how deserving they are, shows an awareness that you too need God's mercy and not his judgment. And God treats us as we treat others, either acting in judgment against us, or loving us with infinite mercy. We should love others impartially, James says, because mercy is what we need.

That's James's final reason in verses 12–13 [**mini-synopsis, only next verses, 294–96**]: To love impartially, he says, shows your desire for God's grace, that you want his mercy toward you to be greater than, stronger than, triumphing over his judgment of you.

> Speak and act as those who are going to be judged by the law that gives freedom, because judgment without mercy will be shown to anyone who has not been merciful. Mercy triumphs over judgment!

This command to love impartially is the command that liberates you. It's the law that gives you freedom—freedom to trust God's control in your life, freedom to focus on those whom he has chosen, freedom to obey all that he has written in his Word, and freedom to live within his mercy.

So speak and act according to this law of impartial love, for your obedience to this law—to show mercy to others without regard of gain—will determine whether you'll be judged as you deserve or whether mercy will continually stream into your life.

If we fail to love impartially, if we fail to show mercy to others, it means that God will act the same way toward us—we will get what we deserve: justice, judgment, with little sense of his love and mercy in our lives.

But when you love impartially, when you show mercy without judging whether people deserve it, then God's love and mercy toward you will be greater than, and will triumph over, any judgment of you. When you love impartially, you show your desire for God's grace—that you want his mercy instead of his judgment.

[what does it look like, 106–12] Maybe next Sunday you'll find your-self near someone who looks out of place, alone, uncertain. Maybe it's a young couple in the parking lot, struggling to get all their gear and small children together. Maybe it's an elderly person walking slowly with a cane, hoping not to get bumped, trying to open a door. Maybe it's a teenager with skin problems and shirttail flapping. It may be someone who weighs too much, or talks too loud, or smells too strong.

But here, among God's people, they are loved—[take-home truth, 65–83] loved for who they are and not for what they can do.

- Loved, without thought of gain, because God controls all that.
- Loved, because unknown to us, God may be doing wonderful things in their lives.
- Loved, because our greatest desire is to do all that our God has said.
- Loved, because we too are all so aware that though we are unwor-thy, God's mercy and love never come to an end in our lives.

Here, among God's people [take-home truth, 65–83], there's no favor-ing one over another. There's only impartial love.

Scripture Index

NEW TESTAMENT

Mark

Luke

1. What central meaning(s) can modern readers fairly extract from the passage? (always keep in mind the meaning / the passage for its original readers)

What should be done? Who needs to do it? Why do they need to do it? When and where should they do it? How should they do it?

(what do they need to know?)
(why do they need to know it?)
(what do they need to do?)
(why do they need to do it?)

2. if fairly and accurately applied, what impact would this passage have on modern church and society?

3. How might the differences between modern and the biblical setting influence the interpretation and application of the passage?

4. What modern social, political and economic presuppositions or agendas do you have that might influence your understanding and application of the teachings of your passage? (After these notions are identified, remove them from your application process & see what clearly remains of the passages meaning.

5. What picture of God, Jesus and the Holy Spirit is clearly portrayed in your passage? How does the picture help modern christian understand the theology of the passage?

6. What thought, feeling, or behaviour does God, through your passage, require of us? What knowledge about living the christian life emerges from the passage?

Headings   / Proposition / context / Ex
  (main points   prohib
  if the passage)

P113

(applying the take-home truth)   with Satan -
                                          - a piece of spiritual ar
  Relevance : How the message   to wear
              connects to life   - A temptation to res
                                         - A device to recogn
  With God -   - A person to resist
    - A truth to rest in   - A sin to avoid
    - A command to obey   context
    - A prayer to express
    - A challenge to head   (Specific hard times and
    - A promise to claim   hostile places that listen
    - A fellowship to enjoy   might experience) p 12
                                         = How the premise is l
  With yourself -   out... equivalent to
    - A thought or a word to examine   one the bibl
    - An action to take   author is
    - An example to follow   talking about
    - An error to avoid
    - An attitude to change or to guard against
    - A priority to change
    - A goal to strive for
    - A personal value or standard to hold up
    - A sin to forsake

  With others -
    - A witness to share
    - An encouragement to extend
    - A service to do
    - A forgiveness to ask
    - A fellowship to nurture
    - An exhortation to give
    - A burden to bear
    - A kindness to express
    - A hospitality to extend
    - An attitude to change or guard against
    - A sin to forsake.